C000176294

TUDOR CHILDREN

TUDOR CHILDREN

NICHOLAS ORME

YALE UNIVERSITY PRESS
NEW HAVEN AND LONDON

For information about this and other Yale University Press publications, please contact:
U.S. Office: sales.press@yale.edu   yalebooks.com
Europe Office: sales@yaleup.co.uk   yalebooks.co.uk

Set in Adobe Garamond Pro by IDSUK (DataConnection) Ltd
Printed in Great Britain by Gomer Press Ltd, Llandysul, Ceredigion, Wales

Library of Congress Control Number: 2022946473

ISBN 978-0-300-26796-9

A catalogue record for this book is available from the British Library.

10 9 8 7 6 5 4 3 2

FOR VERITY, KEN, AND GRACE

CONTENTS

ILLUSTRATIONS

PREFACE

This book, I believe, is the first general study of childhood in Tudor England. As a result it aims to provide an introduction to the subject rather than a final definitive history. There are still many obstacles to producing a work of the latter kind. Historical sources relating to children in the sixteenth century are far fewer than is the case for adults. Most of what is available relates to the wealthier ranks of society rather than the poorer majority. Modern studies are restricted in the fields that they deal with. My strategy has been to give all the aspects of the subject equal weight, so as to provide the reader with a sense of the range and richness of childhood in this period. Topics more fully examined elsewhere, such as demography, family relationships, medicine, and law, may be followed up in the books and articles cited in the endnotes and the bibliography.

I am grateful to all the published authors who have previously worked in this field. Robert Kirkpatrick and Tamsin Lewis in particular put me in touch with sources that I would not otherwise have found, while Sir John Mummery enlightened me about partible inheritance. I am again indebted to Yale University Press and to Lucy Buchan, Sophie Richmond, and Katie Urquhart in particular for the care and patience of their work on the text and the illustrations.

Nicholas Orme
Oxford, 2023

De sancto sacramento an
Sacrum comunium in
quo xpistus sumitur re
colitur memoria passionis eius
mens impletur gratia et future glo

1. A noblewoman receiving communion. Up to the Reformation, this often
preceded giving birth for spiritual support and in case of death in childbirth.

1

BIRTH AND INFANCY

BIRTH

On All Saints' Day, 1 November 1489, the queen of England, Elizabeth of York, withdrew to her private suite in the Palace of Westminster to prepare for the birth of her next child. Her withdrawal was marked by an ornate sequence of rituals.[1] It began with mass in a private chapel, sung by Richard Fox, the bishop of Exeter. The queen was given communion while two earls held a towel beneath her chin lest any crumb should fall from the sacred wafer: the very body and blood of Jesus Christ. Afterwards she took a sip of unconsecrated wine as an ablution. Then a procession of noble men and women led her to her 'great chamber', the outer of her two principal rooms, where her lord chamberlain asked all those present to pray for her safe delivery.

Next the queen withdrew to her inner chamber, which was hung around with blue cloth of arras powdered with fleurs-de-lys of gold. This background was apparently thought more soothing for childbirth than the pictorial arras that was hung elsewhere. The principal feature of the chamber was a magnificent bed and bedclothes, topped by a canopy of gold, and decorated in various colours embellished with roses and strips of ermine. The room also contained a portable altar furnished with relics and a large cupboard or dresser 'richly garnished', probably with vessels of gold and silver. The queen asked that she might have the prayers of the nobility, and the lord chamberlain drew a curtain and retired. It was the custom that henceforward no man would normally enter the chamber till after the birth; the queen would be surrounded and served only by ladies and midwives. On this occasion the rule was breached soon after the retirement, because an embassy from France arrived with good wishes, and its leaders had to be allowed in to deliver their compliments. And as it turned out, the queen did not go into labour for another four weeks until, on 29 November, she gave birth to a daughter, Margaret, who was to marry James IV of Scotland and become the grandmother of Mary Queen of Scots and the great-grandmother of James I. Altogether Elizabeth experienced this withdrawal between six and eleven times during the seventeen years of her marriage to Henry VII, from 1486 to 1503. The last occasion was fatal: both she and the baby would die.

A royal confinement and birth were far removed in their setting from those of most of the population, but their elements, to a greater or lesser extent, were paralleled widely. The most common was the exclusion of men from the scene. There might be exceptions. Henry VIII was so concerned about the birthing of his third wife, Jane Seymour, that she was attended by male physicians not midwives: a fact that may have contributed to her death soon after the birth of her child.[2] Normally, however, a midwife was the central figure, assisted only by other women. Even in the popular romance of *Bevis of Hampton*, read throughout the sixteenth century, Josian the heroine, who went into labour while travelling, refused help from Bevis her husband. He and their male servant were sent out of the way until her twins were born.[3] Elizabeth of York gave birth in her own house, as most women did, but in some cases a mother-to-be was sent away for the purpose. This may have been popular with the wealthier classes in towns, where there was a constant fear of infections. The London grocer Richard Hill, whom we shall encounter again on our journey, recorded the births of his children in a commonplace book that he kept. His eldest child John was born in 1518 at Hillend near Hitchin in Hertfordshire, whither his wife had evidently retired, although his others came into the world in London.[4]

Up to the Reformation, communion was offered to women before the event. This was preceded by confession, and involved attending one's local church to be given the consecrated wafer or else, perhaps, receiving it at home (Fig. 1, p. xiv).[5] Relics too had an important role, at least among the wealthy. Many monasteries and other churches possessed ones appropriate for childbirth: usually a girdle said to have belonged to the Virgin Mary, or chains ascribed to St Peter's prison experience. These might be accessed before a birth, or lent out for the purpose, and be laid on or perhaps around the abdomen. Scrolls of paper carrying prayers were used in a similar way.[6] The Reformation made a difference here. Relics and talismans fell under disapproval in the late 1530s and most of those relating to childbirth were removed or destroyed. After the new English Prayer Books were introduced, from 1549 onwards, communion services were held only three or four times every year, and the reservation of the sacrament for occasional distribution was forbidden. This did not stop some women continuing to look for super-natural help. Reginald Scot, writing about witchcraft in 1584, noted that they would now tie their girdles or shoe latchets to a bell, and ring it three times, evidently with the same idea that a girdle could somehow acquire the power to relax the womb.[7]

Knowledge of childbirth, and the expertise to help with it, lay in the traditions and experience of hundreds of midwives. Most of the latter were unregulated but some were licensed by the Church authorities, perhaps because they might need to administer emergency baptism to babies in danger of death.[8] From 1540 there was also a detailed handbook in English on giving birth: *The Birth of Mankind*, translated from the Latin of Eucharius Rösslin (d. 1526), a German physician. The translator into English, Richard Jonas, was another German who came to England in the retinue of Anne of Cleves. He probably hoped that the book would help with the birth of the heirs she would bear for Henry VIII. But Henry's failure to consummate the marriage and the swift disposal of Anne obliged Jonas to dedicate it to the next queen, Katherine Howard, only for her to be discarded by the king and beheaded before she could give him a child. Fortunately the book found a better audience outside the royal family. It gained publication in German, Dutch, and French, and Jonas's English translation itself was printed at least eight times during the sixteenth century.

Much of its success must have come from the fact that it drew on tradi-tional and well-known practices.[9] The translator acknowledged that many midwives were 'right expert, diligent, wise, circumspect, and tender about such business' but, he thought, there were also 'many more [who were] full indiscreet, unreasonable, churlish, and far to seek in such things' through

3

whom mothers in childbirth came to grief.[10] His translation guided a woman and her helpers through pregnancy, childbirth, and the care of her baby. It was aimed at the wealthy who would buy the book or receive directions from it from their physicians, so that although the procedures it describes may have been common, its remedies (in terms of diets and medicines) must have been restricted to a minority of women.

Rösslin's work advised what to eat and drink during pregnancy. He recommended avoiding desiccating or sour foods such as medlars, chestnuts, crab apples, choke pears, or overmuch verjuice (vinegar). Sweet foods were better, like apples fried with sugar, wine, and figs. Bathing or washing should be done in the last ten days, the water being infused with herbs.[11] Labour would normally happen in the ninth month, or fortieth week, but babies could survive if born in the seventh month although (oddly) not in the eighth.[12] Labour would be more difficult if the woman was too young (only twelve or fifteen, although the author observed that this was infrequent) or if she was weak, elderly, or obese. The birth of a male was reckoned to be easier than that of a female.[13] When labour began, the room should be of the right temperature: warmed in winter and well aired in summer to reduce the heat. During labour, it was good to sit down leaning backwards, and in France and Germany birth-stools with low seats and sloping backs were used for this.[14] The midwife should sit before the mother and assist with the delivery. It is not clear how often such stools were used in England, but the term certainly came into use.[15]

In a 'natural' birth, the baby's head would appear first, followed by the shoulder and arms, but in 'unnatural ones', the legs would come first or one leg only, in which case the midwife should try to turn the child to ease the birth.[16] Her hands should be wiped with oil of almonds or oil of lilies for this purpose. In the birth of twins, more care was needed to bring them out in turn. When the baby had been born, the umbilical cord (known as the navel-string)[17] should be cut to a width of three fingers above the navel and tied. Some people thought that the length of what was left, in the case of a man, would equal the length of his full-grown tongue or penis. Others asserted that, in the case of a woman, the number of wrinkles in the remaining part would presage the number and frequency of her children in adulthood. If the cord was cut too short, it would impede her deliveries.[18] Next the baby should be rubbed with acorn oil, washed in warm water, the nostrils opened and cleaned, and a little oil wiped round the eyes. The remains of the cord would fall off after the third or fourth day, after which its base should be dried with ashes or red lead (!) tempered with wine. Then the baby should be swaddled and put in its cradle.[19]

A sad minority among the births were those born with deformities. The condition of cleft palate was known as 'harelip', by analogy with the mouth of a hare, and was said to be caused in pregnancy through a mother being startled by a hare or having a desire to eat hare.[20] If the deformities were major and unusual, such as missing limbs or in a case of conjoined twins, the baby or babies born were known as a 'monstrous child', becoming an item of news and commented on according to the notions of the day. There was a cluster of such births in about 1562, human and animal, which attracted contemporary attention and even got into the standard histories of Elizabethan England.[21] Several formed the material for 'broadsides': cheap leaflets printed on one side of the paper (Fig. 2, p. 6). These could be bought at fairs by credulous people, like the one about the usurer's wife who gave birth to money-bags, mentioned in Shakespeare's *The Winter's Tale*.[22] Such broadsides often displayed a woodcut of the deformed child and described the birth in verse for singing or retelling to other people.[23]

Like modern tabloid stories, the accounts mingled the sensational with the censorious. Three of the children had been conceived illegitimately. In one case from Essex, the parents had each had normal offspring in their marriages and produced the deformed child through an irregular relationship. This enabled the birth to be interpreted as 'a terror as well to all such workers of filthiness and iniquity, as to [all] ungodly livers'. 'The babe', another writer admitted, 'is guiltless', but it and its parents are 'both infamous made with sinful birth.' If no guilt could be pinned on the father and mother, the event was explained as a general warning from God to sinners to repent and amend their lives. Of the tragedy for the child and its parents, little was said. In one case the (unmarried) father was said to have fled, no doubt for fear of public opinion and the responsibilities of maintenance. In two others, the parents (or others who inveigled them) exhibited the children in London. One was a case of conjoined twins who had died at birth

The true description of two monsterous childẑen,

lawfully begotten betwene George Steuens and Margerie his wyfe, and boẑne in the parish of Swanburne in Buckyngham shyẑe, the. iiij. of Apẑill. *Anno Domini*. 1 5 6 6. the two childẑen hauing both their belies fast ioyned together, and imbẑacyng one an other with their armes : which childẑen wer both a lyue by the space of half an hower, and wer baptiȝed, and named the one John, and the other Joan.

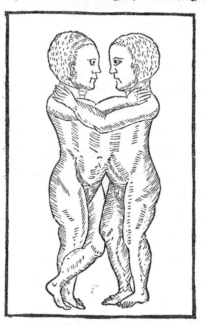

I Read how *Affrique* land was fraught
foẑ their most filthy life,
With mōstrous shapes, confuȝedly
that therin wer full rife.

And thus by these two children here,
foẑewarnes both man and wyfe :
How both estates ought to bewayle,
their vile and wẑetched lyfe.

But to the end Gods gloẑie great,
and miracles diuine :
Might on the earth apparaunt be,
his woẑkes foẑ to define.

2. Infant deformity. Abnormalities, such as conjoined twins, gained notoriety and were publicised in broadsides (news sheets) as God's warning for sins.

and the other a child of fifteen weeks with 'ruffs' of skin on its shoulders. It could be visited at Glean Alley in Southwark.

BAPTISM

In Tudor England up to 1549, almost every baby was taken to church to be baptised on the day of its birth or within a day or two afterwards. This was not a practice of the early Church but one that had developed during the Middle Ages. It was the outcome of the words of Jesus that 'no one can enter the kingdom of God without being born of water and the Spirit'.[24] A child that died without baptism in water would not go to heaven, and in an age of high infant mortality its salvation needed to be assured as quickly as possible. If a newborn child was weak and unlikely to live, the Church regularly instructed lay people that the midwife or parents should do the christening at home by sprinkling on some ordinary water and repeating the words (in any language): 'I baptise you, [saying a forename], in the name of the Father, the Son, and the Holy Ghost.' Should the child survive, it must be brought to church later and have the benefit of a proper service of baptism, omitting the christening itself which could not be repeated.[25]

In normal circumstances a message would be sent to the parish priest that a baby had arrived, and a party of adults would carry it off to the church. The baby was held by the midwife and accompanied by the father and the three required godparents: two of the baby's sex and one of the other. The mother remained at home. Parents liked to choose godparents of status and wealth, if they could. This meant asking them beforehand and perhaps, when the mother went into labour, sending a message that the birth was imminent. We get a sense of the scurry for a godparent at this point from a letter written in the mid-1530s by Ralph Sadler to Thomas Cromwell, to whom he acted as secretary. Sadler's wife, he said, had just given birth to a boy at Hackney outside London. The baptism was to be held in the church there next day, and Cromwell was asked to come as chief godparent and give his forename to the child. He had already acted in this way for another son who had died. Sadler hoped to enlist Mrs Richards or Lady Weston as the godmother, because they were both staying near Hackney. No doubt he thought that the presents these people would give and the assistance they might offer in later life were very well worth having.[26]

Along with the midwife, father, and godparents, one can reasonably assume that neighbours and relatives might also be present. Affluent families brought servants with them to carry water, salt, and candles for the service, and refreshments to distribute afterwards. In some places there was a custom for the candles to be carried unlit to the church, and lighted on the return to the house.[27] Arriving at the church, the baptism party met the priest and parish clerk at the principal church door, most such doors having a porch outside to give shelter. The service of baptism, like all Church worship, was in Latin except where the priest had to give instructions to those who were present.[28] It had its origins in the days when adults were baptised, requiring them to be examined about their belief before they could enter the church for the ceremony. Hence the beginning of the service outside. An oral examination was impossible for a baby, of course, so this had evolved into a series of ritual actions which made the baby fit to go into church. Prayers were said, the priest blessed the child with the sign of the cross, exorcised it with prayers, placed a few grains of salt in its mouth, and anointed its ears and nostrils with saliva, recalling Christ's healing of a blind man in that way. The child was now a 'catechumen', a candidate for baptism, and might come into church for the purpose.

Those present duly entered the building and gathered by the font at the western end of the nave, near the door: the priest, the parish clerk holding the priest's book, and the laity (Fig. 3, p. 9). Fonts were required to be kept permanently full of water: water that had been consecrated with prayers and holy oil, so that baptism could take place at any time. Important families (at least) liked to have fresh water, however, so this would be poured in and the priest then consecrated it with the appropriate series of rituals. If the family was wealthy, the font might be decorated with silken hangings and the high altar at the east end of the church with tapestry. Four or even six servants might be deputed to stand around the font with candles, giving light to the proceedings, but most poorer people could not have afforded such splendours.

The ceremony at the font centred on the making of vows on the baby's behalf by the godparents. They were asked to renounce the Devil and his works as well as to affirm their belief in God. The priest then baptised the baby, calling it by its name and baptising it in the name of the Father, the Son, and the Holy Spirit. The basin of a font was made large enough to dip a baby totally under the water and this was done three times, the priest pointing the baby's head towards the east. During the first immersion the baby was held looking north, during the second looking south, and during the third looking downwards.

Next the baby was given into the hands of the senior godparent of its own sex, who was said to 'raise it from the font'. The priest anointed the baby on

3. Baptism. A priest attended by his parish clerk baptises a baby in a font, in this case a boy. Three godparents are present: two male and one female.

its forehead with chrism (a mixture of oil and balsam, consecrated by a bishop) in the form of a cross. A white cloth, known as the 'chrisom cloth', was wrapped around the baby as a sign of purification of the baby from the sin into which it was born. A candle was then held in the baby's hand while the priest urged it to remain faithful to its baptism until it came to heaven. The godparents were instructed to wash their hands before leaving church, in case they had come into contact with the holy chrism. When the baptism was over, refreshments might be served if the family could afford them: the servants of the wealthy dispensing wine and hot loaves. Again among the rich, money might be thrown to the bystanders or gifts be given so that those present might remember the occasion. The party then returned to the house where, in the higher ranks of society, the godparents and others might give presents to the mother and the nurse.

The mother was compensated for her absence at the baptism with a special service of her own: her purification or, as it was usually known, her 'churching'.[29] Jewish tradition regarded a mother who gave birth as becoming impure and barred her from holy places for several weeks, after which she visited a priest, made an offering, and was pronounced purified. The Christian Church adopted this tradition, associating it with the Virgin Mary who had experienced it, but the Church modified the notion of impurity. A mother was not forbidden to come to church at any time after a birth, but she was enjoined to go there after forty days to give thanks for her delivery. It was customary for her to wear a headdress, to be accompanied by two other mothers, and for them all to bring lighted candles. They were met at the church door by the priest and, after a few prayers, the mother was led inside. She then attended mass during which she returned the chrisom cloth to the church. Its contact with the chrism made it holy, and it could not be used again for any secular purpose. She and her friends gave an offering of money, and afterwards there was a special meal if resources permitted. Should she first meet a man on leaving church, said one superstition, her next child would be a boy; if a woman, a girl.[30]

Immediate baptism not only secured a child's salvation but made it a member of the Church from the day of its birth. Neither the clergy nor most of the laity could conceive of a human being who was not in the Church. Membership was essential not only for the individual but for the well-being of society. It was not voluntary. When the Church of England was created during the 1530s and 1540s, it inherited these views. Early baptism was vital for one's personal salvation and for the existence of a Christian land and nation. On the Continent, the Reformation saw the appearance of Anabaptists, who argued that baptism should take place in adulthood, involving a personal profession of faith. That was seen as subversive everywhere, including England, and in 1538 Henry VIII ordered clergy to keep a register of baptisms in order to guard against evasions.[31]

In 1549 the Catholic Latin services were abolished and replaced by the first Book of Common Prayer in English, which was now imposed for use in every church. The Prayer Book made changes to the service of baptism, chiefly to remove most of the ceremonies. The English Reformers wished to base people's faith on the biblical scriptures rather than on trust in rituals. A major change was made to the timing of baptisms. They were now to take place on the Sunday after a birth, so that they could be done in church within the service of morning prayer at about 9.00 a.m., or that of evening prayer at about 3.00 p.m. This became the most usual day for baptism up to the Civil War of the 1640s.[32] The change enabled the baby to be received into the church community more obviously than before, and the adults present to be reminded of their own baptisms. It remained lawful, however, for a sickly child to be christened at home as soon as it was born, and the Church continued to instruct lay people how this should be done.

The English Prayer Books greatly simplified the form of the service. The 1549 edition did so partially and a second edition in 1552 made further amendments. There was a brief return to tradition under Mary Tudor in 1553–8, after which the Prayer Book of 1552 was restored in an almost identical version in 1559. The 1552 and 1559 baptism services dispensed with the initial meeting at the church doors. Instead the christening party was to gather at the font halfway through morning or evening prayer, after the second Bible reading. The service consisted of instructive readings and prayers in English, but the godparents made the same affirmations of faith as before. The font was filled with ordinary water, no longer specially conse-crated, and the baby was 'dipped' in the water once and without necessarily requiring full immersion. If it was weak, sprinkling of water on its head was sufficient. The only other ceremony was that, after the baptism, the priest made a sign of the cross, once, on the baby's forehead. This simple action, during the reign of Elizabeth I, became controversial among those radical Reformers known as Puritans, who saw it as a superstitious survival from Catholicism. They petitioned against it, but the queen stood firm and it remained a requirement.

Such a simplified baptism must have seemed stark after the elaboration of the Catholic service. Nonetheless there might be more people present at the service than there had been before, and the Prayer Book did not forbid the activities that had formerly accompanied a christening in a wealthy family. It was probably still possible to decorate the font and other places in the church. The child could be brought to church with a procession and in a magnificent dress. Godparents could still be recruited from the wealthy and, if they themselves were unavailable, have 'deputies' to appear for them at the service.[33] In 1562 the London diarist Henry Machyn recorded that the daughter of 'Master Cromwell' was carried to church by 'a fair maid . . . in a white satin gown'. The baby was wrapped in a 'mantle of crimson satin, fringed with gold'. The Master of the Rolls was the godfather, and Lady White one of the godmothers. Afterwards there was a great banquet at the family's home.[34]

The duties of godparents were not meant to stop with the christening. It was their task to make sure that the child was brought up in the Christian faith: to see that it learnt the basic prayers and was taken to the bishop to be confirmed in due course.[35] The Prayer Book of 1549 added that they should ensure that it knew the Ten Commandments and encourage the child to learn more about religion by attending sermons. One godparent should also personally bring the child to the confirmation service.[36] How much contact godparents later had with their charges must have varied. Some supporters of the Reformation in Norfolk in 1556 claimed that 'many good men of forty years, that had been godfathers to thirty children, knew no more of the godfather's office but to wash their hands ere they departed the church'.[37] On the other hand, as we shall shortly see, godparents often gave their own forename to their godchild, which may have set up a closer relationship. Some certainly remembered their charges, years later, when they made their wills: at least with a token sum of money. Thus Henry Bole of North Cadbury, Somerset, 1494, and William Bower of Mells in the same county, 1521, left a shilling to each of their godchildren.[38]

NAMES

Baptism in Tudor England, especially up to 1549, had a significance that it has lost today. It was also a naming ceremony. Nowadays long periods may pass between births and christenings, during which a baby's forename has become well known and often legally registered. In earlier times the name was formally announced for the first time at the baptism, and this became in effect the registration of the name. In the Catholic liturgy the name was repeated some sixteen times, but this was reduced to three times in 1549 and to once (at the moment of baptism) in 1552 and thereafter. The forename was almost always a single one. An early exception was Henry Algernon Percy, earl of Northumberland, born in 1478, unless his second name was an informal addition. The historian William Camden, who wrote a pioneering and perceptive study of English names in 1603, commented that 'two Christian names are rare in England'. He cited the new king, James I, who had been christened Charles James, and his eldest son Prince Henry Frederick. Otherwise he could think of only two instances. One was Thomas Maria Winfield (*c.* 1516–57), perhaps named after Thomas Wolsey and Mary Tudor, formerly queen of France, who seem to have been his godparents. Winfield had two sons, Thomas and Edward, with the same second name. The other example was Sir Thomas Posthumous Hoby (1556–1640), so called because he was born after his father's death.[39]

Another difference between now and then was the choice of the baby's name. Today it is almost always made by the parents. In Tudor times this was not necessarily so. Some Tudor parents, or fathers at least, did select their children's names. Henry VII must have decided on Arthur for his first-born child and eldest son because it was not a recent family name. Instead it was meant to link the new Tudor dynasty with a great king of the past from whom the family claimed descent. A few years earlier, in 1480, Edward IV or his wife Elizabeth Woodville must have thought of Bridget (another new family name) for their youngest child, suggesting that they had a devotion to St Bridget of Sweden. Some of the gentry seem to have sought distinction or to be faithful to their ancestry by giving less usual names to their children, especially the sons. The Digby family used Everard and Kenelm, the Constables and Lumleys Marmaduc, and the Pauncefoots Grimbald.[40]

The other influence in naming, not normal nowadays, was that of the godparents. 'Who gave you [your] name?' asked the catechism which all children were required to learn after 1549. The answer was, 'My godfathers and godmothers at my baptism.'[41] It was they, or more exactly the senior godparent of the child's own sex, not the father, who announced the name to the priest at the christening service. There is plenty of contemporary evidence that the godparent concerned had a claim to give his or her own name to the child. This was not invariable, because the Digbys, Constables, and Lumleys mentioned above would have found it difficult to get godparents with their unusual family names, but it was very common.

The practice can be seen in operation in the family of Richard Hill, the London grocer mentioned above. He and his wife Margaret, daughter of a London haberdasher, had seven children between 1518 and 1526: five boys and two girls. Richard noted down their births in the commonplace book in which he collected songs, carols, romances, and other items that interested him (Fig. 4, below). He also recorded the names of their godparents. Of his seven children, only John the eldest was not named after a godparent, perhaps because the name was that of a forebear which needed to be given. All the others bore the names of their chief godparent, male or female, except for Robert, the youngest, who was called after the man who was to later to fill the comparable role of sponsoring him at his confirmation. Perhaps that man was not available for the christening.[42]

What was the impact on naming of the godparent's role? Names in large families of children were usually all different. To take a single example,

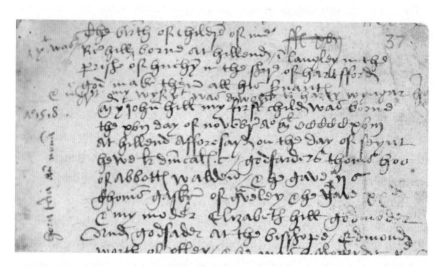

4. Richard Hill's notes of the births of his children. As well as recording the dates, he listed the godparents and sometimes the gifts they gave at the christenings.

14

Sir John Kingsmill of Kingsclere in Hampshire, who died in 1558, and his wife Constance, had seventeen children. The boys were named William, Richard, Roger, Edward, Henry, George, John, Andrew, Thomas, and Arthur; the girls were Constance, Jane, Alice, Anne, Katherine, Margaret, and Mary.[43] Either the parents chose a wide range of friends or dignitaries as their godparents, who gave their own names, or the parents suggested the name they would like in some cases. However there are also instances, although they are less common, when two siblings received the same name. In another big family, that of Richard Calthorp, esquire (d. 1562), of Antingham in Norfolk, and his wife Anne, two of the eleven sons were named John and two George.[44] The same feature is found among the children of John and Jane Alline of Wixford, Warwickshire (she died in 1587): two sons named John and two daughters named Annis (Agnes). There are numerous other examples.[45] One explanation could be that the second to be named followed the death of the first and that the parents wanted to preserve that name, perhaps because it belonged to an earlier relative or godparent. However, there are cases of siblings with similar names growing up to adulthood, notably John II and John III in the Norfolk family of the Pastons in the fifteenth century. So the doublets are equally likely to reflect the fact that one godparent gave the name twice, or that two people with the same forename were involved in doing so.

The majority of the names given to children in Tudor England were common ones.[46] They were used by families in all ranks of society. There seems to have been little concern by the nobility and gentry as a class of society to adopt special names to differentiate themselves from the populace, except for the traditions that have been noticed in certain families and the greater openness among some of the wealthy to using new names. Henry, John, Robert, Thomas, and William were widely given to boys of all social ranks, as were Anne, Elizabeth, Jane or Joan, and Mary to girls. As with us, they were often abbreviated in everyday life to Jack or Jenkin for John, Dick for Richard, Moll for Mary, or Bessie for Elizabeth. These common names were not universal, and plenty of others were in use but in much smaller numbers. Moreover unusual names in gentry families could also be matched lower down in society. In Devon, for example, the names of two local female saints are found among

15

girls: Sidwell and Urith. In Cornwall other saintly names were used. Boys occur called Gerens, the patron saint of Gerrans, Madern of Madron, Perran of Perranzabuloe, and Petroc of Padstow. In the case of girls there are Dilecta, the saint of Landulph, and Minefred of St Minver.[47]

During the sixteenth century the traditional names retained their popularity but there were changes in that of the less common ones. Some new arrivals reflected the rebirth of interest in the classical world and its literature, which began in schools in the 1480s.[48] Camden noticed a revival of classical names especially for girls, such as Diana and Cassandra; one might add Atalanta, Cynthia, Penelope, and Phoebe, usually in the higher ranks of society.[49] A greater influence was that of the Reformation. Its leaders disliked the veneration of anyone other than God: Father, Son, and Holy Spirit. In 1536 churches were forbidden to hold festivals of their patron saints unless these were commonly venerated, and in 1549 the number of saints' festivals in general was cut down to those of the New Testament. As time went on, church dedications ceased to be remembered, at least in the countryside, and some of the local saintly names gradually ceased to be used.

In their place a larger number of biblical names came into fashion. Early examples of this occur in the families of two merchant brothers: John and Otwell Johnson. John's children included Rachel (born 1544), while Otwell called his Israel (born 1547) and Abigail (1548).[50] Other cases from about 1550 were those of Samuel, son of Robert Ferrar, bishop of St David's, and Joseph, son of Simon Heynes, dean of Exeter Cathedral.[51] Camden mentions Barnabas, Daniel, Jacob, Josiah, Malachy, and Zachary for boys, and Abigail, Judith, Sarah, and Susanna for girls.[52] But even biblical names did not satisfy some evangelical Christians: those who came to be known as Puritans. They adopted the names of virtues. Here John Johnson was again a pioneer with Charity (c. 1542), Faith (1548), and his first son Evangelist (1550).[53] Camden refers to Temperance for women, and Prudence occurs as well. Others were to follow in the seventeenth century. More bizarrely Puritans, especially of the middle orders of society, gave even stranger names to boys and girls. Camden's examples include Free Gift, Reformation, More Fruit, Tribulation, Joy Again, and From Above.[54] These aroused amusement among other people, and Ben Jonson satirised them in his Puritan characters:

Tribulation in his play *The Alchemist* (1610) and Zeal of the Land in that of *Bartholomew Fair* (1614).

Finally there was a genealogical influence, reflecting the deep interest in family history and traditions among the wealthier classes. This led to surnames being given as forenames, so that the recipient would become a memorial and representative of a family other than that of his surname. The device of hyphenating two surnames had not yet come into vogue. One of the earliest examples of the practice is Guildford Dudley (*c.* 1535–54), son of Robert Dudley, duke of Northumberland, and later the ill-fated husband of Lady Jane Grey. He was named after his mother's family. Most of those so named were boys, but not invariably: Radcliff Gerard (died 1601), of a Lancashire family, was given her mother's maiden surname.[55] Camden observed that the practice was not found elsewhere in the Christian world and that 'many dislike it'. However, he felt, 'it seemeth to proceed from hearty goodwill and affection of the godfathers to show their love, or from a desire to continue and propagate their names to succeeding ages'. This suggests that godparents were often responsible for it, giving their surname rather than forename at baptism. 'We now have', he concluded with a touch of irony, 'Pickering Wotton, Grevill Varney, Bassingburne Gawdy, Culthorp Parker, Peesell Braces, Fitzralph Chamberlaine, who are the heirs of Pickering, Grevill, Bassingburn', and so on.[56]

BABY-CARE

Rösslin's book provided advice about the care of babies after birth. He recommended that a mother should breast-feed her child because it had bonded with her in the womb. Feeds should take place two or three times a day. If a mother could not do so, a 'wet nurse' should be chosen from a woman of good physique who had given birth to a male child at least two months before, but not too many more.[57] Maternal breastfeeding was recommended by educational writers too: by Juan Luis Vives, the Spanish scholar influential in England, in 1529, and Sir Thomas Elyot in the following year.[58] In 1553 Thomas Cranmer tried to make the practice official in a new code of Church law submitted to Parliament. Pronouncing it to be the natural order

17

of things, he criticised those women who deputed it to others through 'a kind of lax indulgence towards their own bodies'. The code was never sanctioned, however, so that the practice remained unregulated.[59]

Women normally did so themselves with the exception of those in the wealthier ranks of society: the royal family, the nobility and gentry, the wealthy of the towns, and the professions. Pierre Erondelle, a leading teacher of French in London, when describing a nursery scene in his book, *The French Garden*, in 1605, assumed that the affluent mothers of his pupils would employ a wet nurse.[60] The practice of doing so is confirmed by the many noblewomen and gentlewomen who had large numbers of children, like the Aldriches, Cobhams, and Corytons mentioned in the next chapter. Breastfeeding delays the return of fertility and would have produced smaller families. Elizabeth Clinton, dowager countess of Lincoln, whose own childbearing took place in the 1590s, wrote a short work called *The Countess of Lincoln's Nursery*, published in 1622.[61] She identified wet nurses as the usage 'of the higher and the richer sort than of the meaner and poorer'. The specious reasons for not breastfeeding oneself, she thought, were that it was 'troublesome', 'noisome to one's clothes', 'makes one look old', endangered the health of those who were weak, and gave social cachet to 'nice and proud idle dames who will imitate their betters', presumably from the middle orders of society. Against this she argued that God intended women to do so, as demonstrated by Eve, Sarah, Hannah, and Mary in the Bible (Fig. 5, p. 19). It was comforting to a mother emotionally, and helped her to bond more closely with her child.

The countess admitted that she had borne sixteen children without nursing them herself. That was because she had been both advised and commanded not to do so, the latter presumably by her husband. She herself regretted her failure to nurse. She felt that she might have lost one or two children through poor nursing, and believed that only two of the many nurses she had employed were thoroughly willing and careful. She dedicated her book to her daughter-in-law, Bridget, the next countess, who broke from tradition and embraced breastfeeding. There was certainly a male prejudice against doing so at the higher social levels, for which we can imagine several reasons. It went against social convention, was thought

5. The Virgin Mary breastfeeding Jesus herself. In practice, many wealthy mothers deputed the task to a wet nurse.

to age the wife, and delayed her next pregnancy. In some citizen families, not doing so gave the wife more time to supervise household or business tasks.[62]

When Anne Newdigate, daughter of one knight and married to another, decided to nurse her own child in 1598, her husband did not prevent her but she received discouragement from other people. Her father wrote: 'I am sorry that you yourself will nurse her.' A family friend, chosen as godfather, said that he would not have liked his own wife to do so. It would be a trouble, and she would regret it if the child died through her own nursing. She persisted nonetheless and nourished all five of her children, yet even in 1603 another male friend reproached her, arguing that it kept her from the company of other people and would age her. However, she cannot have been alone in her determination because in 1605, when James I's queen was pregnant, several gentlewomen including herself were suggested as wet nurses for the child. Presumably a woman of lower status was not thought proper.[63]

Except in the royal family and among some of the high aristocracy, the wet nurse did not move into the baby's house. Instead the infant was sent to live with her and her family. It was the custom in London, and perhaps other towns, to choose a nurse in the countryside which was deemed to be healthier and less subject to epidemics. This was done even for the poor foundling babies rescued by the charitable institution of Christ's Hospital in the capital.[64] Parents who lived outside towns could find nurses closer at hand. Dr John Dee, the Elizabethan mathematician and astrologer, belonged to the ranks of people who employed wet nurses, and mentions several of them in his diary in the 1570s and 1580s. Based rurally at Mortlake in Surrey, his babies were sent shorter distances to Barnes and Petersham. In at least one of these periods, Dee's wife made monthly visits to see the nurse and pay her. The usual fee in Dee's case was 6s. a month, plus money for soap and candles.[65]

When a wet nurse was employed, Rösslin advised that care should be taken about her diet. This, he advised, should include fresh cheese, milk, bean soup, and fine bread: items again appropriate to a household of high rank.[66] The medieval physician Avicenna had recommended breastfeeding for two years, but Rösslin's book observed that 'among us' a single year was common. Dee recorded the dates at which some of his children began to be weaned: Arthur after thirteen months, Katherine after fourteen, and Margaret after only just over seven.[67] A year seems to have been usual among the general population, and two years in many cases.[68] Weaning, said Rösslin, should be done gradually, beginning with little pills of bread and sugar.[69] 'Pap' was a common kind of early infant food: bread or meal mixed with water or milk, and often heated.[70] Plenty of cows' milk during childhood was reckoned to make boys especially grow taller.[71] No doubt other foods were served mashed up. The thirteenth-century encyclopaedia of Bartholomew Glanville, still read in Tudor England, observed that nurses did this by chewing the food themselves.[72]

A wealthy household might have a special staff or room called the 'nursery'. The royal family made the largest provision in this respect. Its nursery stayed in royal manors, independently of the royal court but sometimes moving about, with a lady of status in charge. Prince Arthur's was directed by Lady Elizabeth Darcy, who had looked after the children of Edward IV; those of Elizabeth I and Edward VI by Lady Margaret Bryan. As well as the wet nurse employed for breastfeeding, there would be a 'dry nurse' responsible for general nursing, with two or more women assistants called 'rockers' because their duties included rocking the cradle.[73] The earl of Northumberland in 1512 employed a nurse and two rockers, with a 'child' or boy to do general tasks.[74] His nursery, and doubtless that of other great families, was given special dietary arrangements for the benefit of the nurse and young children.[75]

The furniture in a wealthy family's nursery centred on a cradle. Illustrations show this to have been a wooden structure resting on curved runners at the head and the foot, so that it could be rocked from side to side (Fig. 6, p. 22). There might be a lacing arrangement above the baby, to keep it secure. An account of the contents of a nursery room survives from the house of a gentleman, Sir William More of Loseley, Surrey, in 1556. It had a fireplace for warmth and contained a bedstead and bedclothes, presumably for the nurse and perhaps also for children of a few years old. Other equipment consisted of a cradle and pillow, a cupboard, two chests, a wicker hamper, and two small close-stools or potties for children. The room was decorated with a blue hanging cloth and a curtain of red and yellow.[76]

The layette for a baby could be extensive, which does not mean, of course, that this was the case outside wealthy households. No doubt among the population as a whole recourse was had to what was available, had been handed down, or could be borrowed. In *The Gentle Craft*, written in the late 1590s, the novelist Thomas Deloney sketched out the costs of having a baby, evidently with a well-to-do family in mind. They began with 16*d.* a week, presumably the cost of a wet nurse, together with soap and candles (as in Dee's arrangements). A long list of other items followed: 'beds, shirts, biggins [caps], waistcoats, head-bands, swaddle-bands, cross-clothes, bibs, tail-clouts, mantles, hose, shoes, coats, petticoats, cradle and crickets [small stools], and beside that a standing-stool [walking frame] and a posnet [metal pot on feet] to make the child pap'. Some of these items, however, looked forward to the baby becoming a toddler.[77]

The basic clothing for a baby consisted of a shirt of a simple T-shape with an open front, while a clout or tail-clout, meaning a nappy, was wrapped or tucked around the child's hips.[78] A larger cloth might be folded over the shirt

21

deus salutis mee cvexultabit lingua
mea iusticiam tua

omine labia mea aperies et
os meum annunciabit laude tuam

uonia si voluisses sacrificiu
dedissem vtiqs holocaustis non de
lectaberis.

acrificium deo spiritus con
tribulatus cor contritum & humi
liatum deus non despicies.

enigne fac domine in bona
voluntate tua syon vt edificentur
muri iherusalem

unc acceptabis sacrificium
iusticie oblationes et olocausta tua
imponent super altare tuum vi
tulos.

equiem eternam. añ. Exulta
bunt domino ossa humiliata. añ. Ex
audi deus. Psalmus

E decet hymnus deus in sy

6. A baby in a cradle. The mother or a nurse warms food by the fire while
other children play.

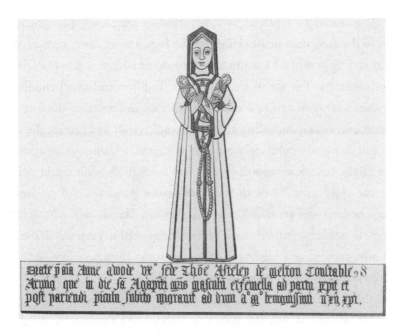

7. Swaddling, showing the characteristic criss-crossed bands used to hold
the baby clothes together, from the memorial brass of Anne Asteley (1512),
who died in childbirth with her twin babies.

and clout, and then all the underclothes were secured by swaddling bands, at
least in families other than the poorest. Swaddling bands were narrow strips
of cloth, wound round the baby in a criss-cross pattern (Fig. 7, above).
Rösslin advised that swaddling should be done tenderly and not crookedly,
so as to help shape the child. Bad swaddling might lead to deformities. The
child's arms should be laid at its sides for this purpose, and included in the
swaddling.[79] It was a common enough practice for illustrations of babies in
this period usually to portray them wrapped up in the criss-crossed bands.
The baby's head would be covered with a cross-cloth or headband, and a
biggin or baby's cap on top of it.

The clothes thus mentioned were sufficient if the baby was in a cradle
under bedclothes; if it was taken out, an outer coat such as a mantle would
be used to keep it warm. Swaddling was gradually modified after about three
months as the baby became more mobile. Once it was able to crawl, the

swaddling would be replaced by a petticoat or long undergarment going down to the feet, hose or stockings on the legs, and an outer coat or kirtle usually ending in skirts. Viscountess Lisle ordered a kirtle and bonnet for her granddaughter at the age of five months.[80] Toddlers and small children of both sexes were customarily dressed in petticoats and coats for the first years of life. A bib, usually including an apron, would cover and protect the outer coat, and drawers would replace clouts once toilet training was achieved. Coats might have leading-strings attached so that an adult could help to guide the child as it learnt to walk, while the standing-stool (at least in affluent houses) was another aid in this process. The women who acted as 'rockers' in noble households were probably expected to keep watch over the child as it crawled and learnt to climb and walk. In poorer families, older children must have been deputed to help in this way.

Further information about baby-care is forthcoming from Rösslin's book. He prescribed that the baby's eyes should be frequently wiped and cleaned with a cloth of fine linen or silk. The body should be washed two or three times a day in a bath, after waking from sleep. In winter warm water should be used, in summer lukewarm. Water should not be allowed to get into the ears. When the baby was taken out of the bath, it should be wiped and dried with a warm soft linen cloth, then laid on its front and stroked with the hands, then swaddled and laid to rest in its cradle. Its head should lie somewhat higher than the body. The cradle should be put in a dark place so that sunbeams or moonlight did not shine on the baby's face.[81]

Erondelle's book gives another description of the kind of care to be expected in the nursery of a wealthy mother. She is imagined coming to supervise the wet nurse in waking up her young son in the morning. The baby lies in a cradle with a pillow, pillow-case, and coverlet. The nurse should take him out, undo his swaddling bands, and wash him carefully all over. His nails should be pared when necessary. The mother is worried that his thumb and little finger are flea-bitten. Are there any fleas in the room? How many teeth does he have?[82] When a little older, the swaddling bands are discontinued and he seems to wear a shirt, a petticoat, and a coat of taffeta with satin sleeves, protected by a bib and an apron on which a handkerchief is hung. He has a biggin on his head and a (piece of) coral to bite against when he is teething. This is fastened to his clothes in some way with a small gold chain.[83]

Three paintings of infants from Elizabeth's reign give further help to understanding baby or toddler clothing, albeit among the aristocracy.[84] All are formal posed portraits and therefore do not reproduce how the children might have looked in everyday situations. The earliest, the small son of Lady Katherine Seymour, painted in about 1562, is shown with his mother. He wears a linen under-cap, a cap with a feather over it, a sleeveless coat ending in skirts, detachable sleeves, and a long bib-apron under the coat, the coat perhaps being on top because of the formality of the occasion. Two years later a son of Sir John Thynne of Longleat House, aged six months but shown standing up, is dressed in a hat, a sleeveless coat with a collar, and separate sleeves. His status is indicated by a double chain around his neck, supporting a pectoral cross. In his hand he holds a rattle including small bells and a coral (to assist teething), all fastened to him with a light chain. A third undated picture of one of Thynne's daughters, aged twenty months, depicts her in a cap and a bib-apron over what is probably another sleeveless coat with detachable sleeves. Again her rank is indicated by a chain, a pectoral cross, and a similar rattle and coral.

Poorer families might care just as much for their children but had far fewer resources to maintain them. The cradle may have been a basket hanging from a beam, or merely a box. There was a temptation in poor crowded homes to put a baby into a bed with adults, in which case it ran the risk of injury or death by overlaying. The Church had warned about this for centuries, and the role of a godparent including ensuring that the parents kept the child safe until it was able to look after itself. In one church during the fifteenth century they were told not to allow a child to sleep with adults until it was old enough to say '*Ligge outer*', in other words 'Lie further off'.[85] Nevertheless overlaying sometimes happened, and it could bring the adults concerned into a Church court for admonishment.[86]

The worst plight for a parent was that of a single woman, made pregnant without the support of a spouse or family. This was especially an issue in London with its large population of female servants and migrants. The

Commissary Court of the bishop of London, which dealt with cases of illegitimate pregnancies and births, recorded forty-four cases in 1471, twenty-
four in 1481, and forty-nine in 1490.[87] By this period at least three London
hospitals offered to give help to expectant mothers for short periods.[88]
St Bartholomew's took them in and allowed them to stay with their babies for
forty days after birth. It also observed confidentiality. St Thomas's provided
eight beds for them, endowed by Richard Whittington with a similar promise
of secrecy, although there was a complaint in 1535 that the hospital favoured
the servants and mistresses of rich men rather than the poor. A third institution, St Mary without Bishopsgate, had a parallel ministry, at least in earlier
times. These remedies fell short of providing a long-term solution for poor
single mothers, however, causing some (and even poor parents without
resources) to abandon their offspring. This did not necessarily imply lack of
care or a wish for a child to perish. Favourite places to leave a baby included
churches and rich people's doors, with the assumption that help would be
forthcoming there. Some foundlings were left with a small amount of salt, to
indicate that they had not been baptised, so that this could be done.[89]

During the sixteenth century some progress was made towards dealing
with this problem in London. In 1552 Christ's Hospital was founded in the
former Franciscan friary, and placed under the control of the city authorities.
It provided long-term care for over 400 children in need, both girls and boys.
Infants and small children were boarded out with nurses and foster-carers.
Older children from about the age of six were maintained in the hospital
itself, where they received some education or practical instruction. In their
early teens apprenticeships were found for them, or places in domestic
service.[90] An analysis of the hospital's admissions by Valerie Fildes indicates
that between 1552 and 1599, 312 of the children whom it took in had
been abandoned, ranging in age from two days old to nine years, of whom
266 were aged from birth to two.[91] More of these can be identified as boys
(52 per cent) than girls (48 per cent), partly but not wholly reflecting the
greater number of boys being born.[92]

Even so this help was not sufficient to solve the problem of foundlings
in the capital. Fildes's study of eight city parishes in the 1590s has recovered
statistics of babies who were baptised, having been abandoned. While

this was a small proportion, with a mean of just under 1 per cent of baptisms per annum, it would amount to several hundred if all the parishes in London were considered, not counting those who were thrust onto the world in later stages of their childhoods.[93] The burden of responsibility for maintaining foundlings was laid on the parish authorities during the mid- and later sixteenth century, as we shall see in the following chapter. On discovering an abandoned child, their officers had to try to identify the mother and father, and if they were resident in another parish, to transfer the duty there. Otherwise the officers were bound to arrange for babies to be nursed and pay the costs of this, as well as the boarding out and maintenance of older children until they were of age to work.[94]

SURVIVAL OR DEATH?

Not all those born would survive. There was a high mortality among children through infections aggravated, in much of the population, by poor food and poor housing. It has been estimated that, towards the end of the sixteenth century, about 17 per cent of babies died in the first year of life, the deaths of boys slightly exceeding that of girls. In the age group between one and four mortality fell by about half to around 9 per cent, with a further falls in percentages between five and nine and again between ten and fifteen. Altogether, the number of deaths between birth and fifteen around 1600 has been reckoned at about 30 per cent of births.[95] This is a very high figure by modern standards, but compared with mortality in England across a wide period from 1600 to 1800, it was less than would become the case in the late seventeenth and early eighteenth centuries. Survival was not necessarily worse the further back in time that we can trace it. Children made up a significant proportion of the population even in Tudor England: up to a third if we count them up to their mid-teens.[96]

Richard Hill and his wife Margaret had seven children between 1518 and 1526: five boys and two girls. When Richard recorded their births in his commonplace book, he wrote down the dates on which they were born and in most cases where this took place and at what time of day, perhaps in view of its astrological significance. There were many superstitions relating to the disposition of the planets at the time of a birth, conferring anything from wealth and happiness to blindness, deafness, death in prison, and hanging by a rope (Fig. 16, p. 61).[97] Richard also listed his children's godparents, what each godparent gave as a present, and who acted as their sponsors when they went to the bishop for confirmation. The children were born at intervals of a year to a year and a half. Despite the fact that the parents were prosperous, but perhaps because of infection or pollution due to living in London, Simon died after about a year, Robert when a little older, and Elizabeth at the age of seven and a half. The entries for Thomas and William have also been struck through, for whatever reason. Wealth and comfort were no secure bars to the coming of death to the young.[98]

Plenty of other records tell a similar story, even in families of status. Some monumental brasses on gravestones in churches list not only the number of a father's children but the total of those who were alive at his death. Thomas Burrough, a yeoman of Eastwood, Essex, who died in 1600 at the age of forty-five, had ten children but only six were living at the time that he died.[99] Alexander Bence, a leading inhabitant of Aldeburgh, Suffolk, aged sixty-five at his death in 1612, had nine sons and two daughters, but only four of the sons had survived by that date, along with both the daughters.[100] The royal family itself was not exempt; indeed its losses were even more considerable. Four Tudor queens gave birth to children. Elizabeth of York may have had as many as eleven pregnancies over the seventeen years from 1486 to 1503. But only five of her children lived for more than a few days, of whom Edmund survived for less than a year and half. Four alone reached adolescence or adulthood: Arthur, Margaret, Henry VIII, and Mary.[101] Henry VIII's first wife, Katherine of Aragon, gave birth about five times, but in all cases save one the infants were stillborn or soon died. Only Queen Mary I grew up to maturity.[102] Henry's next, Anne Boleyn, bore only Elizabeth I, and had two miscarriages.[103] His third, Jane Seymour, had one child, Edward VI, and died herself twelve days later: like Elizabeth of York, probably of an infection contracted during the birth.[104]

It was once supposed that the high proportion of deaths in childhood would have made parents less concerned about their children and possibly less loving and empathic. There were indeed cases of newly born children being killed. These were chiefly associated with unmarried mothers, such as female servants. When such women became unintentionally pregnant, they faced frightening consequences: loss of employment, social disapproval, and little likelihood of future marriage, not to mention the bringing up of a child without the support of a partner and family. A pregnancy in this situation might be concealed and methods of abortion be resorted to, but if the process ended in birth, this was likely to take place alone or secretly and the baby be smothered or drowned, sometimes with the assistance of a family member or well-wisher.[105] Church teaching, public opinion, and the law all worked to make such actions unusual. Traditionally infanticide was treated as murder and as a capital offence. This was endorsed by a statute of 1624 which confirmed that any woman accused of destroying a child should incur such a penalty. The statute, however, conceded that at least one witness could be brought to affirm that the child was dead at its birth, which opened a potential loophole for the defendant.[106]

But these cases were exceptions. Children's deaths were taken seriously. Any death by misadventure was investigated by a coroner's inquest.[107] Every baptised child was given a funeral in church and a burial in a churchyard or (for those of high status) in church. Wealthy parents, as we shall see, put up memorials to children, even to ones who died while in swaddling clothes (Fig. 8, p. 30).[108] School exercises from Oxford in the 1490s give two glimpses of family emotions. In one, a schoolboy tells how, 'When I came home to my father and my mother, we wept for joy, each to other, and no marvel, for the beholding of the child comforts the old fathers and mothers as much as the pleasant words of the physician comforts the sick body.' In the other, the boy speaks of the death of his sibling. 'A great while after my brother died, my mother was wont to sit weeping every day. I trow [think] that there is nobody which would not be sorry if he had seen her weeping.'[109] When John Shorlond of Woodbridge, Suffolk, died in 1601, at the age of seven, his family placed a monumental brass over his grave with his effigy and an inscription praising him as one 'whom men did love for grace and wit' (Fig. 33, p. 121).[110]

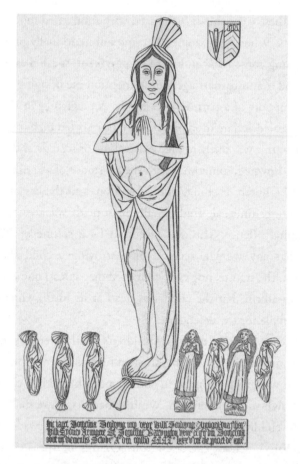

8. Another memorial brass of a mother who did not survive giving
birth: Thomasine Tendring (1485).

We shall encounter other examples of adults worrying about sick
children or sorrowing for dead ones.[111] Parents in Tudor England often had
different ideas about children's development and discipline from those of
today. But there is no reason to think that most of them lacked love for their
children or failed to grieve at illness or at death.

2

---◇---

THE HOME

FAMILIES

Into what kind of family was a child born in Tudor England? It varied greatly, of course, depending on rank and wealth (Fig. 9, p. 32). Marriages were permissible from the age of puberty, calculated as twelve for girls, fourteen for boys.[1] That made it possible for a baby to have young parents in their teens. But marriages like these were rare and restricted to wealthy families, who married off their children in order to acquire property. Even then, such families might wait to arrange their offspring's marriages until a couple of years after puberty. In the gentry family of the Temples of Stowe in Buckinghamshire, girls were typically married at fifteen, although two were younger.[2] Among the whole population, marriages took place much later.

In 1538 Henry VIII, the new head of the Church of England, and his minister Thomas Cromwell, ordered all parish clergy to keep a register of births, marriages, and deaths.[3] Not many registers now exist from so early a date and even later ones are often poorly kept, but there are enough with sufficient accuracy by the late sixteenth century to compile statistics about the size of families and the ages of their members. These show that most people at that time remained single until their twenties. The mean age of first marriage in England around 1600 was about twenty-eight for men and twenty-five for women.[4] This meant that most children, as they grew up, had parents in their thirties and forties. The expectation of life at the age of thirty was just over another thirty years for a woman and just under thirty for a man.[5] That usually gave enough time to bring up children to adulthood, but a child's life would not necessarily overlap with those of its parents for much more than thirty

31

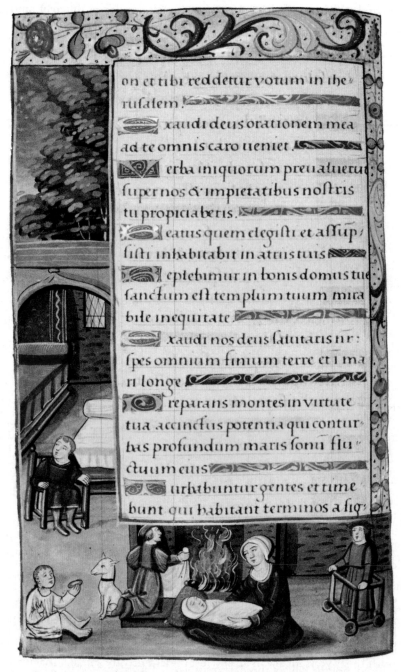

on et tibi reddetur votum in ihe
rusalem.
  xaudi deus orationem mea
ad te omnis caro ueniet.
  erba iniquorum preualuerut
super nos & impietatibus nostris
tu propiciaberis.
  eatus quem elegisti et assup/
sisti inhabitabit in atriis tuis
  eplebimur in bonis domus tue
sanctum est templum tuum mira
bile inequitate.
  xaudi nos deus salutaris nr:
spes omnium finium terre et i ma
ri longe
  reparans montes in virtute
tua accinctus potentia qui contur
bas profundum maris sonu flu
ctuum eius
  urbabuntur gentes et time
bunt qui habitant terminos a siq

9. A nursery. The nurse holds a swaddled baby while clothes are warmed at a fire. A toddler (right) is in a walking frame while an older boy (left) sits in a child's chair.

years, and with any grandparents for very much less. It was different among the wealthy where men and women married earlier. In their case grandparent-ship could begin much earlier, in middle age. John Greene of Shelley in Essex, who died in 1595 at the age of eighty-nine, and his wife Katherine who lived to be seventy-one, had thirteen children and 111 descendants by the time of his death.[6] John Fosbroke of Cranford St Andrew, Northamptonshire, who died in 1602 aged about eighty, had twenty-four children by two wives, and over seventy grandchildren, or so his tomb boasted. In these families even grandparents had ample time to see their descendants grow up.[7]

Most children would also have siblings. The usual age of women at marriage meant that they had about fifteen years to bear offspring, forty being as late as was normal to do so. Breastfeeding slowed down conceptions to an interval of about thirty months, so that each mother could give birth to a maximum of six or seven children at most.[8] Deaths in childhood, as we have seen, might reduce this number to nearer four. Again, the wealthy were an exception. Younger marriages and greater fertility, due to the use of wet nurses, enabled more children to be born at shorter intervals. The monu-mental brasses on the tombs of gentry and merchants often show small images of each of their children, and these suggest that totals of half a dozen or so were quite common. Even larger families are recorded, although they were not typical of the whole population. John Brooke, Lord Cobham (d. 1512), had eight sons and ten daughters with his wife Margaret. In the next generation his son Thomas (d. 1529) had seven and six, and in the third George (d. 1558) had ten and four.[9] The most numerous to be shown on brasses include the families of William and Agnes Aldrich of Burnham, Buckinghamshire, and Peter and Jane Coryton of St Mellion, Cornwall. The Aldriches produced nine sons and fifteen daughters, the Corytons seventeen and seven respectively.[10] One superstition linked with large families was that a seventh son had the same ability as the monarch to cure scrofula, the 'king's evil', by touching the afflicted part.[11] The evidence of brasses, however, is misleading in one respect. They usually show all the children that the marriage produced, not the tally of those who survived. The infant who died is equated with those who grew up. Nevertheless Thomas and Hester, the Temples of Stowe, had at least fifteen children, of whom thirteen survived.[12]

10. A Tudor family: John Corbet, his wife, four sons, and six daughters at
Sprowston, Norfolk (1559).

The depiction of families on brasses conveyed a message about them
(Figs 10, above; 60, p. 225). The father was shown to be potent and the mother
fertile. They and their children were clothed appropriately for their rank, and
the children were well cared for. The larger size of the parents proclaimed their
authority, while the smaller size of the children and their placement in a subordinate position expressed their deference. Similar statements were made in
another newer medium: the commissioning of paintings to show adults with
their children, or the children alone. These had similar motives to the brasses
in displaying a family in an idealised way, but differed by recording a single
date in time rather than a range of dates. They thus anticipated photographs.
In one case a painting of William Brooke, Lord Cobham (d. 1597), his wife,
and six of their children made in 1567, now at Longleat House, was even
copied later on to include a seventh baby.[13] The earliest known English portrait
of a child comes from just before the Tudors in about 1480: that of Sir John
Donne, his wife, and their young daughter Anne, painted by Hans Memling
while Donne was in the Netherlands.[14] Individual pictures of the teenage

11. Lord Cobham, his wife, his sister, and his family of three boys and three girls (1567). Their rank is indicated by their clothes, the grapes on the table, and the pet parrot.

children of Henry VII: Arthur, Margaret, Henry VIII, and Mary, survive from round about 1500 or later. Single portraits of aristocratic children were being commissioned by the reign of Elizabeth I, as we have seen, as well as family groups depicting parents too.[15] The six children in the first Cobham portrait include a boy aged six, twin girls of five, their sister of four, and two small boys of two and one (Fig. 11, above). All sit at a table, each in front of a plate, with their parents standing behind them. The table is plentifully supplied with fruit including grapes: a sign of affluence.[16] Two years later, a group of the family of Edward Lord Windsor features four boys, aged eight, six, three, and two (Fig. 22, p. 82). All have ribbons around their necks holding medals. The two eldest are playing chess, and the two youngest hold playing cards.[17] Here again, the lifestyle is clearly that of the nobility.

Two similar paintings of a high standard were executed by the Dutch artist Marcus Gheeraerts the Younger, who visited England in the 1590s.

Lady Anne Pope, in 1596, is shown in pregnancy with the offspring of her first marriage: an older boy with a sword, a younger girl, and an even younger second boy still in the skirts of an infant (Fig. 14, p. 43).[18] In the same year Gheeraerts depicted Barbara, countess of Leicester, standing alone behind six children: an eldest girl, a boy holding his hat and wearing a sword in a belt, three younger girls, and a baby boy.[19] Not all families had so many children to display or wished to do so. The National Portrait Gallery contains the likeness of Sir Walter Ralegh in about 1602, with his only son at that date: Walter, aged eight, again with a sword (Fig. 12, p. 37).[20] The image of deference of children to parents, however, is apparent in each of the last three pictures. Not only are they all shown obediently sitting or standing to attention, but the eldest boy in every case is bare-headed, observing the correct behaviour of a child or adolescent in the presence of their parents and seniors.

THE DISADVANTAGED

As pictures of families imply, there was an expectation that parents would look after their children in terms of housing, clothing, and feeding them according to their rank. They should be brought up to behave appropriately, learn the skills needed for adult life, and gain knowledge of the Christian faith and its duties. Alexander Barclay wrote a charming description of the biblical Eve in the 1510s as a housewife of his day, with her babies and children around her. She hugs and kisses them, delouses and combs them, and puts butter on their necks to soothe dry skin.[21] Poverty and fecklessness did not always achieve this. People in Tudor England were concerned about adults who became beggars, and with the children they might have. Beggars had been a problem since medieval times, and they had long been seen as falling into two groups: the deserving and undeserving. In the first category came the very young, orphans, the sick, wounded soldiers, the infirm, prisoners, and the elderly; in the second, those who were able-bodied but preferred to be idle or beg. The former were to be helped, the latter to be made to work.[22]

Help for the deserving, up to the Reformation, depended on a strongly held ethic of charity rather than on a developed system. Great households were

12. Sir Walter Ralegh and his son Walter (1602). At that time Walter was
Ralegh's only child.

expected to give surplus food to the poor. The royal household had an almoner
with a small staff in charge of doing so.[23] Its lead was followed in others. Anne
Boleyn is recorded instructing her almoners to give to needy poor people
including pregnant women and 'impotent householders overcharged with children'. She is said to have told her ladies-in-waiting to make shirts, smocks, and
sheets to give to the poor.[24] A ballad on the death of Henry Hastings, earl of
Huntingdon, in 1595 praised his charity to widows and fatherless infants, and
thought that a thousand poor children would requite the fact with prayers.[25]
Monasteries, which were also great households, had an ancient custom of

providing alms of food to the neighbouring poor: sometimes daily, sometimes every few days.[26] Ordinary people were constantly urged by clergy and writers to be generous with food or money. The private accounts of Sir Henry Willoughby of Middleton in Warwickshire, list the odd pence that he gave in alms while at home or in travelling the country during the 1520s, as do those of William Cavendish of Hardwick in Derbyshire around 1600.[27]

The problem of poverty may have been, or have seemed, worse after the Reformation. That event involved the closure of the monasteries as well as the chantries and some hospitals, many of which had offered charity in small individual ways. Accordingly the authorities in Tudor England came to realise the need to set up a national system of poor relief, including the support of needy children. In 1549 voluntary collections of money for the poor were introduced into the Sunday morning services in all parish churches.[28] In 1563 a statute of Parliament confirmed the church collections and ordered two able persons in each parish to administer the money and dispense it to the poor.[29] Another statute in 1572 allowed 'honest men' to take beggars' children into service from the age of five upwards, subject to the approval of the local justices of the peace. Such children could be bound to their service until the age of eighteen if women, or twenty-four if men.[30] Four years later further legislation tried to deal with the issue of children born out of wedlock who might have no secure and settled home. It complained that they were often left to be a charge on a parish where they were living. Accordingly two justices of the peace were authorised to punish the mother and the reputed father, and to provide for the child to be maintained (by implication in a normal family) at its parents' expense. If they defaulted, they could be imprisoned.

A final Tudor statute in 1601 established the churchwardens and four substantial householders of each parish as 'Overseers of the Poor'. They were empowered to set to work the children of those parents who were not thought able to provide for them, in effect from the age of seven.[31] This completed the creation of a system to maintain poor children. Those under seven, who were assumed to be with their mother but had no settled residence, were to be sent to where the father was, or had last been, or had been born. If the husband was dead, the mother must go to her own place of birth or last dwelling. If children were abandoned by their parents, they must stay in the place that they were.

Wherever they ended up, the children would receive relief within the parish, but from at least the age of seven they would be expected to work in some way.[32]

We can follow the arrangements made for needy children in the annual accounts of parochial churchwardens. At Ashburton in Devon, for example, a poor man named John Barrett died in 1575–6 together, it seems, with his wife. This left two orphans, a boy and a girl. Clothes and shoes were bought for them, and the boy at least was boarded out in the parish for 7d. a week, at the wardens' expense. By 1577–8 there were three children 'on the parish': the Barrett boy, another boy curtly described as 'the bastard', and Honor Yolland, a girl. The second boy was boarded for 8d. a week (perhaps he was older than Barrett) and Honor for 6d. All were provided with basic clothes or the materials for having their clothes made for them. Subsequently the parish paid 5s. for a local woman to take Honor into service, but this seems to have miscarried because she was later maintained by the parish again.[33] There is a complete account of the costs paid by St Peter's parish, Hertfordshire, for a lad called John Mylward, probably a teenager, who was sent there from Hatfield in 1573. He was boarded for 1s. a week, provided with clothes (cap, jerkin, doublet, slops [breeches], stockings, and shoes), and indentured as an apprentice.[34] Such children were not necessarily neglected, but the accounts tell us nothing of the difficulties and sorrows they experienced in their childhoods.

A further group of the deprived were the illegitimate. This was not a large section of the population. It has been estimated at a little under 4 per cent of births at the end of the sixteenth century, but those involved often faced social disapproval as in the case of the 'bastard' above.[35] In at least one influential institution (the royal household), preference was given to recruiting young men of 'clean' meaning 'legitimate' birth.[36] As far as the Church was concerned, those born outside marriage were normal human souls entitled, indeed obliged, to be baptised and to grow up as normal Church members. They suffered only one religious disability, and that one only until the Reformation in 1550, in being barred from ordination as clergy unless they obtained a special dispensation, which was not hard to acquire for a fee.[37] In terms of the secular law, they had standard rights but were not entitled to inherit parental property or status.[38]

As usual, more is known about illegitimacy in the wealthier classes.[39] Some fathers refused to acknowledge their responsibility, like Sir Henry Pierrepoint whose will of 1489 disowned Edmund 'that calls himself my bastard son'.[40] Others made provision for their children, usually in the form of annuities or gifts of money since transferring land was less easy. The sums of money involved, however, were typically modest ones unless the father had no legitimate heir.[41] Then he might do like Philip Furse, from a Devon family of minor gentry, who 'had no issue but a base son to whom he [left] . . . all his lands and goods'.[42] Cardinal Wolsey fathered two illegitimate children, a boy and a girl, by the shadowy 'Mistress Lark'.[43] Thomas (who took the name Wynter) was given ecclesiastical preferment from his childhood, and was at various times a cathedral dean and an archdeacon. He survived his father's fall but his career petered out thereafter. Dorothy (surnamed Clansey) was less favoured. She was sent to be a nun at Shaftesbury Abbey.[44]

Those who did best were born into the highest social ranks, where fathers had enough wealth and influence to establish a boy in a career or arrange his marriage with a female ward. Girls could be paired with men of lesser status whose linkage to the father was worth having for both parties. A few such boys had spectacular careers. One was Thomas Poynings (c. 1512–45), son of a councillor of Henry VII without legitimate children, who took part in the capture of Boulogne in 1544 and was made a baron in the following year.[45] His success was surpassed by Thomas Egerton (1540–1617), son of a Cheshire knight, who rose to high office under Elizabeth I as a lawyer and diplomat, became lord chancellor in 1603, and ended his life as a viscount (Fig. 13, p. 41).[46]

Most favoured of all were members of the royal family. Charles Somerset (c. 1460–1526), from its Beaufort branch, was made a baron in 1504 and earl of Worcester ten years later.[47] Arthur Plantagenet, son of Edward IV (c. 1472–1542), was accepted as a nobleman by both Henry VII and Henry VIII. He became a knight of the garter and a viscount, although he spent some time in the Tower of London as the victim of court intrigues.[48] The greatest recognition was given to Henry VIII's illegitimate son, Henry, duke of Richmond and Somerset (1519–36), whom we shall meet in Chapter 5. He was sent as a boy to be the figurehead of the Crown in the north of

13. Sir Thomas Egerton (d. 1617), who rose despite his illegitimate birth to become lord chancellor and a viscount.

England and, until his early death, may have been viewed by the king as a possible heir to the throne (Fig. 39, p. 144).[49]

Shakespeare conveys something of the equivocal status of such people in his plays. Two of his villains were illegitimate: Don John in *Much Ado About Nothing* and Edmund in *King Lear*. On the other hand an heroic young man of this kind appears in *King John*: the Bastard of Faulconbridge, who is identified as the son of Richard Lionheart. He becomes the spokesman for the nation during the play and speaks the stirring lines with which it ends: 'This England never did, nor never shall, lie at the proud foot of a conqueror.'[50]

DAILY LIFE, CLOTHES, AND FOOD

Once children were a few years old, they began to live a daily routine approaching that of adults. It started earlier in the day than now, reflecting a world in which most human activity was regulated by daylight in view of the costs and limitations of night-time lighting. Children, like adults, rose at dawn or soon afterwards, as we shall see that they had to do while at school.[51] Breakfast took place after getting up, or a little later; midday dinner was at 11.00 a.m. or noon; and supper in the late afternoon. Bedtime came at or soon after nightfall, often involving more than one child in a bed. The boys of Christ's Hospital, London, slept in pairs, as did those of Winchester College until they were fifteen, when they each got a bed to themselves.[52] At Wells Cathedral the choristers were placed in threes, with two small boys facing one way and a larger boy the other way, between them.[53] Erasmus felt it worthwhile to tell those who shared their place of rest to lie still and not to pull the bedclothes.[54] Children could also share the bed or bedroom of an adult of the same sex. There is an example of a boy sleeping with his school-master, and another doing so with his uncle, a priest.[55] This was not regarded as dangerous in the way that it would be today.

Clothes for children could be made at home or ordered from tailors, who worked in villages as well as towns (Fig. 14, p. 43). As we have seen, toddlers after babyhood were dressed in long clothes including a petticoat and a skirted coat above it. These helped protect from falls and enabled cleaning until toilet training was established. At about the age of seven (the accepted end of infancy) or a year or two younger, gender differences began to affect clothing.[56] Boys were put into clothes more like those of men, a process that came to be known as 'breeching'.[57] A shirt and drawers were worn as under-clothes, a closer-fitting coat or doublet on the body, and breeches (often wide and known as 'slops') on the thighs. Shins and feet were covered with stock-ings, originally of linen but more often knitted as the sixteenth century progressed. Outdoor wear for wealthier boys included gowns in the early Tudor decades, and schoolboys are depicted wearing them. Later in the period gowns became less popular than cloaks, either short or long depending on the activity. Caps were worn on heads and removed as a polite gesture.

14. Anne Lady Pope and her children (1596), by Marcus Gheeraerts
the Younger.

Girls, in contrast, stayed in longer clothes. They too wore shirts, often
known as smocks, drawers, petticoats, and stockings. A kirtle or long garment
was placed over these. During the Tudor era, the upper half of the kirtle
became a closer-fitting bodice, and the lower half a skirt. Above the kirtle,
for warmth or formality, a gown would be put on, usually sleeveless, with
additional detachable sleeves. Hoods were worn on the heads of the wealthier,
replaced during the period by hats or caps: at first for travelling, later for
normal use. Working girls wore aprons for protection and kerchiefs (head-
scarves) on the head. Shoes for both sexes were of leather, flat or low-heeled,
reinforced underneath, and with square toes until the middle of the sixteenth

century when rounded ones became popular. Boots were put on for riding rather than walking. Night clothes for boys and girls consisted of shirts or smocks, sometimes those worn during the day, and often night caps.

Among the gentry, the children of the Cavendish family of Hardwick (a girl and two boys) had shirts and stockings bought or made for them, with doublets, coats, gowns, hats, gloves, and shoes, the latter frequently renewed. Colours are sometimes mentioned: green stockings and red leather shoes. Once three white feathers were purchased, probably to decorate hats.[58] An inventory of the clothes of the Tollemache family of Helmingham in Suffolk in 1597 describes the daughters (aged eight to fourteen) as each having several gowns, while Lionel (the son and heir, aged six) possessed two hats, a cloak, two doublets, a belt and hose (or stockings).[59] Ordinary children were dressed in more basic ways. The Ashburton orphan boys were provided with caps, shirts, coats, hose or stockings, and shoes. The girl had a kerchief for her head, a neckerchief to wear round the throat, a smock, an apron, hose, and shoes.[60] One can also assume the wearing of drawers. Among the poor, clothes might be ragged or lacking. 'Many children', wrote the author of a school exercise in the 1490s, 'wear no shoes till they be thirteen, or twelve years old at least.'[61]

In families with sufficient resources there could also be ornaments and accoutrements, at least for formal occasions. Two portraits of the Thynne children have already been mentioned as showing them wearing neck chains and crosses.[62] James Basset, a schoolboy of about twelve in 1538, hoped for a gold chain from his wealthy parents, Viscount and Viscountess Lisle.[63] However in the godly family of Sir Henry Sharington in Wiltshire, in the 1560s, the young daughter Grace later recalled that her mother 'said she could give me' jewels and pearls but 'she would not until I were furnished with virtue in my mind, and decked inwardly'.[64] Belts or girdles would be needed for both sexes. Knives were commonly carried by men and boys and these would be used at meals. Schoolboys required pen knives to sharpen their pens, and also pen cases and inkhorns.[65] Portraits of older boys of gentry rank show them girded with sword belts and swords: no doubt for special occasions.[66] The ten-year-old Edward Manners, son of the earl of Rutland, had a sword and dagger bought for him in 1558 for 24s., and a further 6s. was spent on 'dressing' his rapier and that of his younger brother. They also had lessons from a fencing master.[67] A list of customs duties on imported goods in 1550 mentions 'bags for children', presumably satchels, and another of 1583 includes purses for children and 'knives with velvet sheaths' for their use.[68]

Food for children, like clothes, must greatly have varied, as it did for adults, depending on wealth and, in the case of the poorest, on availability. In theory they benefited in comparison with adults in one respect, since they were not required to fast until they reached the age of puberty or even later.[69] Up to the Reformation adults were expected to avoid eating meat on numerous days in the year. These included every Friday, the vigil (or day before) about forty important religious festivals, and the three Ember days which came about once a quarter. In addition, during the six weeks of Lent up to Easter, they had to abstain from dairy foods (eggs, milk, butter and cheese) as well as meat. Only fish or shellfish were allowed. The requirement was somewhat reduced in the 1540s to allow dairy foods in Lent, but remained in principle throughout the sixteenth century.

In practice this also affected children's diet to some extent. Household catering (except perhaps in the richest families) was chiefly designed for adults and in the case of older children there was probably a wish to prepare them for adult fasting. School exercises from Oxford in the 1490s portray a boy complaining 'how weary I am of fish' in a season that is evidently Lent.[70] This suggests that his family, or the college in which he was lodging, applied the fish rule to all of its members. In the household of the earl of Northumberland in 1512, the children too ate fish during Lent although they were allowed butter.[71] James Basset, already mentioned, was sent to study in Paris when he was about twelve while his mother and stepfather were ruling English Calais. Fish did not agree with him (perhaps he had an allergy), so he was sent during Lent from the college where he was staying to a private household where a more varied diet was available.[72]

William Harrison, writing in 1587, claimed that the English ate only twice a day: dinner (eaten in the late morning) and supper (in the late afternoon or evening), although the young were permitted breakfast as well.[73] In reality most adults too had a drink and a snack at the beginning of the day.[74] Three years previously Thomas Cogan, in a popular work of advice about human diets and health, agreed that the young should be fed 'more largely' than adults, and should be given breakfast.[75] In the Northumberland household, the earl's two eldest sons (one eleven, one younger) were allowed a breakfast each day of basic household-bread, a small loaf or manchet of fine wheat bread, beer, and chicken or mutton bones. Their two smaller sisters had a manchet, beer, and mutton bones. The choristers of the earl's chapel were served with ordinary bread, beer, and boiled beef for breakfast, with salt fish in Lent.[76] Other meals are not mentioned, probably because the children had portions of what was produced for the adults.[77] There are several references to the young being given bread and butter as snacks, perhaps especially for breakfast. An Italian visitor to London in about 1500 mentioned this, and said that the kites (birds) of the city were so tame that they would take the food from the children's hands.[78] Cogan's recommendations for children's breakfasts included bread, drink, fish, and dairy products such as butter and eggs.[79]

A more extensive account of food is given in a book of dialogues to teach English pupils foreign languages by the schoolmaster Claudius Hollyband in 1583.[80] This was evidently the food appropriate for boys or girls of the wealthier classes who were learning the language in a private London school: the food that was eaten in their homes or the houses in which they boarded. Breakfast is described as comprising a small piece of wholemeal bread, butter, and fruit when in season. Midday dinner included a bowl of pottage made of wheat, barley, turnips, and cabbage, sometimes with eggs. On fish days (such as Fridays) there were porringers of bread and skimmed milk with fish (fresh if available or else salted).

Supper comprised a salad flavoured with salt and oil together with mutton stewed along with prunes, small root vegetables, or chopped herbs. On certain days of the week the mutton was replaced by roast veal or kid, while on fasting days the menu changed to eggs, which might be roasted, fried, poached, or made into pancakes. Two eggs were allowed for each child as well as cheese, nuts, and sometimes a little fish. Fruit is mentioned being eaten in summer (but only as a treat when visiting a country farm, of which there were plenty near London) and fresh milk, curds, and cream. The beer drunk was 'small' (or thin) beer. The advantage of beer or ale was its purity compared with that of water, but the poor may have had no alternative to water and Cogan, while thinking it bad for adults, felt that it did less harm to the young, 'and sometimes it profiteth'.[81]

This evidence gives no insight into the diet of children in poor families, especially in times of scarcity. The author of *Piers Plowman* (written in the fourteenth, but still read in the sixteenth, century) described the limited food available for a poor peasant farmer to give his children, apparently in early summer when last year's harvest of grain had been consumed. It included no meat or eggs but was limited to curds, unripe cheese, vegetables (leeks and cabbages), and bread made up of oats or even of beans and bran.[82] In 1586, a year of high prices for grain, local people in Gloucestershire attacked a barge on the River Severn at Framilode, which was taking a cargo of the stuff to Wales. When pursued by the authorities, they claimed that they were forced to do so by necessity. 'They were driven to feed their children with cats, dogs, and roots of nettles, with such other like things.'[83]

BEHAVIOUR

Medieval writers, followed by their Tudor successors, thought of life as a series of stages: 'the ages of man'. They differed in reckoning the number of the ages, some fixing it at three, others at four, seven, or higher numbers. The three ages consisted of youth, maturity, and old age, without specifically identifying childhood, but the four ages distinguished childhood from young adulthood, and the seven ages went into more detail. Infancy, the first age, lasted from birth until seven, childhood from seven to fourteen, and adolescence from fourteen upwards.[84]

In practice many people in Tudor England seem to have thought in terms of the seven-age division, with seven and puberty as the milestones of youthfulness. For boys of status, seven was the age at which they would be taken from the nursery and the control of women to the school and the rule of men. Infant dress was, or already had been, changed for that of manhood. Up to the Reformation, it was possible for a boy of seven or more to receive the first stage of ordination: the cutting out of a tonsure or circle of hair on the top of the head. In earlier centuries boy singers and scholars were often tonsured in this way, but the practice seems to have been dying out in the later Middle Ages. In any case it did not signify any intention of becoming a cleric permanently, and could be followed by a lay career and marriage.

Infancy was traditionally regarded as a time for growth; childhood one for learning and activity. The nature of childhood, however, was believed to be characterised by play, requiring parents and guardians to ensure that play was moderated and that learning behaviour and skills became a priority. All Tudor writers emphasised the need for parents to impose discipline on children. Hugh Rhodes, updating an older popular treatise on children's manners in 1545, urged parents both to do so themselves and to ensure that the schoolmasters to whom they entrusted their children would 'punish sharply', although patience was also important. Children should not be shown too much familiarity; as we shall see, they should learn to respect their parents as subjects did their rulers. They should not be allowed to go wherever they would. Parents should keep abreast of the company they were keeping and what they were doing. They must not be indulged in fine clothes, which increased pride and obstinacy. Idleness should be rebuked.[85]

Discipline at home could include corporal punishment, for boys or girls. The Elizabethan play *July and Julian* features a mother beating her daughter for failing to carry out some instruction.[86] The Elizabethan diarist John Dee recorded how, in 1589, his wife hit their daughter Katherine on the ear when she was a little short of her eighth birthday, causing the child to suffer two outbreaks of nose bleeding.[87] A more picturesque account of paternal discipline comes from the reminiscences of the Devon soldier Sir Peter Carew (1514–75), narrated to the Exeter historian, John Hooker. Peter, the son of Sir William, a knight in the east of the county, was sent to school at Exeter and boarded with Thomas Hunt, a draper and alderman. The boy disliked his lessons and played truant. Hunt searched for him and found him on the city wall. Peter climbed onto a turret and threatened to throw himself off if approached. 'I shall break my neck and thou shalt be hanged.' Hunt reported this to the father, who on his next visit had the boy tied to a rope, led round the city like a dog, and so brought home. When they reached there, he was tied to one of the family's dogs and kept in that way for a time.[88]

Alongside such advice and practices, there was criticism of parents for being too indulgent, especially those of the wealthy classes. School exercises from Oxford in the 1490s complained that most rich men's children were spoilt. Their mothers pampered them and allowed them to run astray. When a boy had been beaten at school – 'after his master has driven away the fleas from his skin' – the mother would look at his buttocks. If she found weals, 'she weepeth and waileth and fareth as [if] she were mad . . . [and] complaineth of the cruelty of teachers'.[89] The same exercises imagine a boy of eleven comparing his schooldays with the tolerance of his earlier childhood. Formerly he slept in a chamber with wall-hangings, lying in bed well into daylight, and having his breakfast brought to him there. Now he must rise at 5.00 a.m. and study his book, and if the master comes to wake him, he brings a rod, not a candle.[90] The subtext is that the comforts of early childhood must be laid aside for the serious business of learning skills and self-discipline.

Other writers preferred to ascribe indulgence to the lower orders of society. Erasmus, in a book published in English in 1532 contrasted the good manners that were appropriate to the higher orders with their alleged absence among 'churls', 'carters', and 'ploughmen'.[91] His view was shared by William Harrison, who deprecated the indulgence shown to children by 'the poorer sort of [women]', adding that 'the wealthier do seldom offend herein'. Poor women, he thought, being themselves undisciplined, were careless in the bringing up of their children, 'wherein their husbands also are to be blamed'. Many poor children grew up 'neither fearing God, neither regarding either manners or obedience' and came to grief. If they had been corrected in youth, they could have become good members of society.[92]

Both authors were writing for the upper ranks of their era, and did not consider that lesser folk might also have ethical standards and codes of behaviour. Indeed, among the poor, the need to use children for domestic tasks and eventually wage earning must have imposed restraints on their lives, even if not moral or educational ones. Schooling too (as the boy above discovered) entailed long hours of classroom discipline. Growing up for everyone is a process of understanding the expectations of adults and in learning strategies to accord with or avoid them. Families have their own ways of doing things, and customs that they observe. These seem natural to their own children until they encounter contemporaries with different observances and learn the variety of human life. Exactly what behaviour was learnt and followed in Tudor homes is now almost impossible to trace, and the variations between one household and another must have been increased by the social differences.

The fullest evidence, at least in terms of ideals rather than norms, relates as usual to the nobility, gentry, and merchant classes. These had long been the recipients of advice about good manners for children. The writing of manuals on behaviour for young people began in the twelfth century and owed much to the wisdom literature in the Bible, such as the books of Proverbs and Ecclesiasticus in which the subject is handled.[93] The manuals had a distinct context and audience. They were directed to boys of rank between the ages of about seven and fourteen who were being educated in a great household or a grammar school. They consequently had a social bias. The behaviour that they taught, as Erasmus had intimated, formed a child to belong to the governing orders of society. It was one way in which the governors defined themselves, just as they did through their wealth and privileges.

The most influential text in the later Middle Ages was the Latin poem *Stans Puer ad Mensam*, generally attributed to Robert Grosseteste, bishop of Lincoln (d. 1253) and read in most grammar schools. Its title, in English 'O boy, standing at your lord's table', was followed by the rules that a boy in a household should observe while waiting on his master at meals or when eating himself with other members of the household (Fig. 15, p. 51). The poem was translated into English by John Lydgate (d. *c.* 1450), printed by William Caxton in 1476, reissued several times in this form, and modernised by Hugh Rhodes in 1545 after which it went on being published until 1577.[94] Also influential was Erasmus's treatise *De Civilitate Morum Puerilium*, turned into English by Robert Whittington, schoolmaster in the royal household, with the subtitle 'A little book of good manners for children'. This appeared at least four times between 1532 and 1554, and was retranslated by Thomas Paynel in 1560.[95] Although its author was not English and wrote for western Europe, he was aware of English practices and the translations would scarcely have been made unless the work was thought suitable for England.

Less advice of this kind was produced for girls. There is a group of English manuscript poems in the fifteenth century typified by 'How the Good Wife Taught her Daughter', which give instruction about morals, deportment, religious observance, and household tasks.[96] More substantial works include *The Book of the Knight of the Tower*, printed by Caxton in 1483, and *The Instruction of a Christian Woman* by the Spanish scholar Juan Luis Vives, published in

15. A youth of high status doing the traditional task in great households of serving his master at the table.

English in 1529. These are discussed in Chapter 5.[97] They are more concerned with virtues than manners, but Lydgate's translation of *Stans Puer ad Mensam* was gender-neutral, so that it could have been imparted to girls as well. And their code of behaviour must have had much in common with that of their brothers. Grace Sharington, born in 1552, described how her father disliked seeing a woman who was 'light in her carriage'. This meant one who held 'her head one way and her hands another, and her feet a third way, her eyes tossing about in every place': the same advice that Lydgate gave to boys.[98]

The literature of behaviour for boys aimed to hit three targets. One was personal hygiene, in both a spiritual and a physical sense. Rising at about dawn at 5.00 or 6.00 a.m., a child should kneel and pray to Christ by saying well-known prayers, reading from the simple prayer book known as a Primer, or (up to the Reformation) doing so from the similar book called the Hours of the Virgin.[99] This should be followed by making one's bed, washing hands and face, and putting on clean clothes according to one's rank. Clothes should be brushed and sponged, shoes cleaned and laced on, and head combed. Nails should be pared and hands washed again before meals. The nose should be kept clean and blown into a handkerchief, never wiped on a sleeve or a cap. One should turn aside to sneeze, and (when with other people) take off your cap and ask pardon. To someone else's sneeze one should say 'Christ help!' Nose picking should be avoided in public. One should go to urinate regularly, not delay doing so, and if breaking wind was necessary, walk away from other people and disguise the sound with a cough. Prayers should be said again before going to bed.

Next the writers of behaviour turned to meals. They envisaged boys in two situations. One was that of a boy of rank ceremonially waiting on his master at the table. He should carry himself well, not slouching or leaning against the wall, and not looking round the room. He should know how to lay the table, hang a napkin over his shoulder while serving, learn how to carve meat, and place and remove dishes. The other situation was that of boys eating with the family, or in a hall with fellow members of a large household or a school. In the first case they might have a table of their own at the end of the adult table, especially if they were younger.[100] In the second they would be older and could be held to full adult standards. Here they should defer to others when taking a seat, rather than sitting where they wished.

Meals customarily began and ended with a child saying grace in Latin or English, so boys should be prepared for this if requested.[101] It should be done with hands raised, presumably together in the usual mode of praying.[102] At the table there would be a wooden plate or 'trencher' in front of each place. Bread should be put to the left of this, and one's cup to the right of it. There would also be a napkin, which could be used for wiping the mouth but not for blowing the nose.[103] Elbows should not be placed on the table and, while seated, boys should sit upright without shifting their bodies about.[104] When a dish was placed, they should again defer to their neighbours and be considerate in helping themselves so as not to take all the choicest parts. Their knives would be those that all men carried, and should be clean. A spoon would be provided, and Erasmus also talked of forks.

The etiquette books envisaged the eating of 'pottage' such as soup, porridge, or stew, and it was permissible to crumble one's bread into it. Such a dish was eaten with a spoon, which should not be overloaded so that the contents slipped off. The spoon should be wiped after use, and not left in the dish but laid down by the trencher. Solid food should be cut into small portions, and salt be taken from the (open) salt-cellar with the point of the knife, not by dipping food into it. One should not hold food in one's fingers, gnaw bones, blow one's pottage to cool it, eat with an open mouth so as to reveal its contents, gulp or slurp one's food, or lick one's fingers. Drink should be taken in moderation, and Erasmus envisaged drinking in two or three sustained draughts during the meal, rather than continuous sipping. Dogs should not be fed or fondled. During the meal one should avoid scratching oneself, spitting, or picking one's teeth with a knife or the fingers. A toothpick should be used. At the end of the meal, hands should be washed and grace again be said.

Finally, the literature sought to teach good manners towards other people. Parents and employers should be treated with reverence and courtesy. At home, after getting out of bed, one should bow or genuflect to one's parents, greet them, and ask for their blessing.[105] At meals children should be silent unless addressed or invited to speak. When doing so, they should rise, genuflect, and face the person concerned. The English method of genuflection, according to Erasmus, was to flex the right knee first and then the left. When talk at the table was humorous, it was permissible to smile, but laughter should be repressed and ribald comments ignored. A stranger sitting nearby at the table should be helped with food, but disputes with one's neighbours should be avoided, as should swearing. While walking in the street, one should go soberly: not gazing around, scoffing or scolding others, or getting involved in violence. Meeting an adult, a child should remove his cap and hold it in his right hand, with his left hand across his abdomen. Alternatively he could hold his cap with both hands across his abdomen to screen his codpiece.

Altogether the advice on manners reflected the ethics considered proper for those at the top of society. Children should be brought up to be humble to parents and employers, moderate and restrained in their way of life. They should be aware of their status and of the need to display it in dress and behaviour, while remembering the obligations that status carried with it. In families with servants or tenants, the children, however subordinate to their parents, received deference like that towards their parents. They were given titles, in an age when only the privileged had them. A boy would be called 'Master' or 'young Master', like his father; a girl 'Mistress', like her mother. Even Honor Basset, a baby of five months in a gentry family in 1539, was 'Mistress'.[106] The shorter word 'Miss' for girls came into common use only in the seventeenth century.[107]

TROUBLES OF CHILDHOOD: ACCIDENTS, SICKNESS, ABUSE

Inevitably children's lives did not always go well for one reason or another. Deaths of parents in childhood could be devastating, emotionally and economically. Fatherless heirs to property were subject to wardship.[108] If they held lands by feudal tenure from the Crown or one of the aristocracy, their custody, the profits of their land, and the right to arrange their marriage belonged to that person or to someone else to whom it was transferred. Wardship lasted for boys until the age of twenty-one, and for girls until marriage, although the custody of heirs could be regained by their family for a substantial sum. Those of lesser rank who held property in towns or by what was called 'socage tenure' in the countryside also had guardians appointed for them. The orphans of the poor, as we have seen, became dependent on charity from their parish with a requirement to work and, perhaps, to enter into a long period of servitude.

Children are vulnerable to accidents. We seldom hear about these in Tudor England unless they were fatal and led to a coroner's inquest. A rare recorder of his children's lesser injuries was John Dee in the 1570s and 1580s. Arthur, aged three, fell down the steps to a London ferry and cut his forehead. Later, a little boy cut Arthur's nose unwittingly with a razor, and when Arthur was twelve he wounded himself on the head when throwing up a half-brick and not getting out of its way in time. Michael, at about the age of three, poked a sharp stick into his eye, apparently without serious results. Theodore, when two, had a fall and hurt his mouth.[109] Although Dee had eight children, only Arthur and his sister Katherine are known to have survived into adulthood, but that seems to have been the result of illnesses rather than accidents. And as we shall see, medical remedies existed which could at least try to patch up injuries.

Worse than these were the ravages of sickness and the substantial mortality they caused among children, especially the youngest.[110] For most of the population, living in the countryside away from professional physicians and not able to afford their services, illnesses had to be treated as best as could be. Traditional medicines might be used, along with charms, visits to holy wells, and (up to the 1530s) prayers at saints' shrines or holy images. A satirical account of such procedures is given in the play *Thersites*, published in 1562.

Ulysses sends his young son Telemachus to a wise woman to be cured of worms. The boy lies down on his back, she blesses him, and recites a long rigmarole, invoking such things as:

> The virtue of the tail of Isaac's cow
> That before Adam in Paradise did low,
> Also the joist of Moses' rod
> In the Mount of Calvary that spoke with God,
> *Facie ad faciem*, turning tail to tail,
> Cause all these worms quickly to fail.

This, she promises him, ensures that the worms will all be gone by tomorrow.[111] George Gifford, in his *Dialogue concerning Witches* (1593) relates a similar story. A man with a sick daughter aged five takes some of her clothes to a wise woman, who advises him to burn them. If they burn black, it is a sign of bewitchment and the witch will appear. The clothes are duly burnt and an old woman enters the house on some errand. The father attacks her, draws blood, and the child recovers in two days. The author condemned the episode, however, pointing out that the advice of the wise woman could itself be the work of the Devil.[112]

The wealthier had access to physicians and, given the fact that parents worry about their children's health, any doctor would have needed to treat such cases when asked. There was already some generally accepted knowledge about child illnesses in the thirteenth century, when Bartholomew Glanville wrote the encyclopaedia that was still current in Tudor England. He listed conditions in babies and gave them names, called in later translations 'whelks, blains, pimples in the mouth, spewing, fevers, cramps, the flux', and ascribed them to impure breast milk.[113] During the sixteenth century writers began to give fresh attention to children's health. In 1539 Sir Thomas Elyot's book on diet, *The Castle of Health*, offered advice on their food, which should be modest in amount, varied, moderately hot and moist, and excluding of wine.[114] In the following year Thomas Moulton's *The Glass of Health*, provided a general medical dictionary with remedies. It gave children passing rather than major attention, but it dealt with injuries to their heads, necks, and bellies, and provided remedies for their fevers and agues.[115]

Two other publications were more important. One was *The Birth of Mankind* by Eucharius Rösslin, first published in English in 1540, which has already been noticed for its coverage of birth. Book II of the work was devoted to the diseases of newly born children and the remedies for them.[116] It dealt with problems relating to respiration (difficulty of breathing, coughs, and sneezing), skin irritations (sore gums, chapped lips, weals, and whelks or blisters), vomiting and flux, swellings of the eyes, temperature and fever, cramp and insomnia, among others. The listing of conditions is impressive, the remedies less so. The prescription for sore gums was to rub with an ointment made of hen's grease, hare's brain, oil of camomile, and honey, and there are others of a similar nature.

Four years later, in 1544, another medical treatise was published in English, *The Regiment of Life* by the Frenchman Jean Goeurot. This was a systematic survey of diseases of the body, proceeding from the head downwards to the heart, stomach, bowels, and feet, as they affected adults. The translator was an Englishman, Thomas Phaer, and the interest of the book for the history of childhood is that Phaer added to it three works of his own, one of which was entitled *The Book of Children*.[117] Phaer was a polymath with a varied career.[118] Born in Norwich in about 1510, he was educated at Oxford and the Inns of Court, becoming solicitor to the Council in the (Welsh) Marches in the 1540s, and writing two textbooks of law. Meanwhile he developed a second vocation as a physician and writer on medical matters and eventually graduated as a doctor of medicine at Oxford. He also served as a justice of the peace, sat as a member of four parliaments between 1547 and 1559, and began a project to translate the whole of Virgil's *Aeneid* into English, of which he achieved only part before his death in 1560. This made him an outsider as a physician, and his perception of the fact is apparent in the introduction to his book. He implied that there was hostility to his work from an unnamed group, apparently the medical establishment, which he accused of hiding its expertise from the public. His intention, he said, was to make work in other languages available in English 'and to declare to the use of many [that] which ought not to be secret for a few'.[119]

After a short account of breastfeeding, Phaer embarked, like Rösslin, on an analysis of forty conditions common among children. He followed Goeurot in proceeding from the head downwards, identifying ailments and providing

remedies with the traditional mixture of chemical, herbal, and fanciful ingre-
dients. His cure for sore gums was similar to Rösslin's, and for earache he
recommended boiling the slough of an adder's skin in oil. He began with
swelling of the brain; scales, warts, and knobs on the head; night fears and
dreams; epilepsy, cramp, and palsy. He discussed bloodshot or watery eyes,
diseases of the ears including worms and tinnitus, and teething and blisters in
the mouth. This led to quinsy and swelling of the throat, coughing, and short-
ness of breath. Internal problems included colic, worms, stones in the bladder,
incontinence, and intestinal injuries. Finally he considered a number of
diseases: smallpox, measles, and ague (malaria), along with the treatment of
scalds and burns, chilblains, and lice. Rösslin and Phaer gave Tudor parents
(and physicians if they so wished) medical dictionaries to identify conditions
in their children and suggest remedies. Phaer's work, like Rösslin's, was printed
at least eight times during the sixteenth century, testifying to the books' popularity and apparent usefulness.

We can follow some children's illnesses: as usual in wealthy families where
records exist and where the care, while not necessarily greater than in poor
households, had the benefit of medical advice and palliatives. One example is
'little Francis', so-called in spite of being in his teens: a boy intended to
become a priest and boarding with the prior of St John in Clerkenwell outside
London in about 1521. His expenses were paid out of charity by the duke of
Buckingham.[120] He had recurrent illnesses, including a skin disease requiring
the shaving of his head and the healing of the 'breaking out' of his neck and
hands: perhaps eczema. Later he contracted ague so badly or for so long that
he was sent on pilgrimage to St Albans and Windsor Chapel in search of spiritual healing. On a third occasion he had an illness of the throat and subsequently yellow jaundice, all of which required expenditure by his guardian.
He survived, however, to go on to study at Oxford.[121]

Two other sick children were Mary and Richard Fermor, the orphan
daughter and son of a gentleman of Somerton, Oxfordshire, in the early 1580s.
Mary was boarded out with a lady of her own rank where 3s. 4d. was paid to
the woman who looked after her when she was ill. Richard was supplied with
2d. worth of sugar candy to bring up phlegm from a sore mouth and throat.
Later a much larger sum of 3s. 10d. was noted for 'syrups, ointments, and other

medicinable things for him in his sickness'.[122] Even greater was the expenditure on a third orphan, Francis Willoughby, in 1552. The costs of his illness included a pound of sugar for 13*d.*, a pound of almonds for 6*d.*, apothecary's pills for 8*d.*, veal to make jelly for him, 'pollyng' (perhaps cutting or shaving his hair), flax seed to make a bath for him, and sausages (perhaps to tempt his appetite).[123] The correspondence of Joan Thynne of Longleat in Wiltshire with her husband John in London in 1602 adds a parental dimension to such illnesses. Their daughter Dorothy, aged ten, needs tincture of saffron. Her mother fears she will not get well 'unless you get better help than is available here'. It then turns out that she and her younger sister Christian have smallpox. Joan worries that they will be disfigured: 'their faces are very full of sores'. 'Doll takes it very heavily and mourns very much . . . neither can I without mourning look upon her.' They recover, 'but Doll is now troubled with an ague'. Two days later, she is better, and her fits have left her.[124]

Diseases were not the only dangers to children. Knowing what we do today about the abuses that they may encounter, it is impossible to discount such mistreatments in Tudor England, and traces of these turn up from time to time. Children of vagrant men and women were exposed to risk. Thomas Harman, in his 'exposure' of beggars' practices, *A Caveat for Common Cursitors* (1567), described small girls being carried about on their mothers' backs, and small boys being bred up to thieve. 'Some of [the mothers] go with children of ten or twelve years of age. If time and place serve for their purpose, they will send them into some house at the window to steal and rob, which they call in their language "milling of the ken"'.[125]

There were cases of sexual abuse. Monks and friars faced accusations of this, relating to boys, up to the Reformation and, in invective, for long afterwards. Henry VIII's commissioners, visiting monasteries in 1535, met with cases in Leicestershire and Nottinghamshire.[126] Nicholas Udall, the headmaster of Eton, was committed to prison and had to resign in 1541 for sexual relations with one of the boys.[127] Girls under the age of puberty were another target. In 1576 an act of Parliament, trying to tighten up the penalties for rape, was prompted to order that any such crime involving a girl under the age of ten should be considered a felony deserving of capital punishment.[128] Allegations of rape have been collected for the period 1558–1625 from five counties close to London. The number involving women altogether was 128, of which 52 (about 40 per cent) concerned girls under the age of fifteen. The alleged victims stretched as far down as children who were only toddlers, and there were twenty-one cases among those who were aged from ten to eleven.[129]

There could be sheer physical cruelty. In 1552 Henry Machyn recorded the public humiliation of a woman in London for scarring her young maid with a metal 'card' of spikes, endangering her life.[130] Later, in 1563, he described how a schoolmaster beat his pupil with a leather belt, causing terrible physical harm. The man was put into the pillory and whipped; the boy's injuries were then exhibited.[131] These cases came to light because of their enormity, or because people noticed them: in those situations action was taken. There must have been many others, especially behind domestic walls, where the victim suffered in silence without intervention.

MENTAL HORIZONS

The sixteenth century is not now rich in autobiography or in evidence of what adults remembered thinking in their childhood. Such memoirs as we have, like those of Grace Sharington, Thomas Tusser, and Thomas Whythorne, tell us more about the studies of their early years than their thoughts and feelings. A few reminiscences survive in which adults compared their childish selves with their maturity. Robert Ashley, born in 1565, recalled his fondness as a boy for reading romances.[132] Thomas Nashe, who was two years younger, remembered listening to old dames discussing superstitions about birth dates, unlucky days, and physical characteristics. 'I was a great auditor of theirs, and had all my witchcrafts at my fingers' ends.'[133] Best of all, Edward Herbert, born in 1583, revealed a little of what he thought in his infant years. When he understood what was said by others, he refrained from speaking in case he said anything imperfect or impertinent. 'I found myself here indeed [in the world] but from what cause or beginning, or by what means, I could not imagine.' When he asked where he had come from and why, his nurses laughed and said that they never heard a child ask such a question before.[134]

For the most part, however, we can only conjecture children's mental horizons from the circumstances in which they lived. In the following chapters we shall explore four of these: what they learnt at play, in church, at school, and in reading or sharing in oral culture. Here let us ponder two others: time and place. What would children have known about time in relation to their own lives? The recording of birth dates began among the wealthy during the Middle Ages, so that Richard Hill's practice in this respect was not unusual.[135] John Dee, one of whose professions was the making of horoscopes, could access detailed information about the dates and times of day of the births of his clients, who came from the upper ranks of society.[136] These, as has been mentioned, were regarded as significant pointers to later life (Fig. 16, p. 61).[137] Even non-literate people, it seems, could remember the date of a birth if it coincided with a major Church festival. Shakespeare envisaged this in *Romeo and Juliet*. Juliet's old wet nurse claimed to be able to 'tell her age unto an hour'. She was born on Lammas Eve (31 July), at about the same time as the nurse's own daughter Susan, and would be fourteen on the next such eve. In comparison the nurse's knowledge of the current calendar is less clear: she does not know when that day will fall, and has to be told.[138]

Some young people needed to understand their age for practical reasons. Children in wardship wished to know when they were entitled to succeed to their property. Apprentices who were bound to service for a period of seven years must have kept watch on time, as would their employers. Winchester College recorded the ages of its incoming scholars from the 1420s, so that either the parent or child had to report the fact on arrival, at least approximately.[139] In one school exercise of the 1490s, a boy explains that he is in his twelfth year.[140] At the same time, the fact may have been lower in many children's consciousness than is the case today. Birthdays do not seem to have been greatly celebrated, so that they formed less of a marker of time than with us. Outside property holders and apprentices, age mattered less than physical development into puberty and the ability to work. In another exercise of the 1570s, a boy is asked how old he is and replies that he does not know but that his father has noted his birth in a Bible.[141] Ages may also have been falsified: downwards in cases of crime, upwards to try to escape from others' control. Pride could also lead to obfuscation in adulthood. Dee encountered one lady who insisted that she was twenty-seven, although he judged from her birth details that she must have been two years older![142]

16. Birth on a particular day of the week was thought to influence one's life. Wednesday's children are endowed with skills such as writing books, organ playing, and clock making.

Turning to place, or topography, how far would girls or boys in Tudor England come to know the world beyond the house or settlement in which they were born? Age was clearly a factor here. Young children had to be left at home for the most part, even if their parents engaged in travel. As they grew older, there was more probability of them going too. It seems likely that the children of the nobility and richer gentry could eventually have accompanied them on journeys to different estates, to London, or to stay with friends: particularly once the children reached their early teens. There was also movement for reasons of education. Admittedly most boys and girls under education learnt only to read, which would be done at elementary schools nearby, because such schools were very common. Even at the next stage of learning, in the Latin grammar schools restricted to boys, there was a place of this kind in most English towns by the sixteenth century at which they could study from home.

But this was not always possible or desirable. In the countryside, a gentleman's or yeoman's son might need to lodge for his schooling in a town some miles away, as Peter Carew did, because it was not feasible to go to and fro every day. Alternatively a father might choose a school a long way from home because it had some apparent advantage. The agricultural writer Thomas Tusser, son of a minor gentleman in Essex, was sent to Wallingford in Berkshire.[143] Tudor England was also coming to have schools of countrywide repute. Eton and Winchester, both boarding schools, gave preference in offering scholarships to boys from their estates, often far away. Other wealthy parents placed their sons in one or other of the two schools as private pupils because of their reputations. St Paul's School, London, was a third institution well-known nationally. Both Carew and Tusser went there after spending time in other places.

Most of the population could not have moved about in these ways. Nevertheless, even the poorest were not always bound to a single place during childhood. There were the beggars whom we have encountered travelling and taking their offspring with them. Older children and adolescents must have become familiar with the nearby market town where they went to visit markets and fairs, or were sent to do chores.[144] Drovers and boatmen travelled by land and water, very likely taking young assistants with them. Illness provided another motive for children to travel. Up to the 1530s it was still a practice of some people to visit shrines of saints or holy images in search of healing, including that of their children, as well as holy wells. The shrines and images were suppressed in that decade, but the wells remained and went on being sought out for centuries.

An additional medical reason to travel was prompted by epidemics: outbreaks of the plague and the dreaded sweating sickness. Wives and offspring might be sent away to safer places during such outbreaks. The merchant John Johnson moved his whole family from one Northamptonshire village to another in 1546 during an outbreak of plague.[145] John Dee recorded how his baby daughter was sent home from her wet nurse in 1581 when the nurse's maid fell ill.[146] Whole schools might relocate themselves for the same reason, as happened in the case of Magdalen College School, Oxford. Its teachers and scholars migrated to places in the countryside on numerous occasions in the sixteenth century, including Brackley (Northamptonshire), Highworth (Wiltshire), Wallingford (Berkshire), and Witney (Oxfordshire).[147] So while most children's lives were geographically restricted by modern standards, this was not true of all, and some would have come to know rivers, roads, inns, and towns away from their own homelands.

This does not mean that children in Tudor England perceived their neighbourhoods in the same way as their adults. The ground is closer when we are small, making spaces seem greater and distances further. Young people have ways of demarcating territory and exploiting it that are different from those of adults. Children in a settlement may regard its surroundings as theirs, and then discover that their counterparts a mile or more away have claims on it as well. There may be battles over territory, and territory may identify a child to others. There are hints in medieval and Tudor England of an awareness of difference between town and countryside and between one parish and its neighbours.[148] Equally, children and adolescents may use space in ways that their elders did not intend. Churchyards were disputed areas from ancient times, the Church trying to keep them as consecrated ground and young people as places for recreations.[149] Tennis, which in Tudor times could cover a variety of games involving a ball and the hands or a racket, is recorded being played by young people in streets and alongside buildings, causing disruption or damage to the annoyance of adults.[150] And surroundings, for all children, would have a freshness and stimulus that they lacked for adults. Their details would be more minutely noticed and committed to memory, to be recalled in memory and dreams across the whole of a lifetime.

3

---◇---

PLAY

People in Tudor England, as we have seen, thought of life as a series of phases. Each had distinctive features. Infancy was a time of growth, childhood had a craving for toys and games, while youth was marked by energy and wayward-ness. Writers and artists, when they depicted the ages, did so with these traits in mind (Figs 17, p. 65; 51, p. 191). Thomas More, portraying childhood in about the 1490s, created a picture of a boy whipping a top, with the lines,

> I am called Childhood, in play is all my mind,
> To cast a quoit, a cock-stele [throwing stick], and a ball.

Could all my schoolbooks be burnt, he muses, 'then might I lead my life always in play'![1] The author of the drama *The Worlde and the Chylde*, published in 1522, did the same. He featured childhood as a boy called Wanton, holding a top and a whip and boasting how he teases animals and children.[2] A third writer, William Wager, in his play *The Longer Thou Livest, the More Fool Thou Art* (1569), sketched an identical boy: Moros ('a fool'), with a whipping top, a bowling ball, and a fresh list of the mischief that he does.[3] The image even lurks within Shakespeare's famous description of the ages of man in *As You Like It*. His portrait of childhood may seem to be different – a boy 'creeping like snail unwillingly to school' – but the creeping shows us that, like More's boy, he would much rather play with his friends.[4]

Adults in Tudor England did not forbid children to play, especially younger children, and toys were made or bought to give them pleasure.[5] At the same time, it was agreed that play should be kept within limits. Children

17. Boys shooting at birds. Birds were both a source of food and objects of sport.

needed to be disciplined, otherwise they would grow up to be idle and criminal. They should learn, while young, the knowledge and skills essential for adult life. So play tended to be circumscribed as children grew older and went to school or were introduced to the world of work. Religious and moral considerations came into the matter as well. For adolescents in particular, games that involved both sexes might be regarded as improper or dangerous. Gambling or rough sports attracted condemnation for the idleness, profligacy, or injuries that they were alleged to cause. The history of play in Tudor England is therefore not only one of youthful enjoyment but of criticism and attempts at restriction by adults.

It is also a history that, by modern standards, contained a stratum of insensitivity towards birds and animals with which it is hard now to sympathise. The naughty boy Wanton in the play of *The Worlde and the Chylde* boasted:

> Yea, sirs, I can well geld a snail,
> And catch a cow by the tail . . .
> I can spy a sparrow's nest.[6]

His counterpart 'little Dick' in John Heywood's *The Play of the Weather* asked Jupiter to send snow to the world, not only for snowballing but for snaring birds:

> All my pleasure is in catching of birds . . .
> And to hear birds how they flicker their wings
> In the pitfall [trap], I say it passeth all things.[7]

Their counterpart Moros in William Wager's play sang songs about robins and nightingales, but agreed:

> I will bring you a pretty bird's nest;
> Verily I think it be a redshank.[8]

As bad as nest robbing was cruelty to adult birds. Cock-fighting was a popular activity throughout society. An account of a fight at Winwick in Lancashire in the early sixteenth century described how both adults and children were present to the number of about fifty, and how some of the children carried the cockerels there.[9] Shrove Tuesday, the day before Lent began, was a traditional day for boys at school to bring such birds in order to make them fight. The dead bodies were the perquisite of the schoolmaster. School poems were written on the subject, and the term 'cock-fighting' appeared in school dictionaries.[10] One influential Tudor figure, John Colet, dean of St Paul's London and the re-founder of its grammar school in 1508–12, forbade cock-fighting there and his lead was followed at Manchester Grammar School in the 1520s. Whether this arose from dislike of cruelty or of disorder is hard to say.

Cock-fighting was associated with 'riding about of victory', apparently meaning the hoisting of the victorious boys in an unruly procession.[11] Yet despite these prohibitions, the practice continued elsewhere: widely, so it seems.

Equally callous was the practice of half burying a cockerel and aiming missiles at it. The 'cock-stele' mentioned by Thomas More was a throwing stick for this very purpose, and a pupil in another school exercise from Oxford in the 1520s describes seeing people shooting arrows at such a bird.[12] In that case the organisers were adults who paid for each shot, but a boy could still be an onlooker. Other sentences for translation in an Oxford school in the 1490s describe a bear-baiting attended by 'all the young folks, almost, of this town'.[13] Such practices reflected their social context. In an age so heavily reliant on its own agriculture and stock raising, men and women were in competition with birds and animals for the benefits of their labour, and both were sources of food in themselves. Human beings were equally harsh to each other. Beggars were punished with whipping, murderers with hanging, and heretics with burning. It was not so instinctive to feel respect for other creatures in such an environment.

TOYS

Play may be imaginative (primarily in the mind), practical (using objects), and physical (requiring exertion, with or without the help of objects). It can also involve more than one of these elements. We know little about imaginative play in the sixteenth century, through a lack of adults who recorded having done it in later life or described their offspring doing so. The innumerable games that must have been played, singly or in groups, by boys pretending to be knights or outlaws or girls imitating queens or mothers, are lost beyond recall. One stray reference comes from Sir Thomas Elyot in 1531. 'We behold some children, kneeling in their game before images, and holding up their little white hands, do move their pretty mouths as they were praying; others going and singing as in procession.'[14] Another was noted by John Dee in 1582 when his small son Arthur was playing with a girl of similar age. 'Arthur Dee and Mary Herbert, they being but three year old the eldest, did make as it were a show of childish marriage, of calling each other husband and wife.'[15] But much of the practical play that we shall now explore would have been imaginative too. Toys such as dolls and miniature utensils would have led those who played with them to create a mental world, in which adult life was visualised and imitated.

The word 'toy' first came into common use during the sixteenth century. It did not initially mean a plaything, as it does today, but any kind of 'trifle' meaning frivolity.[16] Nevertheless toys in the modern sense existed then and had long done so. They may be defined as objects to play with, created by children themselves, by their parents or friends in an ad hoc way, or by professional toy-makers. All three kinds of production would have existed in Tudor England. Children's own creations are the least well recorded in human history, but their manufacture had already been noticed in the fifteenth century by a Scottish gentleman named Rait in a poem about the ages of mankind that he called *Ratis Raving*. Talking of children's love of playing, he observed that their will is always:

> With flowers for to jape and play,
> With sticks and with spales [splinters] small
> To build up chamber, spence [buttery], and hall,
> To make a white horse of a stick,
> Of broken bread a sailing ship,
> A bunweed [ragwort] to a burly spear
> And of a sedge a sword of war,
> A comely lady of a clout [piece of cloth]
> And be right busy thereabout
> To dight it featously [dress it handsomely] with flowers,
> And love the puppet paramours.[17]

Many of the playthings that we shall encounter were objects of these kinds: universally available and costing nothing. They included little stones and pebbles, animal bones, cherry stones, nuts, and discarded metal items. Plants were another source. Shepherds were traditionally associated with making and playing pipes from straws or hollow stalks, and the writer Nicholas Breton describes boys doing so too.[18] We hear of one reference to a word 'powpe', which may refer to a pop-gun made from an elder branch or balsam stem, while there are several references to playing 'at blow-point'. The latter also popular with adults: apparently involving the puffing of pointed darts or arrows through a tube at a target.[19] A herbalist in 1633 noted that it was easy for children to be poisoned by blowing down pipes, if they used the stems of noxious plants like hemlock.[20]

Babies have been given rattles since ancient times. The word is not found in English, however, until 1519, when William Horman's *Vulgaria*, a book of exercises for boys to translate from English into Latin, included the sentence 'I will buy a rattle to still my baby for crying.'[21] Metal rattles were manufactured or imported by the sixteenth century.[22] They are shown, as we have noticed, in portraits of Tudor children.[23] A common type had a handle attached to a sphere-shaped grid containing a ball to make the noise. But they were not all small or confined to babies and toddlers; older children too might use them in a game or activity, as happens in the last act of *The Merry Wives of Windsor*.[24] Young people in York were accused of disturbing the peace by sounding them inordinately in the three days before Easter. On these days church bells were silent and people were summoned to worship with rattles, which some children or youths evidently took to extremes.[25]

Dolls must have been commonly played with by girls, although here too the modern word, a diminutive of Dorothy, is not recorded before the seventeenth century. The earlier terms were 'babe', 'baby', 'poppet', 'popyn', or 'puppet'.[26] One Tudor dictionary defined the equivalent Latin word *pupa* as 'a small image which maidens are wont to make in the form of girls and to wrap in clothes'.[27] Elizabeth, daughter of the earl of Rutland, had a 'puppet' bought for her in 1558 for 10*d*.[28] However, not all dolls were female. Manufactured ones could be given male features, and playing with them was by no means confined to maidens. When the son of the merchant John Johnson was two in 1552, his mother wrote to his father in London asking him to bring 'some baby' for the child.[29] The Johnsons' gentleman counterpart, William Cavendish of Hardwick, bought dolls for his children in 1599–1601, including his young son James.[30] Boys could also play with dolls together. A sentence in a children's Latin dictionary of 1584 contains the sentence, 'Thy puppets bring with thee, if thou wilt play with me.' This implies boys, since the book was one for a school classroom.[31]

Dolls could be made of several kinds of material. Cloth was probably very common, and any mother or child could have formed them from scraps of fabric. The writer Philip Stubbes referred to 'puppets and maumets [small images] of rags and clouts, compact together', and Shakespeare to a 'babe of clouts'.[32] However by the reign of Elizabeth I well-dressed dolls were being produced commercially. A book illustration of a Native American woman and girl of about 1590 shows the girl holding two imported toys, evidently brought in by early explorers or traders. One is a manufactured rattle and the other a female doll dressed like a lady. She wears a hat, a ruff round the neck, and a long gown reaching her feet.[33]

Earthenware figures in the shape of a cone or tube and bearing a face are attested on the Continent, forming a basis on which clothes could be added. Wooden dolls of a similar kind, like a truncheon with a head, are recorded in Tudor England, and a list of customs duties in 1562 includes 'little puppets . . . which come to be sold in England in boxes'.[34] Such dolls, also known as 'babies' and made perhaps in the Netherlands or Germany, were imported in large enough quantities to feature in the rates at which duties were paid. The duty in 1545 was 3s. 4d. for a gross (144), later rising to 6s. 8d.: roughly a farthing or a halfpenny each, which suggests that they were sold for only a few pence.[35] Wax dolls may also have been available, since similar small human figures were produced for offering at shrines until such practices were forbidden in 1538.[36] Dolls of one kind or another were available in shops or from traders. Two shoppers could be imagined concluding their purchases by saying 'Let us buy some babies for our children', and a pedlar could be assumed to carry them in his pack as he travelled around the countryside.[37]

Small models of objects used by adults are now known to been widely manufactured in Tudor England. They were commonly made of pewter, a mixture of tin and lead, by pewterers and 'whitesmiths' who worked in soft metals, as a sideline to their main business of producing utensils for adults. The chief source of these objects hitherto has been the city of London, where they are preserved and found in the mud of the foreshore of the River Thames, but they have been discovered in other places such as Yorkshire (Figs 18–19, pp. 71–2).[38] Since they are accidental survivals, they have no social context and it is possible that some had adult purposes, but their appeal to

18. Mass-produced metal toys from Tudor London. They include a male
figure, a pikeman, and a galleon.

19. Other London metal toys of the period: part of a buffet or dresser (originally a three-dimensional model), a standing bowl, and a pewter jug.

children must have been great. Many, if not most, were suitable to serve as toys for parents to buy for their offspring, or the latter to do so with their own pocket money. It is reasonable to consider them as toys, at least in many cases.

Finds of this type from the Thames in the sixteenth century include a hollow bird with a moveable tongue. More common are flat human figures dressed as gentlemen and gentlewomen with widely splayed arms. Fingers could be inserted within the splays to manipulate the figure, or it could be suspended from a ribbon and made to 'dance'. Other miniature copies survive of cauldrons, skillets, cups, ewers, and dishes. More elaborate models include buffets, that is to say dressers used for serving food and displaying dishes. These were stamped out on sheets of pewter which could be bent or slotted into a three-dimensional form. Coaches of a similar kind have been found, together with flat horses to pull them. A 'little coach' bought for James

Cavendish in 1601 at a cost of 14*d.* may have been such a thing.[39] A two-dimensional galleon has been found, with three masts, guns, and a crew member blowing a trumpet. Fairs would have been places at which such toys were sold. An author writing in 1631 mentions that children could buy 'quills' at Bartholomew Fair in London, meaning specially manufactured tubes 'out of which they can shoot a snake to fear their fellows'.[40] Playing with dolls and miniatures also leads to a wish for small buildings in which to place them. Medieval princes had castles made for this purpose, and it is likely that these or dolls-houses were produced for the wealthy in Tudor England. For ordinary children, a small disused box may have been just as acceptable, and it would not have been difficult for them (or for a sympathetic adult) to turn a box (or make one) into an identifiable house, perhaps with a roof thatched with straws.

Another group of toys were those that needed physical effort. One was the tiny windmill to run with or wave about, described by Thomas Blundeville in 1561 as 'a whirligig ... made like windmill sails'.[41] The linguist John Florio characterised it in 1598 as 'a piece of card or paper cut like a cross and with a pin put in at the end of a stick which, running against the wind, doth twirl about. Our English children call it a windmill.'[42] A variant of this contained a string which, when wound up, caused the vanes to spin as the string was pulled.[43] Then there was the hobby-horse: a natural attraction in an age when the horse was so essential for transport and riding one such a mark of social status. A simple stick to hold between the legs could go some way to satisfying a 'rider', but illustrations in books show that sticks were also manufactured with a modelled horse's head at the end to give them more authenticity (Fig. 20, p. 74).[44]

Finally there were tops, produced in several kinds and sizes, ranging from small ones for spinning with the fingers to the larger that were whipped to revolve them, culminating in versions that could be used by adults for exercise or as a competitive sport. Shakespeare refers to a tipsy man as whirling about like 'the parish top'.[45] The English-to-Latin dictionary, *Promptorium Parvulorum*, compiled for use in schools in 1440 but printed in England as late as 1528, lists four kinds of tops which it says were used in children's play: 'top', 'prill', 'spilcock', and 'whirligig', although the latter, as we have seen, could also mean a windmill. One form of whirligig, preserved in the London finds, was a pierced metal disk with cogs.[46] This was threaded on to a double

solennitate beatorum martyrum
dyonisii rustici & eleutherii passio
ne decorasti concede nobis famuli
tuis digna veneratione eorum me
moriam celebrare vt quorum do
ctrina exeplo tibi gallorum sub
didisti colla fauertica ipsorum i
teruentione assidua mereamur
adipisti gaudia sempiterna. Per.
De Sancto Martino. Antipho.

Bea
tu
virum cu
ius anima
paradisu
possidet
vnde ex
ultant angeli letantur archangeli
chorus sanctorum proclamat turba
virginum inuitat mane nobiscum
ineternum. ꝟ⁹ Amauit eum dns

20. Boys on hobby horses, the heads specially manufactured for realism.

string which could be wound up and flexed indefinitely to make the disk whirr with a buzzing sound. Other words, 'scopperil', 'spilcock', spilquern', and 'whirlbone', are found in school texts, testifying to the variety of spinning toys and to words that circulated almost wholly among children themselves.[47]

GAMES OF SKILL

A vast number of games of skill were played by children and youths in Tudor and early Stuart England. A single play, *Apollo Shroving*, performed by the scholars of Hadleigh School, Suffolk, on Shrove Tuesday 1627, mentions (as being known to the boys) blind man's buff, blow-point, check-stones, dice, football, hide and seek, leap-frog, morell (nine-men's morris), mumble-the-peg, mumchance, nine holes, quoits, scourge-top, span-counter, spurn-point, tick-tack, trap-out, and truss.[48] Some were also adult games, others more specific to children. Many were still current in the nineteenth century, when they were catalogued in great detail by the folklorist Alice Bertha, Lady Gomme.[49] The following account must necessarily be a more abbreviated one.

Children's games in Tudor England can be divided into those involving skill (manual dexterity or mental power) and those requiring physical strength. In the first category there could be actions using parts of the body alone: whistling, bird calls, popping noises, or tricks with the fingers. One of the latter, 'handy-dandy', in which small items are moved from hand to hand while the onlooker tries to guess where they are, is mentioned in the fourteenth century and gained an entry in Florio's Italian dictionary of 1598: '*bazzicchiare*: to shake between the hands, to play "handy-dandy" '.[50] A rare reference to another occurs in a school Latin dictionary of 1553, where the word *scloppus* (gun) is translated as 'a pot [popping sound] made in the mouth with one finger, as children use to do'.[51]

More interactive was 'cherry-pit' or 'cherry-stone': the competitive game most closely associated with children and the least likely to be played by anyone much older.[52] It involved throwing or flicking cherry stones at a hole or target which enabled scoring and competitive play, perhaps with the forfeiture of the stones that missed. 'Buckle-pit', mentioned by Sir Thomas More in 1532, may have been a variant word, implying a contest to hit a pit.[53] 'Penny-prick' consisted of aiming at a penny, perhaps to win it.[54] Cob-nuts (large hazel-nuts) were similar items of play.[55] They could be used like cherry stones. Claudius Hollyband, in a book to teach Italian in 1583, describes boys saying 'We will make a pit-hole and there cast our nuts.' The nuts were also the currency which the winner took and ate, because Hollyband's boys complain that they have only rotten ones.[56] Other ways of playing with nuts may have been in a kind of miniature game of bowls or throwing them individually to try to knock down a pile of themselves, again with the winner rewarded.[57]

Marbles could have been used in the same way. As objects they existed by the 1550s, as we shall see, but the common words used for them in later times – 'marbles', 'alleys', or 'taws' – are recorded only from about 1700.[58] They must have had an earlier name: perhaps merely 'stones', the name given to the tiny balls being rolled by a boy in a seventeenth-century engraving (Fig. 21, below).[59] 'Check-stones', meaning smooth round pebbles, is another possibility.[60]

21. Children's games from Comenius's *Orbis Sensualium Pictus* (1659). They include bowling at skittles, whipping tops, shooting, and swinging.

There are also likely to have been games like 'conkers', using a nut or plantain to strike that of one's opponent. The boy who became the famous knight William Marshal played 'knights' with plantains against King Stephen in 1152. Something similar was still being done by children in the nineteenth century: holding the plantain near the top end and trying to knock off the opponent's head with one's own.[61]

A game must have existed, too, like the later five-stones in which small bones, stones, or marbles are tossed or picked up deftly with the hands. That term is not found in Tudor England but the word 'knuckle-bone' appears in a school dictionary in the fifteenth century, and Wager's play *The Longer Thou Livest* refers to a boy having learnt to play with a sheep's joint.[62] The latter source mentions a game called 'span-counter' in which counters or small balls may have been thrown at some distance to a hit a target or to come within a distance of it equivalent to the span of a hand.[63] A further game of dexterity was the one known as 'shove-board' or 'shovel-board', played with discs or worn fourpenny-pieces called 'shove-groats' and 'slip-groats', or worn shillings.[64] The discs were propelled by the hand from the edge of the board to reach a target coin, or to knock rival coins out of the way. This was a popular adult pastime: Falstaff in Shakespeare's *Henry IV Part II* ordered his retainer Bardolph to throw the obstreperous Pistol downstairs 'like a shove-groat shilling'.[65] That being the case, it is likely that children copied what their elders did, with counters or pieces of wood which were more easily obtainable.

Of games that required more mental ability, 'merels' is the one most closely associated with childhood.[66] The best description, by Randle Cotgrave in 1611, called it a 'boyish game called *merills* or five-penny morris, played here with stones but in France with pawns or men made of purpose'.[67] It required two players and needed no more than a grid of three concentric squares which could be scratched on any stone slab. The pieces were small stones which were moved around to make groups that allowed one's opponent's stones to be removed. Alternatively the game could have been played with pegs on a board and, at least among adults, with logs on a marked-out piece of ground, hence Shakespeare's comment that 'the nine-men's morris is filled up with mud'.[68]

Dice playing was popular throughout society, and there were various forms of it including 'gresco', 'hazard', 'mumchance', and 'passage'.[69] Horman mentions it in his *Vulgaria* as being practised by children: 'Men play with three dice and children with four dalies'.[70] 'Daly' seems to have been a word for a primitive children's die or knuckle-bone equivalent.[71] Another dicing game was 'even and odd' (or 'odd and even'), presumably scoring according to the dice numbers. Richard Huloet, in a dictionary of 1552, called it 'a game much used nowadays among children'.[72] The play *Jack Juggler* (1565) describes boys casting dice at a street corner, and one simple-minded player losing his money in doing so.[73] At the same time there was an ancient tradition of hostility to dice playing, traceable back to Chaucer's 'Pardoner's Tale', for allegedly leading to gambling and immorality.[74] One school author, John Withals, tried to have the best of both worlds in his popular elementary Latin dictionary. After listing dicing terms and their Latin equivalents, he included the comment: 'Dicers be the worst people of all.'[75]

More sophisticated games included 'tables' or backgammon, 'tick-tack' (a similar game), chess, and draughts, each of which required a special board, as well as the use of playing cards. All five of these must have come within the knowledge of boys in grammar schools. Horman included the sentence: 'I have bought a playing table with twelve points on one side and chequers on the other.'[76] Tudor moralists often criticised the use of playing cards, but Sir Thomas Elyot, writing on the education of noblemen in 1531, thought that playing backgammon, chess, and cards all developed one's 'wit', and recommended them to that extent.[77] Many of the nobility and gentry seem to have taken the same view. Edward Lord Windsor, as we have seen, thought it acceptable for his sons to be shown holding cards in their portrait of 1569, and one of the earl of Rutland's sons was given 20*d.* to play cards at Christmas for stakes.[78]

There is a rare description of schoolboys playing with cards in a French-and-English phrase book of 1586. When their master sanctioned a break from lessons one afternoon, four of them decided to play 'trump'. This was a popular and easy game: a later observer thought that 'every child almost of eight years hath a competent knowledge' of it.[79] They cut to deal, and each player got nine cards. The top card of the residue was turned up and its suit became trumps. The boys played to gain tricks and win currency in the form of pins, a medium to be explained presently. They valued a king at six pins, a queen at four, a knave at two, and the other cards at one apart from the ace of trumps which counted against all. The boy who won the game demanded payment for six cards.[80]

Other games of skill were played on a larger scale and needed more physical effort. These too were mainly adult pursuits and involved apparatus beyond the means of most children, although they could be copied in cruder ways. They included bowls: very popular among men in Tudor times, although Elyot considered the heavy balls as liable to injure the muscles.[81] 'Loggats', first mentioned in 1541 and therefore a new game or a new name for an old one, involved throwing logs at a target in a similar manner to bowling.[82] 'Quoits', a third such game, used discs of stone or metal for the same purpose and could be imagined as played by children, as it was in the verse of the young Sir Thomas More. 'Mumble-the-peg' was a knife-throwing game. The first player whose knife did not stick in the ground had to draw out with his teeth a peg driven into the earth.[83] Skittles was a very common amusement, although that word is not attested in Tudor England. The names then in use were 'kayles', 'skayles', and 'pins', played either with nine pins or ten pins.[84] Finally there was closh, which is recorded in the fifteenth and sixteenth centuries up to 1588, but disappeared thereafter, at least by that name.[85] It appears to have been a gentle diversion like croquet (Elyot thought it too gentle for noblemen) in which a ball was propelled by a bat through a hoop, and must have been widely played in view of the danger it was thought to pose (like kayles) to the practice of archery.[86]

The problem about understanding children's games in the distant past is that we know so little about how they were played, by whom, where, and with what result. In Tudor England there is a strand of evidence that explains one aspect of this: the playing of games for rewards. In the 1960s and 1970s, excavations were made on the site of the Carmelite friary in Coventry, whose building was used for a short period in the mid-sixteenth century to house a local grammar school. In the former choir of the church, which served as the classroom at that time, a large trove of little items was discovered which had fallen through the floorboards. These were the kind of objects that boys kept in their pockets or brought out for amusement. They included a few marbles made of stone, brick, and clay, along with a Jew's harp that is played with the mouth. The vast majority of the finds, however, which numbered hundreds, were tiny metal things: aglets (or tags) from the ends of laces, pins, beads, and discs and jetons of metal or stone.[87] These are revealing about how games were played. Some of the discs are the counters that were needed in games where pieces had to be moved around. Others are the currency used in playing. Contests of skill or chance need a coinage to measure winning and losing, and most children did not have access to money. Instead they had recourse to common objects.

This reading of the evidence from Coventry is confirmed by documentary and literary records, including the game of cards described above. In 1583 the schoolmaster Claudius Hollyband imagined schoolboys saying 'Let us play for points.' 'What shall we stake?' 'For every point a pin.'[88] Somewhat later, the early seventeenth-century tale of Tom Thumb describes how its miniature hero played with other children in the street 'for counters, pins and points, and cherry stones'. These items were won and lost like coins, and when Tom's stock was all gone, he was obliged to dive into cherry bags to get stones until he was captured by a scholar (meaning a schoolboy) and shut into the box where the boy kept his pins, in other words his currency.[89] Such practices are paralleled exactly in the case of the six-year-old Richard Fermor, orphan son of an Oxfordshire gentleman. In 1581 his guardian paid 3*d.* 'for a dozen of points [metal tags] for him to play with' and 4*d.* for 'two little boxes to keep his points and counters in'. A further 2*d.* was spent 'for pins for him to play with at Christmas'.[90] A boy could even be accused of cutting off the points from his laces for the purpose.[91] Such references are precious, because they point to the affection that children might have for their games and possessions. These little insignificant things, and the boxes in which they were kept, testify to the childhood sense of having treasures, which is something that we can all remember and empathise with.

GAMES OF ACTION

There were many games of action, especially for adult men (at least in the records), and as with games of skill, what is said about men can be assumed in most cases to have been done by boys and youths, and in some cases by girls and women. These could include athletic feats and chasing. 'Spurn-point' has been suggested as a form of hop-scotch.[92] 'Leap-frog', jumping over another person's back, is mentioned in Shakespeare's *Henry V*.[93] 'Truss' seems to have been similar, involving one or more players lifting others.[94] The fool Moros in Wager's play boasted that 'I outrun all the boys in the school.'[95] Competitive running is mentioned in Oxford in the 1490s,[96] and 'a running place' occurs in a school Latin dictionary in 1553.[97] Castiglione's *The Book of the Courtier*, translated into English in 1561, recommended the nobility and gentry to practise running, jumping, wrestling, and throwing weights as a valuable part of military training.[98] When James I allowed Robert Dover to institute 'Olympick Games' in the Cotswolds in 1612, running and jumping were two of the activities.[99] Swimming, as we shall find, was recommended by at least two educational writers, and Latin and English handbooks on how to do it were written in the 1580s and 1590s. It seems not have been widely practised, however, since it was wild swimming, done naked, and limited to men and boys in the summer months. Apart from a few enthusiasts, it was probably most common among those involved with boats: sailors, bargees, and their children.[100]

Running could also form part of a game. Crossing a space of ground from refuge to refuge while avoiding a catcher is recorded in medieval times. It included a ritual in which the chased and the chaser chanted a rhyme before the run took place.[101] Both game and rhyme were still in use in Tudor times because they are recorded again by the Oxford scholar Gerald Langbaine, remembering his schooldays in the 1620s:

Chased: Pe, pe, postola,
    How many miles to Beverley?
Chaser: Eight, eight, and other eight.
Chased: Think you I shall get thither tonight?
Chaser: Yes, if your horse be good and light.[102]

Running-and-chasing games were common under the names 'base' or 'prisoners' base'. Shakespeare's *Cymbeline* refers to 'lads more like to run the

22. Boys playing chess and cards, wearing hats with feathers, watched by their father, Lord Edward Windsor.

country base' than to commit slaughter in battle.[103] Such games often involved a prison area, in which those caught were held until all had been captured and a winner identified. A less strenuous version called 'barley break' was also played in the early modern period. It required six participants, three of each sex, one couple of whom were placed in a central area called 'hell' and the game involved them catching the others, and the captives joining them in the task. 'Barley' appears to mean an immunity that was given or could be gained on a particular spot.[104]

Other active games recorded before 1600 included 'king-by-your-leave' and 'blind-man's-buff', both of which involved a player being blindfolded. There is an unusually precise description of the first of these in the 1572 edition of Richard Huloet's Latin dictionary:

King-by-your-leave: a play that children have, where one sitting blind-fold in the middle hideth so till the rest have hidden themselves, and he then going to seek them, if any get his place in the mean space, that same is king in his room.[105]

This leaves us wondering how the king could both defend his 'seat' and capture other players, or why any player should have wished to be the pursuer rather than the pursued. 'Hot cockles' was another variant, in which a player lay or knelt with the eyes covered, and tried to guess which player struck them on the back, possibly then chasing them as was the custom when I played it in the 1940s.[106]

Games of strength for men were common and young people copied them. John Stow, the Elizabethan historian, described youths in London, on holidays, 'leaping, dancing, shooting, wrestling, casting of the stone or ball'.[107] Robert Dover's games gave opportunities for 'throwing the sledge' or 'spurning the bar', the missile being a heavy piece of wood.[108] Wrestling was widely popular for males. It featured in the fourteenth-century *Tale of Gamelyn*, attributed to Chaucer in Tudor times, as well as in the printed editions of the popular outlaw epic, *A Little Gest of Robin Hood*. The Cornish historian Richard Carew, writing in 1602, noted that it was common in the west of England. 'You shall hardly find an assembly of boys in Devon and Cornwall where the most untowardly [awkward] will not as readily give you a muster [display] of this exercise as you are prone to require it.' He gave the rules as he knew them in his part of the world. Bystanders formed a ring, into the centre of which the two combatants came stripped to their doublets and hose. Each took hold of the other, holds being lawful only above the waist, and the object was to cast the opponent on the ground, so that at least one shoulder and one foot made contact with it. The winner was exonerated from playing again with the vanquished, but was expected to take on another challenger.[109] An alternative form was for the combatants to wear collars of fabric, and for each to grip the other's collar to wrestle him down.[110]

There were numerous ball games, which might involve using a hand, foot, or bat of some kind (Fig. 23, p. 84). A particular game might be played with more than one of these. Their more sedate forms have already been mentioned. A more active one was 'stool-ball', recorded from 1475, in which

23. Death taking one of two players in a game like tennis. Epidemics in Tudor towns did not spare the young.

the stool was apparently a wicket, defended by a player from the bowler by holding a bat, presumably with the chance of scoring runs or points. The game was sufficiently harmless to be played by girls or women, and there are several literary references to the fact. Alternatively it might take place around Easter and involve both young men and women, with a pudding as the prize for the victors.[111] 'Trap-out' and 'trap-ball' were probably forms of 'knur and spell', in which a ball is released from a trap and hit with a bat.[112]

Tennis was widespread. The word originally seems to have applied to any kind of game in which two or more players competed by hitting a ball against a wall, the ground, or even one another. One Elizabethan writer called the similar game of battledore and shuttlecock 'tennis'.[113] Hitting could be done with the hand or with a racket. In France the name for tennis was 'the game of the palm', and it is likely that some of its forms used hands and resembled fives, a term that is not recorded until 1636.[114] The games known as 'hand in' or 'hand out' may have been of a similar kind.[115] Equally a racket could be used by the sixteenth century, or both racket and hand. King Philip of Castile, visiting England in 1506, played with a racket against the marquess of Dorset using his hand. The king gave the marquess fifteen points to compensate for his advantage.[116]

Tennis playing was liable to cause a nuisance. It could be done against buildings like churches with buttresses, which added variations and possibilities but posed a danger to windows. The dean and chapter of Exeter

Cathedral complained about young people playing it in their cloisters in the 1440s, to the damage of the walls and the glazing.[117] Equally it might be done in a street. At Pershore, Worcestershire, in 1441 a prohibition was made against anyone engaging in 'tennis playing' in the king's highway or in any private places.[118] By the sixteenth century special tennis courts were being built, chiefly in London and the university towns, where an income could be made by charging players. Their keepers provided soft shoes, rackets, and balls for a fee, but these places were the resort of adult courtiers, gentlemen, and scholars, and are unlikely to have been available to any but the wealthiest children.[119]

The courts developed what has become known as 'real tennis' in which the ball is bounced off walls. By 1600 it already had much of the modern terminology: 'deuce', 'advantage', 'set', and scoring in fifteens.[120] But by the end of the sixteenth century there was also a form of the game like modern lawn tennis, played across a rope or a net. When the earl of Hertford entertained Queen Elizabeth at Elvetham, Hampshire, in 1591, the queen watched from a window as ten of the earl's servants marked out a square court beneath her, with a dividing line. The game that followed was known as 'bord and cord', perhaps because each player had a board or racket and played across a cord. The men divided into teams of five, and the match lasted for an hour and a half.[121] But the emergence of elite forms of the game, of course, does not rule out the persistence of more basic and individual versions in other places, especially at schools like Eton where distinct forms of fives evolved.

Other handball and football games gathered in large numbers of boys or youths, and were therefore popular rather than aristocratic sports. They probably took different forms from place to place. Carew described one variety, which he termed 'hurling' and was, in fact, chiefly a form of handball since he does not mention kicking. It could be done in two ways. 'Hurling to goals' was played by teams of fifteen, twenty, or thirty players on either side. It took place in a limited area with two goals, each having two goalkeepers. Each player formed a pair with an opponent. On getting the ball, the player could hold or throw it, at which point his opponent could tackle him by holding him and be fended off with punches. If he fell on the ground, he had to yield the ball. Having escaped the opponent, anyone could try to stop him. There were recognised rules, including an offside convention. Carew gives these for east Cornwall, which he knew, but others no doubt prevailed in other places. The matches in his own county commonly took place after weddings, which brought together enough youths or men to form teams.[122]

Carew describes a second form of the game as 'hurling to the country', which was a larger and less structured activity. It was organised by two or more gentlemen who brought together men from as many as six parishes to play it. The goals were houses three or four miles apart, and there was no restriction on the number of players or much in terms of rules. A ball was used, small and of silver, which could be held or thrown, and the player could be attacked by any number of opponents but, if forced to the ground, had to surrender the ball. It was even possible to riders to join in and seize the ball if they could. The struggle went 'over hills, dales, hedges, ditches, yea, and through bushes, briars, mires, plashes, and rivers, so as you shall sometimes see twenty or thirty lie tugging together in the water'. Carew commended the game for the manliness and courage required, but admitted that the result was often 'bloody pates, bones broken and out of joint, and such bruises as serve to shorten their days'.[123]

The resemblance between handball and football of this kind with military fighting is confirmed from other sources. One name for such a game was 'camp-ball' or 'camping', from a verb 'camp' which means 'to fight'. The commotions that broke out in England in 1549 were called by contemporaries 'camping' or 'the camping time'.[124] These were the rising in Devon and Cornwall against the new Book of Common Prayer, and that in Norfolk caused by economic grievances. Tudor writers who noticed football disliked its freedom from restraint, its potentially subversive violence, and (probably) its egalitarianism. It did not allow any respect for rank, and Elyot declared it should 'be utterly abjected [rejected] by noblemen'.[125] Richard Mulcaster, writing in 1581, called it the activity 'of a rude multitude, with bursting of shins and breaking of legs . . . neither civil nor worthy the name of any train [passage] to health'.[126] Two years later, the Puritan writer Philip Stubbes added his condemnation of it as more of 'a bloody and murthering practice than a fellowly sport or pastime'. Men lay in wait for their enemies and attacked them, 'so that by this means sometimes their necks are broken, sometimes their backs, sometimes their legs, sometimes their arms'. He dismissed it as having any place as a Sunday recreation (and by implication at any other time) because, so he claimed in a fine array of synonyms, it leads to 'envy, malice, rancour, choler, hatred, displeasure, enmity, and what not else'![127]

It was indeed possible for communal games of action to turn into mimic wars, under the inspiration of contemporary events. Children in London had chosen kings and fought battles in 1400, six months after Richard II was overthrown by Henry IV.[128] In 1548 the boys of Bodmin School in Cornwall, who were accustomed to divide into sides for their games, formed two religious parties: the old religion and the new. This was at the time that the Protestant Reformation under Edward VI was being enforced across the country. The division, so Richard Carew remembered long afterwards, led to rough conflicts, 'each party knowing and still keeping the same companions and captain'. It ended when one boy made a gun from an old candlestick, charged it with gunpowder and stone, and succeeded in killing a calf, after which the schoolmaster intervened with a good whipping of those concerned.[129] This affair had a sequel in London in March 1554, after the failure of Wyatt's rebellion against Mary Tudor. Boys gathered in Finsbury Fields outside the city 'to play a new game, some took Wyatt's part and some the queen's and made a combat in the fields'. The city authorities took immediate action over such a sensitive matter, and many of the participants were arrested and shut up in the Guildhall.[130] Disturbances like these were not far away from the unruliness of teenage apprentices and others, which we shall encounter in Chapter 7.

It remains to observe that play, for children and adults, had something of a calendar framework.[131] The twelve days of Christmas were especially popular for recreations of any kind and, as we shall see, attempts by the Tudors to steer people away from games to practising archery had to make an exception for that season. Shrove Tuesday had its cock-fighting as well as football matches, and March was also a month associated with football.[132] The six weeks of Lent in this season, up to Easter, were characterised by the whipping of tops.[133] This may have been because the weather was improving and children were able to play out of doors, but there may have been a link with the scourging of Jesus on Good Friday. Another feature of Lent was the 'Jack-a-Lent': a figure of a man set up to be pelted, something said by Ben Jonson to have been done by boys.[134] Spring and summer were appropriate times for all kinds of outdoor games and, if we extend recreation to include food gathering, then autumn was an opportunity for children to go out seeking fruit and nuts (sometimes illicitly).[135] The dark days of November and December were marked by the customs of St Clement's, St Katherine's, and St Nicholas's days when children (at least up to 1540) dressed up and went around asking for food and drink at people's houses.[136] Meanwhile the slaughter of pigs in November made available a supply of bladders for ball games. Play, one may conclude, could adapt itself to all classes, all surroundings, and all seasons.

ADULT ATTITUDES TO CHILDREN'S PLAY

Hitherto we have approached play chiefly from the viewpoint of children and adolescents. It is also relevant to consider how adults regarded their play, because adults had the power if not to stop it entirely at least to oppose, restrict, or regulate it. Apart from parents and employers, whose role in this respect is little recorded, there were three public agencies whose concerns were affected by play: schools, the Church, and the Crown.

Schools, as will be shown, educated a large (although still unquantifiable) proportion of the junior population, at least for parts of their youth. Writers on education in the sixteenth century considered that it should include the body as well as the mind. Sir Thomas Elyot, whose work *The Governor* (1531) was widely read in the sixteenth century, recommended a range of physical exercises: riding, archery, training in weapons, hunting, wrestling, swimming, and dancing.[137] A similar view was taken by Richard Mulcaster, headmaster of Merchant Taylors' School, London, in his treatise *Positions* (1581). Mulcaster's view of education was that, in principle, it could include anything not obviously inappropriate, and that most activities were potentially of human value. He not only endorsed the games that Elyot listed but added playing with tops and ball games such as handball, football, and 'armball' including tennis, although we have noted his criticism of the rough football played in his day.[138]

In an aristocratic household, young people (especially boys) could undergo schooling and have time for physical activities as well.[139] In schools this was rarely the case. They concentrated on teaching reading or Latin, working long hours by modern standards from early morning to late afternoon, and did not provide for games or sports within their timetables. If boys wanted to play during the school day, they had to do so while coming to school, during the midday break (if they went home for dinner), and when lessons were over (Fig. 24, p. 90). The Tudor play *Nice Wanton* (1560), a work of stern morality, contrasts the obedient boy Barnaby with his disobedient siblings Ismael and Dalilah, who linger on the way to school and eventually play truant altogether.[140] Hollyband could imagine play in these intervals as including whipping tops, playing cards or dice, throwing stones, and (in winter) snowballing or sliding on ice.[141]

Nonetheless schoolteachers were inclined to tolerate play at least as a topic in class, because it interested their pupils and could be used to make learning attractive. Sentences translated from English to Latin at Magdalen College School, Oxford, in the 1490s included such activities as archery, hunting, fishing, bear-baiting, and a sports day with archers and runners competing for prizes.[142] William Horman, who taught at both Winchester and Eton colleges, gave fourteen pages to games in his book of Latin exercises, *Vulgaria*. He mentioned running, wrestling, archery, swimming, hunting, dancing, and tennis playing, as well as sedentary games like chess, backgammon, and dice.[143] Other times for schoolchildren to play came with holidays. Up to the Reformation there were many holy days in the calendar when school was either suspended or abridged. The number was much reduced in the 1540s, but there were still two or three dozen that schools might observe, perhaps with attendance at church followed by a cessation of lessons. Occasional extra holidays, known as 'remedies' or 'playing days', were also granted either by the teacher or at the request of some influential person, although usually more influential than the dim but wealthy young Abraham Slender who solicited one in *The Merry Wives of Windsor*.[144]

A few schools boarded their pupils and therefore had to make arrangements for what their charges did outside the classroom. These included cathedral choristers (at least up to the Reformation), the two large boarding

24. Boys arrive at school, bringing toys with them.

schools of Winchester and Eton, and small private schools of whose practices we know very little. A description of life at Winchester in about 1550 states that time was allowed on Tuesdays and Thursdays for recreation, known as 'Hills', on the neighbouring ridge of St Catherine's Hill. The boys were required to go in pairs and were supervised by a prefect to see that order was kept. Their games included quoits and ball games played with the hand, the foot, or a bat.[145] An account from Eton in 1560 points to similar practices. Four prefects were assigned to watch over the boys 'in the field, when they play' to guard against fighting, torn clothes, or black eyes. An hour was usually available after 3.00 p.m. to go to the surrounding fields. Play-time was increased in the summer from midday dinner until 3.00 p.m., and again for an hour in the evening. Holy days brought further relaxations, even after the Reformation: on 14 September, for example, which had been the old Holy Cross day, the Eton boys were allowed to go searching for nuts.[146]

The Church was another potential restriction on play. Officially this mattered less to children than it did to adolescents. Up to the Reformation, as we shall discover, there was no obligation for anyone to go to church until they reached puberty, at which point they were regarded, and required to behave, as adults and keep regular Sunday attendance. Even after the Reformation, there was no statutory requirement to do so until the age of sixteen.[147] Nevertheless Richard Whitford's popular guide to religion, *A Work for Householders* (1530), urged adults to ensure that those in their charge (children and servants) came to church on Sunday morning, and spent the afternoon in appropriate pastimes. These were not to include tennis, closh, bowling, card playing, or dicing.[148] A common image in parish churches up to the Reformation was the 'Sunday Christ': a wall painting of Christ wounded by the tools and playthings used by those who breached the rules of keeping Sunday holy.[149]

This view of Sunday continued after the Reformation among Puritans, who often had a critical and sometimes a hostile view of games. John Hooper, bishop of Gloucester, wrote in 1550 that all games played for money were forbidden by the Eighth Commandment,[150] and Philip Stubbes, in his *Anatomy of the Abuses in England*, denounced not only gambling but games more widely. All were to be avoided on Sundays, many on other days apart from the Christmas season, and football (as we have seen) on any occasion at all.[151]

91

Neither Hooper nor Stubbes mentioned children in particular, but their warn-ings were likely to influence how godly parents and guardians brought up their offspring, which may have limited what could be played and when. And once the young reached their early or mid-teens, they were undoubtedly required to undertake attendance in their parish churches. Records of the Church courts and of visitations made by bishops reveal the actions taken, at least occasionally, against those who preferred to use Sundays as times for amusement.[152]

The Crown supported the Church's policy towards adolescents in this respect. It required them to be in church on Sunday mornings and after-noons, especially after the Reformation. The new services of the Book of Common Prayer of 1549 and its successors were important to the Crown for teaching people their duties to God, the monarch, and their neighbours.[153] Even before that time acts of Parliament had been passed in 1477 and 1512 against the playing of games on Sundays and festival days, which drew people away from their parish churches 'to the high displeasure of Almighty God'.[154] Games among those of an age able to work were seen as also leading to idle-ness, beggary, and crimes. A statute of 1495 prohibited apprentices, servants, and labourers from playing backgammon except for a stake in the form of food or drink, and other games were forbidden except at Christmas, and then only in their master's houses. These included tennis, closh, bowls, dice, and cards. Fines were to be levied on both the participants and on any employers who winked at the practice.[155]

The Crown had a more specific concern about games, in that they were felt to distract the male population from the practice of archery with long-bows. Tudor society was still a military one. There was virtually no profes-sional army, and the defence of the realm, the keeping of peace, or the mounting of expeditions abroad depended on amateur soldiers. Until the later part of the Tudor era, when hand-guns became widely available, a supply of good archers seemed essential. The longbow was the weapon that had won the famous victories of Crécy, Poitiers, and Agincourt, as well as Flodden in 1513. It was part of the national heritage and its hero was Robin Hood, whose exploits were so popular in ballads and plays during the sixteenth and seventeenth centuries.

Accordingly, Tudor governments sought to maintain the skill of the male population in archery and saw other games as distractions in this respect. The statute of 1477 complained that the ancient tradition of bow shooting was being undermined by recreational games, and forbade any householder or tenant to allow them on their premises.[156] A more comprehensive act of Parliament in 1512 set out to encourage archery in a positive way. It required all the king's subjects up to the age of sixty to possess a bow and arrows, and to practise using them. Fathers, governors, and rulers of boys of tender age were required to bring them up in the knowledge of bow shooting. Every man with male children in his house was to provide each one, from the ages of seven to seventeen, with a bow and two arrows, and to teach them the skill. At the age of seventeen each youth was to acquire a bow and four arrows at his own expense or that of his family. Targets, known as butts, were to be made in towns for practice, and competing games were to be suppressed. Shooting with the rival crossbow was forbidden, except by substantial landowners.[157]

This policy continued in principle for the rest of the century. Educational writers pronounced in its favour. 'In mine opinion', wrote Elyot, 'none [in terms of exercises] may be compared with shooting in the longbow.'[158] Roger Ascham wrote a whole book, *Toxophilus* (1545), to explain and encourage the use of the weapon among the gentry and yeomanry of England.[159] Schoolbooks mentioned shooting and its variants: at butts, at pricks or wands, or at 'rover marks', choosing a distant target at random.[160] Some adults followed the law. The guardian of 'little Francis', mentioned in the previous chapter, purchased for his use a bow costing 6*d.*, six arrows for 3*d.*, and bow-strings, a shooting glove, and a brace for another 3*d.*[161] Despite this, it remained difficult to enforce the practice as much as the authorities wished. In 1541 the craftsmen who made bows and arrows complained to Parliament about the games that were competing with archery. The provisions of the 1512 statute were re-enacted, with fines on those who kept premises for playing them and a repetition against apprentices and servants doing so except at Christmas.[162]

Despite the statute, a mere four years elapsed before Ascham was moved to protest that the law was being ignored.[163] In 1571 a further statute tried to reimpose all the previous legislation,[164] but six years later the writer John Fit John thought that in the countryside, at least, shooting had to compete as best it could with jumping, dancing, dice, cards, and bowling.[165] By 1603, the Cornish writer Richard Carew was lamenting that longbows were hung up to be smoked above fireplaces. They were, he argued, still valuable for exercise, hunting, recreation, and protection in war and peace, but his frequent use of the past tense makes it clear that the longbow no longer had the support that the Tudor lawmakers and writers hoped to build.[166] Games, in contrast, against all opposition, maintained their popularity among both young and old.

4

RELIGION

STARTING OUT

People in Tudor England still lived in the world created at the end of the Roman Empire. That world believed that society and all its members should be Christian. Every new child should be taken to church and christened on the day of birth or soon afterwards. If it was weak and in danger of death, lay people should give it a simple baptism at home. Only baptism would save it from mankind's original sin, and secure it everlasting life in heaven. The Church's insistence and the beliefs of most people probably ensured that all but a few children, perhaps in marginalised families living remotely, received baptism in this way. When the Reformation came, it made little difference to the practice. The registration of baptism after 1538 sought to ensure that every baby still came to church for the purpose. From 1549 the new Church of England services delayed the rite, but only until the first Sunday after the birth, and the duty to do emergency baptisms at home remained in force.[1]

Having received each child at birth or soon afterwards, however, the medieval Church took little interest in them until they neared puberty. Children often went to church with their parents up to the Reformation and afterwards, as we shall see, but their presence was not demanded there. The only other formal attendance required of a child, up to the 1540s, was to be brought to the bishop for confirmation. Confirmation had originally been part of the baptism service but, during the early centuries of Christianity, the main part of the rite was left to the local priest, after which the bishop confirmed and validated the fact. In the small dioceses of the Mediterranean world, where bishops looked after a city and its surroundings, this caused no problem, but England possessed only seventeen dioceses until the Reformation (when another five were added), which led to difficulties. Lincoln diocese, the largest, stretched over nine counties from the River Humber to the River Thames, and even Henry VIII's addition of bishops at Oxford and Peterborough still left it with six. Making contact with bishops for confirmation was therefore not easy outside their cathedral cities or the villages where they had their country houses.

Up to the Reformation there was no minimum age to be confirmed. A baby could be given the rite immediately after baptism if there was a bishop present, as there might be at a birth in a royal or noble family (Fig. 25, p. 97). Medieval bishops and writers on the subject urged that children be brought to the bishop when young: within three to five years after birth. William Lyndwood, the chief authority on English Church law in the fifteenth century, said whenever the bishop came within seven miles.[2] Up to about the 1550s some bishops had suffragans to help them, but even so, in large dioceses like Exeter, Lichfield, and Lincoln, a bishop's visit to a district might happen very rarely. It was not impossible for children whose parents were negligent to grow up unconfirmed. Church leaders periodically complained about the fact, but found it hard to prevent, and rules about confirmation had to accept that adults (those who had passed puberty) might turn up as well as children.

Until 1549, two preparations were needed when someone was to be confirmed. The candidate had to be presented by a sponsor, similar to a godparent and sometimes known in practice by that name.[3] The sponsor needed to be someone other than a godparent and of the same sex as the child. Richard Hill noted down the names of his children's sponsors 'at the bishop' just as he did their godparents.[4] Candidates for confirmation also were told to arrive having fasted for at least a few hours and to bring a linen bandage. The ceremony was simple and did not need to take place in church: it could be done wherever the bishop happened to be, even while he was travelling. Children or adults were brought to the bishop in turn. Each sponsor was asked the name of their candidate, and it was possible for the name to be changed at this point although this seems to have happened very rarely.

The bishop anointed his thumb with chrism (the mixture of holy oil and balm also used in baptism) and drew a cross on the candidate's forehead,

25. Confirmation could take place at any time after baptism. Here a bishop confirms a baby, evidently a boy with a male sponsor.

saying in Latin that he confirmed the person in the name of the Trinity. The bandage was then tied around the forehead to protect the chrism, and this had to be kept on (or at least around the neck) until one got home. It was then necessary to go to the parish church within a few days, where the priest washed the forehead into the font to remove any of the holy chrism, and the bandage was undone and burnt.[5] The ritual, however, did not give the recipient any new privileges or duties. As we shall see, both before and after the Reformation, receiving communion and entering into the obligations of an adult Christian were linked to age as well as to confirmation.

The reformed Church of England after 1549 kept confirmation as a duty which everyone had to observe. However it took a different view of the ceremony, making it more instructive than had been the case before. It was not quite clear about the appropriate age. One rubric in the new English Prayer Books of 1549–59 recommended confirmation for children once they reached 'years of discretion', meaning puberty. This was the time, said the Prayer Books, when children could understand the promises that their godparents had made for them, and when they became capable of falling into sin through their own frailty and the assaults of the world.[6] The Prayer Books told employers to send their servants and apprentices to be church to be prepared for confirmation, which points to some being then adolescents. However they also talk of children being confirmed once they had learnt and could say the basic prayers, and had been instructed in a new formula called the catechism. This left it open for younger (although not very young) children to be confirmed as well.[7] Parents who were used to children being confirmed as infants were assured that any who died in childhood would enjoy salvation through the virtue of their baptism alone.[8]

The catechism was a series of questions and answers, and was included in all the editions of the Prayer Book. It required one to know the words in English of the three basic texts of the Reformed Church of England: the Lord's Prayer, the Apostles' Creed, and the Ten Commandments. It also involved learning their meaning and significance in a simple way. Bishops were now required to send notice to parishes when they intended to visit the district to administer confirmation. The incumbent of each parish had to forward, with his contingent of young people, a list of the names of those who could say the three basic texts and also a list of those who had mastered the questions and answers.[9] In other words one needed to have been instructed in the catechism and to be able to say the texts, but it was not compulsory to know the questions and answers by heart since they were longer and more complicated. The role of sponsor was now abolished, and one of the godparents was told to bring the child instead. The chrism and the bandage disappeared. In 1549 the bishop, after the saying of some prayers, asked the child's name and said, '[Name], I sign thee with the sign of the cross and lay my hand upon thee.' After 1552 the naming was dropped, as was the sign of the cross, and the bishop merely laid his hands on the candidate's head.[10]

CHILDREN IN CHURCH BEFORE THE REFORMATION

The fact that children were not required to attend church before the Reformation did not mean that they were left to grow up without knowledge of the Christian faith and practices. But the medieval Church authorities assumed that this would reach them through their parents and godparents. These adults ought to teach the children in their care the three basic prayers, which, from the early thirteenth century up to the Reformation, were the Paternoster or Lord's Prayer, the Ave Maria, and the Apostles' Creed. The prayers were customarily learnt and recited in Latin until 1536, when Henry VIII commanded the use of English.[11] Parents and godparents were also considered capable of teaching children about good behaviour in church: to be quiet, when to stand, sit, or kneel, how to hold their hands in prayer, and how to venerate images.

The medieval Church did not make other demands of children. It regarded them as having earned salvation through their baptisms, which could not be compromised until they reached puberty and were capable of sinning. While there are some medieval stories about wicked children being carried away to hell, mainstream theology regarded this as unlikely. St Thomas Aquinas believed that, at the Day of Judgment, the children (already saved) would be spectators at the rewards and punishments meted out to their elders.[12] There was no requirement for children to attend their parish churches, to undergo confession until they reached puberty, or to fast on Fridays and in Lent as adults had to do. Nor were they made to pay any dues to the Church until they reached their teens. In turn they were not allowed the full benefits of Church membership that were given to adults. They could not receive communion except perhaps at the point of death, because communion had to be preceded by confession; nor could they be given the rite of anointing or 'extreme unction' if they were seriously ill, as was done for adults. That was because they were not reckoned able to understand these rites until they reached puberty, and (being innocent) had no need of their benefits.[13]

Nevertheless there is a good deal of evidence, up to the Reformation, about children being present in church at services. Small children might be taken there because it was impossible to leave them at home. In church they might be noisy, then as now provoking hostile reactions from adults. Parishioners at Wymondham and Kirby Bellars in Leicestershire complained in 1519 that 'children there make a noise indecently, so that it is hard to hear divine service', while at Kimpton in Hertfordshire infants 'laugh, cry, and clamour'. Parents might fail to control, or even encourage, their children's behaviour like Thomas Leyk of Gosberton, Lincolnshire, who allegedly 'impeded the service with an infant'.[14] In the years up to 1538, when there were still shrines of saints and holy images in churches, children might be brought to them by parents or guardians in search of healing or in thanks for a cure elicited through prayer.[15]

We should also allow for children coming to church of their own accord, out of curiosity or because it was a place of socialising. In later times, at least, children making mischief in churches could be a problem.[16] Their presence, however, may have varied according to their social status. Wealthy parents would take their offspring because it was regarded as an instructive thing to do. These offspring, like their elders, would have special seats in church because of their rank in society, and those whose families were wealthy might possess a rosary or a prayer book to take with them, as their parents had. In contrast poorer children might be left at home to look after younger siblings, or to carry out domestic tasks. Indeed some parents set little value on church attendance and stayed away as much as possible, in which case their children were likely to do the same.[17]

The medieval Church did not offer a great deal for children specifically, apart from the universal christenings and confirmations (Fig. 26, p. 101). Worship was something that most people watched, rather than had an active part in. The clergy had a use for some boys in their services. In an age when large churches might have several priests saying daily masses, boys were useful in acting as assistants in saying the responses. In all churches they could be valuable helpers in serving at the high (or chief) altar in the chancel, or in carrying candles, holy-water dispensers, and incense boats in processions.[18] During the fifteenth century, as we shall see, the fashion grew for

ntroibo ad altare dei
Ad deum qui letificat

26. A church interior before the Reformation. Children would have
experienced an array of altars, images, and colourful ritual.

having polyphonic music in the larger churches in cities and towns, as well
as in cathedrals and monasteries, for which boys were needed to sing the
treble parts.[19] But as far as children in general were concerned, the medieval
Church did not offer them any more in its buildings than adults. Services,
the chief of which was mass on Sunday mornings, were mostly in Latin,
although there were some prayers and announcements in English, and sometimes sermons in that language as well. Much of the appeal of worship lay in
the surroundings – the imagery, vestments, and candles – and in the ceremonial.[20] There was a procession before Sunday mass during which the congregation was sprinkled with holy water. After the priest had consecrated the

bread and wine, people came out to kiss the pax (a wooden tablet), and when mass was over a small piece of holy bread was distributed to everyone.

Certain days had their own ceremonies in which children could join, but usually without any special role for themselves. At Christmastide most jollifications took place outside church in halls and houses with feasting and singing of carols, the latter not yet a feature of church services. One such carol, which calls on all its listeners to celebrate Christmas, orders every 'groom' and 'page' (man and boy) to bring some sport to liven the occasion.[21] On Candlemas (2 February) everyone was expected to come to church with a candle, and this seems to have included children (Fig. 27, below).[22] They would also have enjoyed what happened on Palm Sunday, the Sunday before Easter. Clergy and parishioners went out of the church in procession to hear the gospel read at the churchyard cross. There a second procession met the first, with boys dressed as prophets, and a hymn was sung by a choir from an external gallery or window, during which cakes were thrown down and scrambled for by children.[23]

Spring and summer saw other processions, especially those of Rogationtide: the fifth week after Easter. On the Monday, Tuesday, and

27. A procession to church on Candlemas Day, 2 February. Children accompany the adults, each with a candle, and dogs go along as well.

Wednesday of that week clergy and parishioners went on long journeys from their parish church to an outlying chapel in the parish or to a neighbouring church. Blessings were pronounced on the fields, mass was celebrated, and was followed by picnics and drinking. Children took part with the adults and shared in the special food.[24] December saw the only church ceremonies in which children had a distinct role: those of the boy bishop, usually chosen from one of the altar boys or choristers who was familiar with the church liturgy. On the 6th, St Nicholas Day, or the 28th, Holy Innocents Day, or both of them, he and a retinue of boy attendants took over the seats of the clergy in church in an act of 'role reversal'. The boys helped sing the services, and the bishop gave blessings. Afterwards they toured the parish, collecting offerings of food or money.[25] But these were special occasions; ordinary Sundays were more uniform and predictable.

Children became adults in the medieval view, as we have seen, when they reached puberty, which enabled them to enter employment and (for a very few) to marry. Some commentators allowed them to receive communion a few years earlier, if they had been confirmed, but from puberty they were expected to enter into the adult life of the parish. There was no formal process or rite of passage for this. It is likely that as puberty approached, children, their parents, godparents, or the parish priest suggested that they should now enter into the adult calendar of Christian observances. That meant going to confession during Lent, when all those past puberty did so, and receiving communion with their elders on Easter Sunday. In doing so they joined the adults but they were not singled out for special attention or celebration at either ceremony. Once this had happened, they were expected to attend church on Sundays and festivals during their teens. Opinions differed about fasting and the making of offerings of money by teenagers. Some authorities extended the exemption from fasting until as late as eighteen, while others demanded at least small offerings at certain times of the year.[26]

CHILDREN IN CHURCH AFTER THE REFORMATION

The Reformation made a good deal of difference to church services. From the late 1530s their environment changed. Shrines and images in the form

28. A church interior after the Reformation: here Parracombe old church, Devon. Children were now part of a static congregation, taught from the Bible, and presented with texts to be learnt.

of statues were removed, and religious paintings were defaced or white-washed over (Fig. 28, above). Altars were taken out in 1550, and vestments were reduced, for most of the time, to a simple white surplice. In 1536 the basic prayers were ordered to be said in English, and in 1549 all church services were translated into that language, apart from during the five years of Mary Tudor's reign (1553–8). Services lost nearly all their former ceremonial. They were simplified in form and became chiefly occasions for prayer, Bible reading, and preaching. Children of the wealthier classes might now possess or be instructed in the new English books of the Reformation. Margaret Willoughby had a copy of the 1549 Prayer Book bought for her in 1550, and one of the revised version two years later along with a small Bible.[27] Oliver Manners, son of the earl of Rutland, got the revised version in 1553, and books of psalms were purchased for three boys in the next generation of his family in 1594.[28]

These changes led to the disappearance of the boys who had hitherto been involved in church services. They were no longer needed to help at the altar or in processions. A single adult parish clerk could do the few tasks required. Polyphony came under criticism. The Reformers disliked it, partly because of its previous Latin nature and its associations with the veneration of the Virgin Mary. Even when sung in English it was felt to obscure the listeners' understanding of the words. Accordingly the parish choirs which had previously enlisted boys went into decline.[29] Nearly all the other ceremonies in which children were involved came to an end. The boy bishop services were forbidden in 1541, while those of Candlemas and Palm Sunday took place for the last time in 1547.[30] An exception was the presence of boys at weddings. The Italian writer Polydore Vergil, who lived in England under Henry VIII, described how English brides came to church 'with two young boys dressed like angels'.[31] The origins of this are not clear. Were they secular or religious, the boys in the latter case being acolytes in surplices? At any rate the practice survived the Reformation, whose leaders wisely avoided challenging folk-customs at baptisms, weddings, and funerals. In the 1590s Thomas Deloney could still describe a bride being 'led to church between two sweet boys', now in secular dress, 'with bride laces and rosemary [sprigs] about their silken sleeves'.[32]

The Reformers set out to improve the religious education of children rather than to give them roles in ceremonies. First of all there were changes in the three basic texts that they were expected to know. The Lord's Prayer and the Apostles' Creed remained obligatory, now in English, but the Ave Maria, a short text praising the Virgin Mary, was replaced by the Ten Commandments, a longer one which contained a set of instructions to be followed. Next, as we have seen, children were required not merely to repeat the three texts but, through learning the catechism, to understand their contents and relevance to modern Christian life. Teaching the catechism could not be safely left to parents and godparents, whose abilities might be limited. It now devolved on the parish clergy. The Prayer Book of 1549 ordered the priest of every parish to announce to his people, at least once every six weeks, that he would hold a catechism class in church for children lasting half an hour before evensong, in the middle of the afternoon. In 1552 he was allowed to appoint someone else to deputise for him. All parents and, as has been mentioned, employers of servants and apprentices, were obliged to see that young people attended until they were confirmed.[33] To legislate was not to implement, of course. A visitation of Somerset by the bishop of Bath and Wells in 1594 found several clergy who were not doing their duty of catechising, some of whom blamed their parishioners for indifference.[34]

After Elizabeth I came to the throne in 1558, the Reformed religion became more entrenched and many of its leaders were more radical than their predecessors. They felt the short Prayer Book catechism to be insufficient and began to write and publish more extensive versions for young people to study so as to form more fully their reformed Christianity.[35] One by Jean Calvin of Geneva, the great Protestant theologian, was published in England in 1560 and reprinted at least seven times during Elizabeth's reign.[36] It covered the Christian faith, law, prayer, and the sacraments, along with a format for examining children before they were admitted to communion. It included prayers for use in private houses, before and after meals, and even one for a child to say before learning a lesson in school. Even more popular was the catechism of Alexander Nowell, dean of St Paul's Cathedral, which came out in 1570 and was reissued on at least nine occasions during the rest of the century, as well as in the seventeenth.[37] In 1571 it was ordered to be used by all schoolmasters. Again it widened its scope by discussing God's laws, the gospel and faith, the relationship of faith and works, how to pray, the sacraments, and even excommunication. Works like these, of course, reached the wealthier and more literate; most children would only have encountered the simpler form in the Prayer Books.

The leaders of the English Reformation were hardly more specific about children's church attendance than their medieval predecessors. The Act of Uniformity in 1559, which established the Church of England for the next eighty-odd years, indeed laid down that everyone should attend church, but that can hardly have been meant to apply to children, who might be too young or absent for the reasons mentioned above.[38] Nevertheless the leaders of the reformed Church seem to have expected those over the age of seven (the end of infancy) to be in church at least occasionally. Godparents were told after 1549 to make sure that their charges 'hear sermons', and Hugh Rhodes, writing about the upbringing of children in 1577, told parents to 'take them often with you to hear God's word preached'.[39]

Full church membership, as in the Middle Ages, continued to start at puberty. That was the age by which children should have been confirmed, and only then could they begin to receive communion even if they had been confirmed at a younger age. The medieval practice of those over puberty taking communion only at Easter was increased during the Reformation to include Christmas and Pentecost as well, to which a fourth Sunday in the autumn came usually to be added. Later in Elizabeth's reign, Parliament felt it necessary to legislate about Catholics, some of whom were now refusing to go to services in their parish churches. Two statutes in 1581 and 1593 ordered everyone aged sixteen or over to attend church unless they had a lawful reason not to do so.[40] This effectively continued the traditional exemption of children from the religious duties of adults.

RELIGION AT HOME

Church was not the only place where children encountered religion in Tudor England. In the upper ranks of society, at least, they met it in the home: either their own home or that of a guardian or employer. Since the later Middle Ages, they had been told to say the basic prayers on rising in the morning. Those who were literate had been encouraged to read the short morning services in the Latin Book of Hours.[41]

In wealthier families up to the Reformation, older children, at least, might be expected to go to mass each day. This would take place in a church or a private chapel. The daily regime set out for Prince Edward (V) in 1473 envisaged him hearing mass before having his breakfast, and it is likely that similar customs were followed in the highest of the early Tudor families.[42] This was certainly so for Henry VIII's son Henry Fitzroy and, at a lower level, for Thomas Cromwell's son Gregory.[43] Juan Luis Vives, influential in England from the 1520s, expected a noble girl to do so, at least on holy days, and advised her to read the epistle and gospel of the day beforehand, with a commentary if she had one.[44] Later in the day, meal times were occasions for prayer. The practice of getting children, especially boys, to say grace before and after dinner and supper was already followed in the fifteenth century and continued during the sixteenth.[45] At night, children were told to ask their parents' blessing before they went to bed. They should kneel and while the parent said 'Our Lord God bless you, child', making the sign of the cross with the right hand and adding, in Latin, 'In the name of the Father and the Son and the Holy Ghost. Amen.'[46]

Wealthy families, up to the Reformation, were likely to own statues, paintings, or even relics of Christ or the saints for veneration. The nobility, most of the gentry, and some merchants had private chapels in their houses with altars, images, and liturgical books. Walls in domestic rooms might be decorated with painted scenes or short religious texts. After the 1470s, printing enabled pictures of the Trinity, Christ, and the Virgin Mary to be mass-produced and sold cheaply. These too could be displayed in people's homes. Those who went to school would learn prayers there as well. In elementary schools, as we shall see, reciting the alphabet was done as a prayer, and the Latin Paternoster was the first text that pupils learnt to read.[47] In early Tudor grammar schools it was common to begin and end the day with Latin prayers (Fig. 29, below).[48] On festival days the school might go to hear mass, perhaps with a holiday afterwards.

29. Religion was also learnt in schools. Here the schoolmaster and pupils of Eton College work beside a Bible text declaring that 'He who spares the rod hates the child'.

Many of these customs survived the Reformation. Its leaders disapproved of formal services in private chapels (which disappeared except as places for personal prayer). They also sought to suppress the sort of imagery associated with Catholicism such as Christ in the arms of the Virgin Mary or on the Cross. But religious art of a kind survived in wealthy people's houses and, for all we know, in ordinary homes since printed religious pictures of a Protestant type continued to be produced. Children and young servants would have seen such art displayed on wall paintings, wall hangings, plasterwork, and woodwork (Fig. 31, p. 114).[49] Texts remained in use for decoration or instruction, especially the Ten Commandments. Imagery merely changed from the crucifixion and the saints to Old Testament stories and parables of Jesus. Surviving examples in Elizabethan houses include the Judgment of Solomon,

30. A Christian family at home. The father is the dominant figure, responsible for the teaching and discipline of his family.

the story of Susannah and the Elders, the parable of Dives and Lazarus, and that of the Prodigal Son. The latter was especially popular, because it was a moral story with scope for representing different scenes, but could not be regarded as superstitious because it did not demand veneration. It could also be found in rooms at inns: Shakespeare mentions it there in two of his plays.[50]

Protestant families, at least of the wealthier kind, retained the medieval practice of saying prayers at home and added, or increased, that of the reading of godly teaching and reading, especially the Bible (Fig. 30, p. 109). The disappearance of masses in private chapels or at the local church on weekdays meant that worship had to be done in other ways. Emphasis continued to be placed on family prayers, often daily, at which parents, children, and servants gathered to hear the reading of a Bible chapter and the leading of the prayers by the father or, in his absence, the mother.[51] Children of status might be given additional instruction. Grace Sharington, who was born into a family of gentry at Lacock in 1552, had her education at home with her sisters, under their mother's supervision and that of a lady cousin, chosen by their mother as their tutor. Their mother taught them prayers and meditations and told them to read chapters of the Bible every day as she had done. The Bible was the 'Geneva' version of 1560, later known as the 'Breeches Bible'.

Mother bought three additional books for the girls. John Foxe's *Acts and Monuments* described the history of the Church and the Reformation from a Protestant standpoint. The *Common Places* of Wolfgang Musculus, a German Protestant writer, was a substantial theological dictionary, explaining everything from the nature of God to the virtues and duties proper to mankind. The third book, *The Imitation of Christ* by Thomas à Kempis, was written by a fifteenth-century Catholic but remained popular after the Reformation because of its spiritual teaching and lack of engagement with matters that had become controversial.[52] The training that Grace received remained deeply embedded in her adult life. It became her daily habit to read four chapters of scripture every day: one each from the Pentateuch, the prophets, the gospels, and the epistles, as well as all the psalms set for the day in the English Prayer Book of 1559.[53]

Children in these kinds of families continued to be taught to pray. The Paternoster, now called the Lord's Prayer, went on being learnt and said.

The Latin Book of Hours was replaced by the 'primer' with prayers in English. An authorised Primer was issued by the authority of Henry VIII in 1545 to be taught to children and others unable to understand Latin.[54] Children, especially boys but not excluding girls, went on being asked to say grace during meals.[55] Henry's Primer, and its successors under Edward VI and Elizabeth, included prayers to say on such occasions, as did the catechisms.[56] Even the lord mayor of London had his son pronounce grace at a dinner in 1599.[57] Prayers were provided for use before and after midday dinner, and before and after evening supper. Some were in prose and based on psalms, and there were examples in verse as well. Two common ones of the latter kind in Elizabeth's reign involved saying, before dinner:

All that is and shall be set on this board,
Be that same sanctified by the Lord's word,

and afterwards,

He that is King and lord over all,
Bring us to the table of the life eternal.[58]

Robert Herrick's well-known later grace, 'Here a little child I stand', belonged to this tradition.

Claudius Hollyband, in his book of 1573 to teach children French, made a story out of the practice. A father comes home for dinner with a guest, and scolds his son, aged nine and a half, for not being on hand to welcome them and being ready to say grace. The son obliges by repeating one that begins 'Our good Father almighty'. The family is accustomed to have the Bible read during the meal, and the boy is told to recite a chapter or two from the New Testament. Having read from St John the day before, he continues with that author. The father criticises the boy for reading too hastily, but the guest politely comments that 'he reads very distinctly for his age'. At the end of the meal, the father calls for 'the children' to come to say grace. The chosen child, a boy, does so with a prayer 'To thee we give thanks'. He is then asked by his father to share something that he has learnt: a proverb, a fable, or an epigram.

He says 'For one pleasure, a thousand sorrows', for which he is complimented.[59] The story shows the extent to which meals could be used for religious instruction and meditation, as well as how children (although usually expected to be quiet at such times) could be given a part to play in the process.

DISSENTERS

What has been said applies to the majority of people in Tudor England who conformed to the religion of the day, Catholic or Protestant. But not everyone did so. When Henry VII became king, there were groups of Lollards who held unorthodox views about Bible reading, the sacrament of communion, the veneration of saints and images, the payment of tithes, and other things. From the early 1520s there were others who embraced the teachings of Luther and of the Continental Reformation.

Such views could not be aired in public and those who held them had to attend church and engage in communal religion sufficiently to avoid suspicion. Only in meetings of like-minded people in private houses could books be read, discussions held, and prayers made according to the beliefs of those involved. Discovery resulted in pressure to recant and to undergo public penance, with the threat of the death penalty for refusal or any relapse. Lollard and Lutheran families included children, and some (as they grew older) must have absorbed the ideas of their parents. In 1514, Thomas Watts of Dogmersfield in Hampshire was charged with having access to religious books in English and reading the New Testament to his wife and family. Six years later, at Coventry, a group of Lollards was exposed whose activities included teaching their children the Lord's Prayer and Ten Commandments in English.[60] Those who grew up in such families had to learn to live in two worlds: the public one, where they conformed, and the private in which they could follow their own convictions, with care to ensure that the private world did not become a matter of public concern.

Children in these families did not figure in arrests and trials, at least up to the age of puberty, but when they entered their teens they became potentially liable, like adults, to exposure and punishments. In about 1530 Thomas More had a 'child' or boy servant who imbibed unorthodox ideas from a priest in London, including disbelief in transubstantiation. This was the doctrine that the bread and wine used in the mass, when consecrated, became the real body and blood of Christ. He shared his scepticism with a young colleague who revealed it, at which More caused a servant 'to stripe [the first boy] like a child before my household'.[61] At least two young men were burnt for heresy in London during the mid-sixteenth century. Richard Mekins, described as a 'child' of not more than fifteen, was put to death in 1540 under Henry VIII's draconian new legislation enforcing traditional Church dogmas.[62] And John Leaf, aged nineteen, apprentice to a tallow chandler, suffered the same fate under Mary Tudor in 1555.[63]

The Reformation gathered most of these dissenters back into the Church, but others emerged as a result of it. Some were radical Puritan Protestants who also formed small household groups in Elizabeth's reign. A larger group were Catholics who found themselves alienated from the Church after 1559 in the way that Lollards had been in earlier times. They too were obliged to live in two worlds, public and private.[64] Their attendance was required at church, on pain of fines, and their Catholicism had to be practised at home. During Elizabeth's first twenty years, up to about 1580, it was not too diffi-cult for them to reconcile their duty with their belief. Many gentry families remained Catholic, and their status gave them some protection from inter-ference. The men in particular kept in touch with the Church of England and attended services in order to maintain their ties with other families and their influence in the community.

The Crown, for its part, wished to win over Catholics to the Church of England, and while masses were forbidden and all adults required to attend their parish churches, the penalty for not doing so was a fine of only one shilling for each reported default.[65] Meanwhile family prayers of a traditional nature could be said at home, and even mass be celebrated in a private chapel or a house room by older parish clergy sympathetic to the ways of the past (Fig. 32, p. 116). The faith could be learnt, if not from a priest, from a Catholic catechism. A simple one, translated from Latin and secretly published in 1593, was intended 'for the use of children and other unlearned Catholics'. It resembled Protestant catechisms in discussing the Creed, Lord's Prayer, and (briefly) the Ten Commandments, but differed by including Latin texts

31. Religious art survived the Reformation in houses and inns where children would have seen it. Here a panel shows Adam and Eve along with the sacrifice of Isaac by Abraham.

of the first two, together with the *Ave Maria* and *Salve Regina* in honour of the Virgin Mary, with English translations as well in some cases.[66] Children could then be introduced to other Catholic books, devotion to the saints, the saying of the rosary, and the keeping of the old Church year with its festivals and fast days within their home environment.

After about 1580, the tension between the two worlds increased. A fresh generation of Catholic priests educated on the Continent, together with those of the new Jesuit Order, came to England to rebuild the Catholic community. Some (but not all) Catholics grew more resistant to the Reformation. They refused to take their children to church for baptism, which involved attending the Protestant service of matins or evensong. Women concealed their pregnancies or moved their dwellings so that their babies would not be subjected to the rite.[67] Parents then used their own priest for the purpose or christened their children personally.[68] The refusal of some Catholics to attend church services became more resolute, for which they were described as 'recusants'. Gentry families, with large houses and faithful servants, could now access the mass from visiting missionary priests. Those with sufficient money and determination sent children, especially boys, overseas to be educated. The chief such places were the Catholic schools at Douay, Eu, and St Omer in northern France, while older boys wishing to train as priests or Jesuits went to seminaries, several of which specialised in taking English students, in France, Spain, and Rome.[69]

The English government struck back with penalties against both Catholic priests and recusants. From 1581 those importing papal bulls or instruments against the English regime were guilty of high treason. The saying of mass was punishable by a large fine and imprisonment for at least one year, while severe penalties were incurred even by those who heard mass. Heavy fines were imposed on anyone over the age of sixteen who failed to attend the services of their parish church.[70] Just after the end of the Tudor dynasty, in reaction to the Gunpowder Plot of 1605, there were further measures: fines for those who refused to have their children baptised in church or to bring their relatives for burial there, and penalties on the importation of Catholic books including primers, catechisms, and missals.[71] Priests were traced and arrested, imprisoned, or executed. Boys being sent to the Continent were intercepted: four brothers of the Worthington family of Lancashire in 1584 and the Jerningham boys of Norfolk in 1593. Attempts were made to have such children brought up by guardians, especially bishops or deans of the Church of England, so that they might receive a Protestant education, although most were eventually allowed to return to their parents. Despite the dangers of Catholicism to the English Crown and Church, the authorities were reluctant to interfere with parents' rights to bring up their children, which left families with a good deal of scope for passing on their beliefs to the next generations.[72]

At the same time, many Catholics felt torn between their religion, their patriotism, and their social relationships with their neighbours, limiting their resistance and non-conformity. As a result there was a mixture of attitudes and practices among them. Catholic women and girls tended to be especially firm in their beliefs and practices because they could observe these safely at home and came less under other influences. Men and boys needed

32. Catholicism survived the Reformation and continued to be taught to children within some gentry houses, like this one, Baddesley Clinton in Warwickshire.

to keep more links with the outside world. Some boys continued to attend the public grammar schools; others had a noble education in the households of Protestant noblemen and gentlemen.[73] What probably united them all was a greater sense of their special status and their vulnerability. As with their Lollard predecessors, the private practice of their religion had to be shaped to their life in the everyday world.

DEATHS AND MEMORIALS

One reason for children to come to church was death. Given the numbers who died in childhood, it was inevitable that their funerals and burials (or those of their parents) would form a significant part of the life of a parish church in the sixteenth century. Up to the Reformation, there was an issue about the status of the stillborn and those who died at birth without the benefit of baptism. The understanding of human development inherited from Aristotle and other classical scientists was that an embryo acquired a soul after forty days. It followed that most stillborn children had souls but, because baptism was not allowed until after birth, St Augustine of Hippo argued that they would be condemned to hell by virtue of mankind's original sin, and this became the orthodox view in medieval times. Scholars came to locate the destination of such children as the 'limbo' or edge of hell, where they were spared the pains of hell but had to suffer the disappointment that they would not be received into heaven.[74]

The stillborn, being unbaptised, could not have a funeral in church or a grave in the churchyard, since these were reserved for Christians alone. Such a doctrine was, understandably, unpopular with grieving parents and disturbing even to some scholars. Jesus had referred to baptism by the Holy Spirit, and learned writers like William Lyndwood suggested that this might be applicable to unbaptised babies. John Wycliffe, the greatest medieval English theologian to question the beliefs of the Church, doubted whether lack of baptism negated salvation. His followers, the Lollards, are recorded affirming that it was not necessary to christen a child to give it salvation. A child of Christian parents would be saved through grace while in the womb.[75] In practice, ordinary people found ways around the problem. Midwives were suspected of baptising stillborn children in order to give them Christian status. Since churchyards were easily accessible, there was little to stop someone burying a dead child surreptitiously at night. In one case of 1496 a midwife ordered a woman to do so in a London cemetery, although on that occasion the fact came to light and those concerned were summoned before a Church court.[76]

For children born alive who were baptised and subsequently died, funerals and burials were permissible and their ceremonies might imitate those of adults. When Edmund, the third son of Henry VII, passed away in 1500 at the age of sixteen months, he was brought from Hatfield where he died 'with an honourable company' on a carriage through Fleet Street, London, to Westminster Abbey. The duke of Buckingham acted as chief mourner (the king and queen did not attend), and the lord mayor and guildsmen of the city stood as a mark of respect in their liveries alongside the road from the Old Bailey to Temple Bar. At the abbey, the traditional burial place of the royal family, the little prince was buried by St Edward's shrine in one of the holiest parts of the church.[77]

The standard funeral, before the Reformation, included the celebration by the parish priest of a requiem mass including prayers for the dead. This was followed by the bringing of the deceased to the grave, ceremonies to sanctify it, the placing of the body within it (usually in a shroud rather than a coffin), and the closing of the grave.[78] That this was done for children as well as for adults is clear from such surviving parish church records as mention funeral offerings. Those at All Saints church, Oxford, in the autumn of 1492 mention the sums given for John Ashleye's son (3½d.), 'a child' (2d.), Wilton's child (2½d.), George Hosiar's child (4d.), David Diar's daughter (4d.), Georgis's girl (5d.), and John Symond's infant (7d.).[79] These show that the children had the benefit of the requiem mass, at which the offerings were made, as well as the burial. The offerings were less than those commonly given for adults, but that may reflect the fact that only the immediate family was present at the event.

In addition to the offerings at the funeral, a charge was made for the burial. At the London church of St Mary at Hill, a child's grave in the churchyard was priced at 4d., half that for an adult. At Exeter, where all were buried in the cathedral cemetery, the fee of the 'bellman' or sexton was 6d.[80] Burials inside churches cost more, since churchwardens charged for the privilege, and even a simple flat ledger-stone over the grave would be a further expense. Internal burials, moreover, were limited to the wealthier in society. A further exaction, for adults, was a mortuary which went to the church incumbent: usually a man's best robe or farm animal. In some places this charge was extended to children, most famously in London in 1511. Richard Hunne, a merchant taylor and citizen, had a son named Stephen who died at the age of six weeks. He was buried in the church of Whitechapel, after which the rector demanded the 'bearing sheet' or robe in which he had been baptised, as a mortuary payment. Hunne objected on the grounds that the robe was his, not the baby's. This dispute was the small stone that started an avalanche in which Hunne prosecuted the rector, the Church authorities accused Hunne of heresy, he was confined in the bishop's prison, and was found hanged there, leading to a popular outcry that he had been murdered. The belief helped to denigrate and weaken the Church authorities on the eve of the Reformation.[81]

The English Reformers of the sixteenth century had both a different understanding of the afterlife and less respect for ceremony than their predecessors. This helped bring about a more sympathetic attitude to the burial of the stillborn and unbaptised. A draft set of new Church laws in 1535 forbade burial in churchyards only to the excommunicated and suicides, and further laws drawn up in 1553 but never authorised made no mention of exclusions.[82] John Hooper, the first Protestant bishop of Gloucester (1551–4), declared his disbelief in the limbo of young children and other such 'follies, mockeries, and abuses'.[83] On the other hand the survival, for a long time, of clergy and laity infused with the beliefs of the Catholic Church may have led to some continuing opposition to the relaxation of the rules. In 1595, a preacher in London, William Hubbock, wrote a short treatise arguing that the salvation of children did not depend on baptism, and that John the Baptist had possessed faith while still in the womb.[84] Ten years later William Hill took the same view in a work called *The Infancie of the Soul*.[85] The fact that both writers felt it necessary to speak on behalf of the souls of the unbaptised may imply that there was still a prejudice that had to be argued against.

Funerals for live-born children remained permissible, indeed desirable, in the new Prayer Books of 1549 to 1559, and such funerals – officially at least – continued to resemble those of adults in the readings and prayers that were said. Moreover the Prayer Books made one exception to the reform of Catholic worship where funerals were concerned. A procession could still be made to church. The Prayer Books instructed the priest to receive the deceased only at the churchyard gate, but in practice wealthy people could organise an informal parade from their houses. Children in London were sometimes enlisted to take part in these, no doubt in return for (and displaying the dead person's) charity.[86] Equally a child's funeral in Protestant England, if the family was wealthy enough, could also be carried out in ceremonial ways. When James Cavendish died in 1602, at an age probably below that of ten, 25s. was spent on cloth for his funeral hearse, 20s. on the clergyman, clerk, and singers at the service, and £6 was distributed to the poor, at a total cost of £8 5s.[87]

We wish to remember the dead, especially dead children, and do so by means of memorials of a temporary or permanent kind. This would have been the case in the sixteenth century. It is easy to assume that churchyards were bare of monuments at that time, because few have survived into the present day. That is the result of attrition and clearances. There is plenty of evidence that medieval and early modern churchyards contained grave markers, sometimes perhaps only unshaped stones but often (at least for adults) upright slabs at the foot or head of the grave, or larger altar tombs.[88] The outdoor graves of children, then, might be marked for remembrance, and those of the wealthy minority who were buried in church could be embellished with stone slabs and brass plates listing the date of their death and bearing a two-dimensional image of them.[89]

Such images, in the Tudor era, might include babies who died at or soon after birth, sometimes alongside the mother who died in childbirth (Fig. 7, p. 23). Others featured older children like John Shorland, already mentioned (Fig. 33, p. 121).[90] Thomas Heron, son of Sir John Heron, treasurer of the royal household, died at the age of fourteen in 1517 and is buried at Little Ilford, Essex. The brass maker supplied an image of a robed man of indeterminate age, but modified it to include a pen case and an ink pot which, by that date, were the equipment associated with schoolboys.[91] John Stonor, who died in 1512, has a brass at Wraysbury, Buckinghamshire.[92] He was probably the son of Sir Walter Stonor of Stonor in Oxfordshire, and his image shows him in a gown with bands of trimming going down the front and along the skirts. His headdress consists of an embroidered hood, topped by a Tudor cap, fastened under the chin, with two swirling tails: perhaps the headdress of a very young boy. Both brasses, being unusual, were specially commissioned, showing that their families wanted them commemorated in a particular way.

For those of the highest status there were standing tombs of stone.[93] Elizabeth, the second child of Henry VII, who died aged three in 1495, received an altar tomb in Westminster Abbey, formerly surmounted by a gilt effigy. A more striking memorial today is that of Robert Dudley, Lord Denbigh, son of Elizabeth I's favourite Robert Dudley, earl of Leicester, in the church of St Mary, Warwick. He died in 1584, aged four or five, and was given a lavish monument with an appropriately sized recumbent sculpture. Other children, some dead, some surviving, were shown on the stone tombs of their parents in a similar manner to those on brasses.

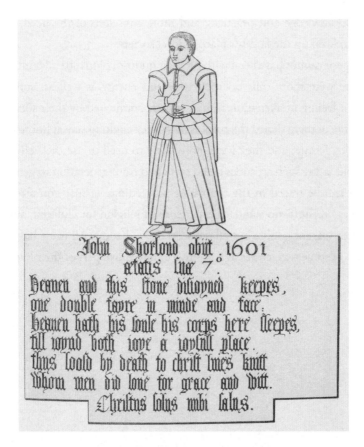

33. A monument to a dead child: John Shorland, aged seven, 1601, in Woodbridge church, Suffolk, with an appreciative epitaph in his memory.

Religion, then, was an important influence on children everywhere in Tudor England. Nearly all were baptised in church in the earliest days of their lives, and most must have gone there at least occasionally up to their teens when they became required to do so regularly. All were free to partake of the Church's worship and pastoral services, and could join in its social activities. All had personal links with their parish church through their baptisms, marriages, and the graves of their parents and ancestors. This does not mean that all adults attended church dutifully or taught their children to do so. Attendance may well have been affected by social status. Wealthier people may have taken their children more often. They were more aware of the advice to educate them in religious knowledge and practices, and more conscious of the need to be in church to keep up the family's place in local society.

The poor cannot have been without their quota of pious attenders at church. But there were more calls on their time and energy as well as, sometimes, perhaps a feeling of alienation from a church dominated by their social superiors. Some of them defied the rules as far as they could to stay at home to work or to enjoy leisure, and they were more likely to need to use their children in household tasks. Such attitudes could be passed from generation to generation, and this can be traced in the records of proceedings against non-attenders.[94] There was, in short, no standard experience of religion for children, any more than there was for adults, but all grew up in its shadow. All must have felt its presence in some way, either as a positive or a negative part of their lives.

5

SCHOOL

Many children in Tudor England went to school, both boys and girls. How many is impossible to say. Schooling was common or universal among the higher and middle ranks of society; less so lower down for the children of artisans and labourers (Fig. 34, p. 124). Nonetheless a census of the poor in Norwich listed seventy-seven of their children at school in 1570: perhaps 16 per cent of those of school age. This was sometimes the case even when the father was out of work.[1]

No law required that children go to school. The Reformation, as we have seen, expected them to learn the catechism, but that did not involve an ability to read it. In 1553 Archbishop Cranmer's proposed new code of Church law ordered the clerk of each parish church to teach children the alphabet as well as the catechism.[2] This code was never approved, however, and the policy was not formally adopted again when Protestantism was re-established in England in 1559. Nevertheless there were strong incentives for parents to have their offspring taught at least how to read in English. The ability to do so gave them a practical skill with which to understand documents such as letters, financial accounts, or legal instruments. It opened access to literary works of all kinds: prayer books, works about religious topics and moral behaviour, the Bible in English from about 1539, practical handbooks, and recreational reading in the form of romances and jest-books. There had long been a hunger to read in England, which helped propel the writing of works in English that is observable from the time of Chaucer onwards. This hunger also stimulated the invention and development of printing in the fifteenth century. Printing made books less expensive and extended the range of topics on which writing could be published and sold.

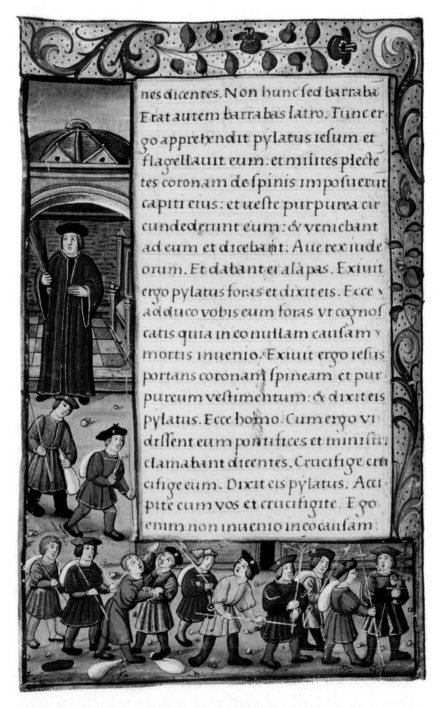

nes dicentes. Non hunc sed barraba
Erat autem barrabas latro. Tunc er
go apprehendit pylatus iesum et
flagellauit eum: et milites plecte
tes coronam de spinis imposuerut
capiti eius: et ueste purpurea cir
cundederunt eum: & veniebant
ad eum et dicebant. Aue rex iude
orum. Et dabant ei alapas. Exiuit
ergo pylatus foras et dixit eis. Ecce
adduco vobis eum foras vt cognos
catis quia in eo nullam causam
mortis inuenio. Exiuit ergo iesus
portans coronam spineam et pur
pureum vestimentum: & dixit eis
pylatus. Ecce homo. Cum ergo vi
dissent eum pontifices et ministri
clamabant dicentes. Crucifige cru
cifige eum. Dixit eis pylatus. Acci
pite eum vos et crucifigite. Ego
enim non inuenio in eo causam

34. A master at the school door, as his pupils leave with schoolbags and,
apparently, weapons.

Another powerful motive impelled parents to have their children taught. Schooling affirmed social standing or provided a means by which it could be improved. Education has always conferred status and been sought after for that reason. In the higher ranks of society it was seen as part of the essence of being a noble or gentle man or woman. It instilled for such people the principles, knowledge, and skills required in a governing elite. Men of high rank were expected to hold public offices in which they had to deal with written material. Their own affairs required them to keep records or supervise the servants who kept them. For the rest of society, education offered a way of improving one's station in life. An educated child might gain a better post or a better marriage. Nor was this merely an investment for the future. Even paying pennies for a boy or girl to go to a reading school distinguished a family that could afford to do so from those who could not, and gave it (or allowed it to feel) an immediate sense of privilege.

ELEMENTARY EDUCATION

Most children who received an education in Tudor England learnt merely to read, and often did so at home or in schools of a humble kind. Some must have been taught by a literate parent, especially a mother who might have leisure during the day to give to the task. In a wealthy household there would be others able to help: tutors, governesses, chaplains, or clerks. Parents who did not have the time or skills to teach could get the job done by a teacher for a fairly small outlay of money. Cranmer's failed attempt to make teaching part of a parish clerk's duties reflected the fact that many clerks already did such work. Francis Clement, whose book *The Petie Schole* (1587) was written to instruct elementary teachers, listed them as doing so along with tailors, weavers, and seamstresses.[3] Roger Ascham had clerks in mind when he talked of boys in a church playing with the bell ropes while their master was absent.[4] Shakespeare imagined the parish clerk of Chartham in Kent as being hanged for teaching boys by Jack Cade and his rebels in *Henry VI Part II*.[5] As for textile workers, they could have pupils with them while they worked at home, interrupting their work to set a task or examine a child, while a seamstress might also teach girls spinning, sewing, or lace-making. The Norwich census of 1570 included one poor sick woman who taught when she was able to do so, as well as two poor men: a hatter and weaver.[6] That women should teach in this way was not a novelty; there had been schoolmistresses of an elementary kind since at least the fourteenth century.[7]

Then as now children might start to learn to read when they were three or four. Clement thought the latter age appropriate.[8] But before education became compulsory in the 1870s, it could begin at any age in childhood and be as long, short, or intermittent as parents wanted or could afford. Edward Herbert, later Lord Herbert of Cherbury, had ear trouble until he was seven and 'my family did not teach me so much as my alphabet until then'.[9] Reading, at least up to about the 1560s, began in Latin. This was true in the sense that the alphabet was Roman in origin and the names of the letters were also Roman. Tudor children reciting the names were following their ancient predecessors. Alphabets were easily available. Some of the prayer books known as primers, up to the Reformation, included one that could be used for teaching at home.[10] Alternatively, any literate person could write out an alphabet, or any non-literate buy a printed copy for a penny. This could be pasted onto a batten with a handle and, by the 1580s, be protected with a sheet of horn, hence known as a horn-book or (later on) as a battledore-book (Fig. 35, p. 127).[11]

The alphabet was presented as a prayer, both before and after the Reformation. It began with the sign of the cross to prompt readers to cross themselves and, or, to say 'Christ's cross me speed'. The letters of the alphabet followed, and after them three abbreviation signs including the ampersand (&) signifying 'and'. Finally the pupil said 'amen'.[12] Schooling began by learning the letter shapes along with their names.[13] This may have been done in groups of letters or in the whole alphabetical sequence. Teaching three or four letters a day, perhaps over a week, seems to have been popular in France but may have been current in England as well.[14] Saying the whole of the alphabet was probably common, at least for children beyond the very beginners. A musical version of this by Thomas Morley survives from 1597.[15]

Pronouncing the names would be followed by learning their sounds. Pupils repeated 'a per se a', b per se buh', and so on, meaning 'a by itself is pronounced with a short a'. The word 'ampersand' is a relic of this process,

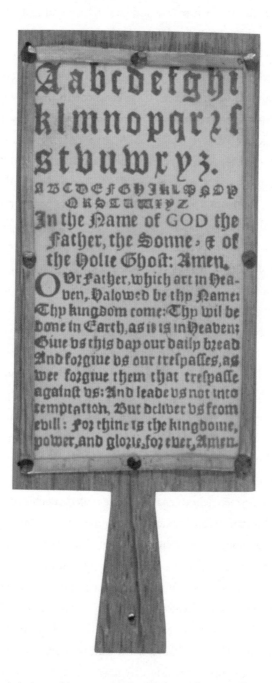

35. An alphabet tablet protected with horn, hence a 'horn-book'.

because at that point the learners said 'and per se and'. Alternatively by the sixteenth century, the horn-book (or a larger elementary book) would display all the syllables, 'ab, eb, ib, ob, ub', 'ba, be, bi, bo, bu', and these would be memorised before going on to words. Then, having mastered the shapes, names, and sounds of the letters, a child learnt to put them together into syllables and words. Traditionally this was done by reading the Latin Paternoster (Lord's Prayer) which often appeared on an alphabet sheet or tablet. One named the letters, pronounced each syllable, and finally gave the whole world: 'p, a, pa; t, e, r, ter; pater'. The Reformation made a large difference here because, from 1536, the king ordered the basic prayers to be said in English.[16] By the second half of the century, primers and simple prayer books would only have them in that form. It was then easy to forget that the alphabet was originally Roman, and it became in effect English, with the addition of the letters 'j' and 'w' which were needed for words in the language.

The reading material in elementary schools was predominantly religious. Children had been taught to read from the psalms in Latin throughout the Middle Ages and this continued when they were translated into English at the Reformation. The seventeenth-century scholar Anthony Wood remembered that he learnt them at the age of five in 1637.[17] Primers of basic prayers had long been used for reading practice too, and these began to be printed in English in the 1530s. Another common reading text in the Reformation period was the catechism. John Colet, dean of St Paul's, produced one in English by 1527,[18] and the version in the Book of Common Prayer appeared in 1549. Later in the century, as we have seen, lengthier and more detailed catechisms were published, especially by Puritan writers anxious to improve the public understanding of religion and behaviour. There seems no evidence as yet that elementary schools encouraged the reading of recreational literature, but once children had learnt to read they could access such literature at home, if it existed there.

It is likely that some elementary teachers taught other subjects, such as basic writing, arithmetic, and simple business skills. Shakespeare portrayed the clerk of Chartham as being able to 'write and read and cast accounts' and as instructing boys to copy text. 'He can make obligations [bonds] and write court hand [the script of legal documents].'[19] Some Tudor grammar schools offered training in writing and composing documents for boys who were not capable of learning Latin. The founder of the grammar school at Rolleston in Staffordshire (1524) advised the schoolmaster to teach such pupils 'reading, writing, and computing', in other words arithmetic.[20] At a higher level, there had long been specialised masters in major towns providing instruction for older boys seeking careers in commerce and administration.[21] An advertisement of such a master in London survives from 1590. In it Humfrey Baker, 'dwelling on the north side of the Royal Exchange', offered to teach arithmetic, accountancy, geometry, and surveying techniques. Children could be boarded at his house.[22]

By Elizabeth's reign, elementary education was common enough to reach at least some children low down in the social order. Thomas Ingelend, in a play of 1570, was able to envisage a cook-maid who had been to school. She had learnt the Book of Hours in Latin, and could remember the opening lines, *Dominus labia aperies* ('O Lord, open thou my lips').[23] And Marlowe's drama *Doctor Faustus*, written by 1594, portrayed a stable-man able at least to recognise and mumble aloud the letters and words in a book of magic.[24] It is not surprising, therefore, to encounter, at a slightly higher level of importance, a cobbler able to read and write in the play called *Locrine*, published in 1595.[25]

GRAMMAR SCHOOLS

Elementary education of this kind was sufficient for most of those who wanted and could pay for it. A smaller proportion of the population, but still a numerous one, wished for more. Here there was a gender divide. Boys of the upper and middle levels of society went on to learn grammar, and a small proportion of them followed schooling with studies at the universities or the Inns of Court in London. Grammar could be learnt from a private tutor in a wealthy household or in a self-contained grammar school. Girls were more likely to be taught at home at this level, although some private schools for girls were in existence by Elizabeth's reign. We shall examine the grammar schools first, before going on to education in households.

Grammar schools had existed since at least the twelfth century, and were common by the Tudor period. Traditionally they taught how to read, compose, write, and speak Latin, with Greek being offered as well in more ambitious schools during the sixteenth century. A grammar school in the countryside might also admit younger boys to learn to read, but in towns where elementary education was otherwise available, grammar masters often expected their pupils to arrive proficient in this respect. Some grammar schools possessed a measure of public status, with buildings, endowments, and governors to appoint their teachers, which gave them a continuous history. Most cities and market towns had places of this kind by the early 1500s. Other schools were private: held in a master's house, smaller in numbers of pupils, and lasting only as long as he cared to teach.

Originally all schools charged fees for lessons and some teachers made additional money by boarding pupils in their houses. This may have been true of most grammar teaching even in Tudor England. However, since the late fourteenth century, wealthy benefactors had been founding new grammar schools or endowing existing ones, especially in towns, so that the master received a salary and charged no fees. The number of such schools increased steadily during the reigns of the Tudors, causing even market towns to have one, and there were several in London. They educated some of the leading authors of Tudor England: John Lyly and Marlowe at Canterbury, Edmund Spenser and Thomas Kyd at Merchant Taylors' in London, Ben Jonson at Westminster, and Shakespeare (we presume) at Stratford-upon-Avon.

Endowment did not make education wholly cost-free, nor open it to the whole population. Sending a boy even to a free school still cost money. While there were no uniforms as such, a decent gown such as pupils wore, 'down to the heels', was necessary for the boy's and family's reputation.[26] Pupils had to provide their own books, paper, pens, ink, and sometimes other things such as candles or fuel for the classroom fire.[27] Richard Fermor, a gentleman's son at school in Islington near London in 1590, needed a Greek grammar, a text of the Latin author Sallust, a pen, an inkhorn, paper, and a satchel to carry his books, costing 6s. 8d. altogether, and these cannot have been his only such expenses.[28] There were other deterrents to attending grammar schools. Sending a boy to one also required an awareness of the value of education by parents and the ability to dispense with the pupil's labour or wages. For the dwindling number of serfs in Tudor England it required the consent of their manorial lord.[29] These obstacles did not deter everyone. William Grene, a boy from Boston, whose father seems to have been a peasant farmer, labourer, and sawyer, managed to learn grammar for two periods of two years in his youth in the 1510s, alternately with working for his father.[30] But the likelihood is that Tudor grammar schools were chiefly filled with the sons of the gentry and yeomen farmers from the countryside or merchants and substantial craftsmen and shopkeepers from the towns.

Grammar school boys were normally aged over seven and under eighteen, although most probably spent only three or four years at school: enough to give them a sufficient knowledge of Latin and the ever important social cachet of studying. School fees could be as low as two or three shillings a year, but if there was no local school, as might be the case in the countryside, pupils had to board away from home in order to access one. This added greatly to the cost of education. There were only two large boarding schools in Tudor England: Winchester and Eton. Most boarding by pupils was done in private houses, either with the schoolmaster himself or with a family of an appropriate rank. Even at Winchester and Eton, only selected boys – the foundation scholars – lived in the school itself, and others who paid fees (the 'oppidans' at Eton) boarded elsewhere. Parents chose a house appropriate to their rank. Peter Carew, the knight's son from east Devon, as has been mentioned, lodged with a prosperous draper and alderman in Exeter.[31]

The typical grammar school building consisted of a single oblong schoolroom, sometimes with an adjacent house for the schoolmaster. Boys entered the room through a door on the outer narrow side (Fig. 36, p. 132). Inside, not far from the door, sat the usher whose name came from the Latin *ostiarius* or doorkeeper. He monitored the entrance and exits of pupils, and taught the junior ones. The schoolmaster occupied a grand seat, sometimes on a dais, at the inner narrow end of the room. Along each side of it, looking inwards, were one or two long rows of benches for the boys, usually without desks. They studied their books or wrote their work on their laps. By the early sixteenth century it was becoming the practice to divide the class into six or seven forms, the forms originally being specific benches. The first form was the lowest, and boys made their way up as their knowledge improved. The master did not normally patrol the classroom, but lectured from his seat or called up pupils to examine their work. In this respect he was like a lord in a hall or an abbot in a chapter-house.

36. A Tudor schoolroom: that of Magdalen College School, Oxford, seen from the master's seat, just before its demolition in the 1820s.

The school day was a long one. Children worked similar hours to adults. They had to arrive by about 6.00 a.m. in summer or 7.00 in winter. An hour or two of work might be done before a short pause for a breakfast snack. There was a longer break at about 11.00 a.m. for another hour or two, allowing boys to go home or to their lodgings for midday dinner. Afternoon school would last till 5.00 p.m. or 6.00, depending on the season.[32] Lateness due to oversleeping or loitering on the way would be punished. To avoid this, a parent might take a boy to school or send a servant to do so.[33] Truancy was not unknown but was penalised. A boy who took a day off 'in the town, walking to and fro into the castle', would be welcomed next day 'in the new fashion': with a beating.[34] During the tedious hours of class-work, boys might bicker and play tricks on one another. The schoolmaster Claudius Hollyband imagined one boy complaining that 'Nicholas has mocked me, plucked me by the hair and the ears, struck me with a fist, and made me bleed'. Another pupil protests that 'John has sworn by God, stolen a knife, lied twice, torn my book, spoken English, and trodden on my cap.'[35]

Failure in schoolwork, bad behaviour, or telling lies were punished in two ways. The minor one involved the ferule or palmer: a flat wooden batten with a spoon-shaped end, pierced by a hole. It was used, perhaps by monitors or prefects, to hit the hand, the function of the hole being to raise a blister.[36] The major punishment was done with the birch, a bundle of thin twigs. This was applied by the schoolmaster himself. The procedure seems to have been the same over a long period. The master cried 'Up with him!' or 'Take him up!'[37] The boy was brought up towards the master's seat by the usher or senior boys, and 'horsed' or held up on the back of another boy. His gown and shirt were pulled up, his drawers pulled down, and he was birched on his bare bottom.[38]

The ritual is described in Thomas Triplett's mocking poem about Alexander Gill, high master of St Paul's School (London) under James I:

> Still doth he cry,
> 'Take him up, sir, take him up, sir!
> Untruss with expedition!'
> Oh the birchen tool
> That he winds i' th' school
> Frights worse than an inquisition.[39]

Gill was notorious for his severity; so, two generations earlier, was Nicholas Udall at Eton (1534–42). Thomas Tusser described how when he was a boy there under Udall:

> Fifty-three stripes given to me
> At once I had,
> For fault but small, or none at all.[40]

Discipline of this kind was deemed necessary to deter children from their natural instinct to play, and to instil in them the virtues and knowledge required for adulthood. But it is by no means clear that all schoolmasters imposed it rigorously, or did so all the time. Some parents complained about beatings and there are cases where this led to lawsuits.[41] One ploy, if a boy left home late and was in danger of scourging, was for his father to invite the schoolmaster to dinner next day, putting him under an obligation to be merciful.[42] Another, at least humorously, was for the boy to claim sickness, although in that case the master might propose to 'drive your malady from you' with his birch.[43]

Some protests survive by schoolboys against their punishments. They include a few late-medieval songs in which the boys narrate their suffering under the birch and the revenges that they plan on their teachers.[44] These have a rather stylised air, however, and for the real misery that discipline could cause, we have just one attestation: from a boy called Robert Yall at Magdalen College, Oxford, in the early 1500s. He was under the supervision of a college fellow, John Molesworth, while he studied at the college school or perhaps as a very junior undergraduate. Molesworth disciplined him, causing him to draft the following remonstration. It needs to be left in the original spelling, so that we hear his voice:

> Master Mullysworth, I wold pray and beseytt [beseech] yow that yow wold be my good master, for syche gere as y lerne, that yow wold sew [show] ytt to me by feer mense [fair means] and ponys [punish] me resnably. Now yow ponyse me houer [over] much, master, and plese yow y cannott byd [bide] this ponysment. Her at fryst tyme yow dyd not ponyse me nott hauff so much; then y dyd lerne more by yowr feyer mense then I doo now.[45]

We are left wondering whether Yall ever finished the letter and plucked up the courage to give it to his master. At any rate it speaks expressively of his misery.

More gentle memories of schooldays come from a book published in 1639 by Richard Willis: a former pupil at the Crypt School, Gloucester, in the 1570s. The school, when he started there, was taught by a master of only moderate ability, but this man was succeeded by an excellent one: Gregory Downhale, a graduate of Pembroke College, Cambridge. The Willis family lived next door to the school and became friendly with the master. 'He made me his bedfellow': presumably to sleep in his room and perhaps do household tasks. 'This . . . begat in him familiarity and gentleness towards me, and in me towards him reverence and love, which made me also to love my book.' Downhale gave up teaching to become secretary to a nobleman, and Willis followed in his footsteps, rising to hold the same office for a trio of high officials of the Stuart kings, ending with Lord Coventry, the keeper of the great seal.[46]

Not surprisingly, pupils left school for the day with relief and often in high spirits. Shakespeare described a school breaking up, and everyone hurrying home or to his 'sporting place'.[47] Francis Segar, trying to teach decorum to boys in 1557, criticised those who came out 'running like a heap of bees . . . whooping and hallooing as in hunting the fox'.[48] But there were also alleviations during the day, as we saw in a previous chapter, when time for recreation might open if the master was called away to other tasks.[49] The school year stopped for holidays as well: both in the form of individual festival days and longer vacations at Christmas and Easter and in the summer. The ends of terms seem sometimes to have been times of festivity. In 1558 we first hear mention of the practice of 'barring out', although it was already said to be an 'old custom'. It seems to have been chiefly observed in the Midlands and North of England, and centred on shutting the master out of the schoolroom, presumably when he arrived to teach. This was done before Christmas and Easter along with Shrove Tuesday: the universal children's day of games and cock-fighting. The master's exclusion was merely ceremonial, however, and the event often continued with some kind of eating and drinking. The tradition lasted in some places until as late as the reign of Queen Victoria.[50]

SCHOOLWORK

Work in grammar schools consisted of the master teaching, the boys learning information from books or writing exercises, and the master examining their knowledge (Fig. 37, p. 136). Examining was known as 'apposing'. Boys would be questioned on their knowledge of grammar, or have their work inspected. Shakespeare described the process humorously in *The Merry Wives of Windsor*, where Sir Hugh Evans, the Welsh priest and schoolmaster, catechises his young pupil, William Page:

Evans: How many numbers is in nouns?
William: Two.
Evans: What is 'fair', William?

William: *Pulcher*.

Evans: What is he, William, that does lend articles?

William: Articles are borrowed of the pronoun, and be thus declined: *singulariter nominativo, hic, haec, hoc.*[51]

William was still at an early stage of learning grammar: in his 'accidence' which dealt with the nature and variations of Latin words and taught one the appropriate linguistic terms. But as *singulariter nominativo* shows, he was already beginning to discuss Latin in Latin, and as he improved his knowledge he would be expected to speak only in that language while he was in the schoolroom.

Willis remembered how the boys in his school learnt to manipulate the system. His first teacher there was 'an ancient citizen of no great learning'. The

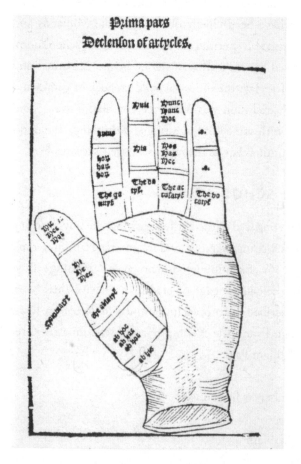

37. A school Latin grammar. John Holt's *Lac Puerorum* (1508) was unusual in containing diagrams, in this case to explain the paradigms of *hic magister*.

master gave out lessons in the evening and examined next morning, beginning with the boys of the first and second forms. Two older boys, known as 'prompters', would mingle among them, learn the right answers, and convey them to the rest, 'so that we escaped correction but understood little'. Willis fell out with one of the prompters who then refused to pass on the information. After that, he had to listen carefully to the examinations, chanced to be given an easy word to parse or identify, and so escaped punishment. By paying more attention, he learnt better, needed no prompter, and later became one himself.[52]

We possess some of the Latin exercises that boys wrote in class up to the early sixteenth century. They reflected the needs of the day, in which Latin was still used for everyday purposes in church services, writing documents, and keeping accounts. These that follow represent work done at Magdalen College School, Oxford, in the 1490s, when the old ways were still being partly observed. The master taught, or the pupil invented, sentences in English and practised translating them into Latin:

The most part of this winter my hands were so swelling with cold that I could neither hold my pen for to write, neither my knife for to cut my meat at the table, and my feet also they were arrayed with chilblains [so] that it grieved me to go anywhere.

Thou wilt not believe how weary I am of fish, and how much I desire that flesh were come in again, for I have eat[en] none other than salt fish this Lent.

Bend your bow and shoot with me. Let us prove which of us be the better archer. I can tell where is a pair of butts made of new turves. Shall we go thither?

My brother hath written to me from London that my father and mother and all my friends fare well, the which letter hath made me right mery, for why [because] the more I love them, the more I rejoice their health and welfare.[53]

Exercises of this kind, surviving from the fifteenth and early sixteenth centuries, provide a varied and interesting window into not only Latin teaching but daily life, both inside the classroom and out in the world beyond.[54]

In the 1480s, at about the time of the battle of Bosworth, schoolwork began to change as the influence of the Renaissance permeated into England. The Italians of the Renaissance rediscovered the great pagan classical authors: Cicero, Horace, Ovid, Virgil, and so on. They were captivated by the topics of these writers, especially classical history and mythology, and by the way that they wrote: Cicero's oratory and the verse of the poets. Studying these writers promised to provide new information and skills, and to reunite the countries of Europe into sharing a common standard of Latin as had been the case at the time of the Roman Empire. The English were obliged to conform to this new standard so as to keep abreast of their neighbours. Between the 1480s and the 1510s, the basic grammars used in English schools were rewritten to accord with what were reckoned to be the usages of classical or 'humanist' Latin as it is also known. Hitherto the texts read in school as literature had included only one late Latin poem, *The Distichs of Cato*: a collection of wise sayings. The other texts were all medieval ones, concerned with wisdom, morality, and good behaviour. History and fiction had been lacking. Now the medieval texts that had been studied as literature were mostly discarded, and replaced by those of classical Rome. Pupils were taught to model their style on its great orators and poets.

This change did not affect the way in which classrooms operated: how they were laid out, how work was done, or how discipline was used. Pupils went on being required to know linguistic categories and definitions as in medieval times. But there were important differences in other respects. Latin moved away from being a language for ordinary practical use. Boys ceased to be taught to write everyday prose of the kind described above. By the 1530s, educationists were asserting that such exercises taught bad Latin. Instead they recommended that a boy should translate a sentence or passage of Cicero into English and then, after an interval, turn it back into Latin and compare the result with Cicero. The aim was now to imitate the classics not, as before, to adapt Latin to contemporary needs. As a result Latin retreated from its everyday uses. English had long been rivalling it for writing letters, keeping accounts, and even some official purposes like acts of Parliament. Now it took over these activities almost completely, and although scholarly works and indeed private letters continued to be written in Latin, others were composed in English or translated from Latin to reach a wider audience.

The Reformation of church services in the 1540s made another great difference. Latin lost its central place to English in everyone's religious life. Instead the language, in its new classical dress, became a more elite accomplishment. It marked off the superior orders of society from their inferiors as distinctly as it had done in the Middle Ages. There were of course gains to set against the losses. Close acquaintance with the classical writers introduced pupils to a huge range of new information: classical history, geography, oratory, mythology, and pieces of great literature. Writers were inspired to create new literary works in English, using the knowledge that they had gained. One has only to read Shakespeare's plays to see how much he knew, and could rely on his audience knowing, about the personalities, events, and stories of the classical world.

ELITE EDUCATION FOR MEN

In the upper ranks of society – of the nobility, gentry, and some of the more aspiring merchant class – there was a sense that education was a duty rather than a choice: an essential process in the formation of noble character. Since the Middle Ages, scholars had written guides for kings, princes, and noblemen, outlining the skills and virtues that they ought to acquire in youth.[55] Literary writers described the attributes of ideal heroes and heroines, both reflecting the ideals of their day and providing models to inspire their readers. Chaucer, for example, who was still widely read in the sixteenth century, described his Squire, aged twenty, as able to ride, joust, and fight. He was courteous, could serve his father at meals, sing, play the flute, dance, and write which implies that he could also read, very likely in more than one language.[56] By the time that we reach Tudor England, there are also documentary references – financial accounts, letters, and autobiographies – which tell us how real children of high status were educated, more fully than we can learn about their inferiors.

Noble and gentle parents in the sixteenth century were given a comprehensive guide to how they should bring up their sons in the book called *The Governor*, written by Sir Thomas Elyot: a man from a knightly family, civil lawyer, clerk of the king's council, and productive author. First published in 1531, it was reprinted at least seven times up to 1580, testifying to its value and appeal.[57] This came about because it blended, in an acceptable way, the traditional ethos of the English aristocracy with the new knowledge about classical writers on education such as Plutarch and Quintilian. As its title suggests, it set out a template for the training of those who formed the governing class in the king's administration, Parliament, and local government. Having defined the ideal political system as a monarchy supported by lesser magistrates, it went on to propose that a boy should be taken from the care of women at the age of seven and put under the care of a tutor, who would be in charge of his general upbringing. The tutor should teach his pupil how to read English and understand grammatical terms, before giving him to a schoolmaster who could instruct him in Latin and Greek. This instruction should continue until his late teens and, Elyot seems to indicate, could be followed either under a private schoolmaster in the boy's own household, perhaps with companions from other gentry families, or in a grammar school. Towards the end of his youth, a boy should learn the laws of England: a practice by then over a hundred years old, by which wealthy sons were sent to study at the Inns of Court and Chancery in London.[58]

Elyot accepted that literary studies should be accompanied by cultural and physical pursuits. Most of these had long been part of the upbringing of young gentlemen, as in that of Chaucer's Squire.[59] In the first category, he included music, both singing and playing on instruments, although this should always be followed as a pastime, not a profession. He also approved of dancing and gave extensive coverage to the virtues which he believed came from doing it, such as concord, prudence, and circumspection. This related not to all dancing but to a particular kind: 'base dancing' which was slow and processional in nature, with two partners taking complex steps.[60] Finally, he recommended painting or carving. This was not a traditional noble pursuit, since although Chaucer speaks of the Squire as able to 'portray', the word in that case is more likely to refer to verbal or literary expression. Elyot's proposal in this case (like a similar one to be mentioned presently) seems to have had little response from the nobility and gentry beyond the study and copying of heraldry.

Physical education, in Elyot's view, should take place chiefly after the age of fourteen, when boys' bodies were sufficiently strong for it. His view reflected the military situation in Tudor England: the absence of a standing army and the need for the nobility and gentry to be trained for war and able to lead the local and national armed forces. Youths, said Elyot, should be trained in riding, hunting (because it replicated war in developing mental strategy and physical endurance), running, and wrestling. He added swimming, because it had been done by Romans like Caesar, although this was not widely practised in the sixteenth century.[61] Finally, all should learn archery: the traditional skill which we have seen that the Crown was so anxious to maintain, despite its growing ineffectiveness compared with firearms.[62]

Thirty years after *The Governor*, Sir Thomas Hoby's translation of *The Book of the Courtier* by Baldassare Castiglione appeared in 1561. This is a more discursive and philosophical discussion of noble education, in the form of imagined conversations between members of the court of Urbino in 1507. It was popular enough to be reissued three times during the Tudor period. *The Courtier*'s view of education for gentlemen was similar to Elyot's, although not argued so methodically. They ought to read the Latin classics and acquire rhetorical skills in speaking and writing. They should cultivate singing, playing instruments, and dancing for recreation, especially in company and when women were present. It was desirable for them to be able to draw and have knowledge of painting. Since their chief role in society was a military one ('the principal and true profession of a courtier'), they must be trained to handle weapons and fight, both on foot and on horseback. This required them to be physically fit, for which running, jumping, throwing weights, wrestling, swimming, and tennis were all recommended.[63]

BOYS OF THE ROYAL FAMILY

It followed that the children of the monarch required a structured education on the lines described by the writers. They needed to be at least the equals of their lay subjects in knowledge and skills and, from the Reformation onwards, to be able to direct the clergy as heads or governors of the Church of England. The records about the bringing up of Tudor princes are fullest in describing their literary education. In part this was traditional. By the fifteenth century, the king's sons were taught reading and Latin grammar in their own household by a professional schoolmaster, as well as learning French. The Latin masters of the young Henry VI and the sons of Edward IV are known by name.[64]

141

Henry VII was the first king, however, whose children are recorded learning Latin of the new humanist kind. Henry may well have encountered it during his exile in France, up to 1485. His eldest son, Arthur (born in 1486), had a Latin schoolmaster by 1491 in the person of John Rede, hitherto headmaster of Winchester College. It is not quite clear if Rede taught humanist Latin, but his successor in about 1496, the blind French scholar Bernard André, certainly did so. André functioned for about three years until Thomas Linacre took over, who was also of the new dispensation since he had studied in Italy. Arthur seems to have been an intelligent pupil (Fig. 38, below). By the time of his death in 1502, he was familiar (according to André) with thirty-three ancient and modern authors in Latin, including Cicero, Livy, and Virgil, and Latin

38. Prince Arthur (d. 1502), the first Tudor prince to learn humanist Latin.

versions of the Greek writers Homer and Thucydides.[65] He also had a French schoolmaster, Giles Duwes, who went on to write a textbook in the language and to teach the king's other children.[66] French had long been learnt by the English aristocracy, men and women, and continued so to be during the Tudor era.[67]

Arthur's younger brother, Henry VIII, born in 1491, was not at first brought up to inherit the throne, but he received a similar kind of education. From about 1495, when he was four, his schoolmaster was the poet John Skelton, who taught him to spell and then to read Latin. The poet produced for his use a collection of maxims in Latin called *Speculum Principis*, 'the mirror of a prince', as a guide for his adult life.[68] Skelton was succeeded in about 1502 by John Holt, who had taught at Magdalen College School and had published a humanist school grammar, *Lac Puerorum*, 'milk for children'. This set out to teach Latin in an original way, using pictures as well as words (Fig. 37, p. 136).[69] When Holt died in 1504, another professional schoolmaster took over: William Hone, a university graduate who had taught at Chichester. For French there was Giles Duwes as there was for Arthur. Henry too was an intelligent pupil and emerged as a confident reader and writer of Latin. He was able at least to appear as the author of a book against Martin Luther, *Assertio Septem Sacramentorum* in 1521, whatever help he had from others, and then to assume the posture of a learned king capable of heading the new Church of England after 1534. This posture was only credible because he had received a good Latin education in its now essential humanist form.

In due course Henry took care that his own two sons should also receive the best possible literary training. The elder of the pair was the illegitimate Henry Fitzroy, born in 1519, whom the king regarded as a member of the royal family, even perhaps as a potential king (Fig. 39, p. 144).[70] Fitzroy had a Latin schoolmaster by the age of six in 1525 in the person of John Palsgrave, who had already taught the king's younger sister Mary. Palsgrave was a competent Latinist and teacher of French, for which he later produced an English–French dictionary.[71] Henry Fitzroy, although reckoned intelligent, seems to have inclined more to physical skills than literary ones, and Palsgrave complained that his lessons were interrupted by courtiers taking him off to

39. Henry Fitzroy, duke of Richmond and Somerset (d. 1536), Henry VIII's illegitimate son who died in his late teens.

ride, hunt, hawk, and shoot. During 1526, Palsgrave was replaced by Richard Croke, a doctor of theology from Cambridge, who stayed for the next three years. He too experienced rivalry from those who lured the boy away to physical exercises, bringing him home too tired to study. Not only that: the officer in charge of Fitzroy's household took it upon himself to set lessons and encourage the boy to write in secretary hand rather than the roman script preferred by Croke. It looks as if Fitzroy would have developed into a nobleman of wide capabilities rather than great scholarship, but he did not live to do so. He died unexpectedly in 1536 when he was only just seventeen.

40. Edward VI (d. 1553), the best-educated of the Tudor princes.

The education of Henry's only legitimate son, Edward VI, was taken far more seriously (Fig. 40, above). Born in 1537, he was given his own household two years later, and had a tutor by 1543 when he was six, in the person of Richard Cox, who was also the dean of his chapel.[72] Cox followed in the tradition of earlier royal schoolmasters in being highly qualified, in his case as a doctor of theology from Cambridge. He had also been headmaster of Eton. In 1544 he was joined and eventually supplanted as Edward's schoolmaster by John Cheke, a graduate of the same university and a scholar of Greek who held the regius chair in that subject at Cambridge.[73] Cheke began by teaching Edward Latin, to which Greek was added in 1549. This was a subject that had gradually been adopted in the best schools during the first half of the sixteenth century. The prince showed himself to be a highly intelligent pupil. He was taken through a wide range of classical authors in both languages, and was capable of translating Greek into Latin and back again.

By learning Greek, Edward updated Henry VIII's status as a learned king. Having a mastery of both classical languages would make him able, as head of the Church of England, to understand and pronounce on matters of religion as well as on government and politics. His education also brought him under the influence of religious Reformers, even while Henry VIII was alive. Richard Cox and John Cheke were both sympathetic to the Reformation, and Cox would become bishop of Ely under Elizabeth I. In addition, Jean Belmaine, a Protestant refugee from France, arrived as Edward's French schoolmaster in 1546 and used their study of French to teach him arguments in favour of the Protestant doctrine of justification by faith alone and against the papal headship of the Church and the practice of idolatry in worship.[74] During Edward's reign, from 1547 to 1553, the Reformation in England was taken much further than Henry VIII had allowed. Edward mentally kept pace with this, and had he not died at the age of fifteen there is every likelihood that he would have been a learned head of the Church like Henry, but of a Church that had entered a new phase of its history.

We do not possess much information about the education of the Tudor princes in matters other than Latin and Greek, but occasional references suggest that similar ground was covered to that mapped out by Elyot. Music – singing and instrumental playing on the lute or virginals – was taught to Henry VIII, Henry Fitzroy, and Edward VI. Henry VIII was capable of composing music, notably 'Pastime with good company' and other songs, but improbably 'Greensleeves' (set in a later style). The princes also learnt to dance. When Prince Arthur married Katherine of Aragon in 1501, he executed two 'base dances' with Lady Cecil, while Katherine did two with one of her ladies, and Prince Henry, then aged ten, danced twice with his sister Margaret 'in so goodly and pleasant a manner that it was to the king and queen [a] great and singular pleasure'.[75] Riding, hunting, hawking, and archery are mentioned in relation to all the princes. Nor can they have escaped an acquaintance with English history or with world geography, the knowledge of which was undergoing such changes in the sixteenth century. Edward VI possessed a map of the world, and he at least was instructed in mathematics and astronomy.

BOYS OF THE NOBILITY AND GENTRY

The nobility and many of the gentry, like the royal family, had their education in households rather than grammar schools for the public. We hear occasionally of noble youths in schools. At least two studied at Eton: Edward Audley, eldest son of a baron, and Richard Grey, Lord Grey of Codnor in his own right, both whom died in their teens while there in 1478 and 1521 respectively.[76] But Eton had the prestige of a royal foundation, and while some gentry were willing to send their boys to schools, others (and the nobility particularly) would have found the egalitarian nature and discipline of a classroom or a boarding house discordant with their status. Even a boy might do so. In 1538 James Basset, mentioned in an earlier chapter as studying at a college in Paris at the age of twelve, complained to his mother that he had to share a bed with a servant and two other boys. An envoy was sent to check, and was assured by the rector of the college that the servant was a gentleman's son and that the other two were 'of great houses', 'clean boys and prettily learned'. The bed was large enough for four adults.[77]

Accordingly some noblemen and gentlemen paid for a private teacher in their household. This avoided their children having to mix and compete with boys of lower rank, as well as enabling them to learn the cultural and physical skills that were not supplied in a school. Contemporaries, however, deprecated the small salaries and lowly status awarded to teachers of this kind. Elyot asserted that fathers hiring a master 'chiefly inquire with how small a salary he will be contented', and gave less attention to the master's qualifications than they would to hiring a cook or a falconer.[78] Joseph Hall, writing in 1598, satirised the poor conditions under which such masters worked. They might be reduced to sleeping in a truckle bed within their pupil's chamber, sitting in an inferior place at table, and needing to ask the mother's permission before chastising the pupil, all in return for £3 6s. 8d. a year and a set of winter clothes.[79]

An alternative practice was to send a boy away from home to be brought up in a greater household, especially once he reached the age of puberty. This was an ancient tradition among both the nobility and gentry, because the household of someone of superior rank would have better resources for learning knowledge and skills as well as bringing contact with people of high status and power. The most exalted families might gain places for their sons in the royal household. The Tudor monarchs maintained a small number of 'henchmen', or pages to the sovereign, who therefore formed part of the household staff. They learnt languages, manners, and physical skills.[80] Alternatively, young men could come into the household during the day as private visitors, partaking of the culture and hoping to be noticed by the grandees. Other parents sent their children to the great officers of state. Cardinal Wolsey's household in the 1520s harboured nine or ten young lords, including the young earl of Derby and the son of the earl of Northumberland.[81] Two speakers of the House of Commons were in demand for the same purpose: Sir Thomas Lovell (d. 1524) and Sir Humphrey Wingfield (d. 1546).[82] William Cecil, Lord Burghley, fulfilled a similar function in Elizabeth's reign.[83] Abbots and bishops were also sought out for this purpose up to the Reformation, after which the former disappeared and the latter were poorer and less influential than they had been.[84] Their role was largely replaced by the growing practice of sending teenage boys to the universities or the Inns of Court.[85]

Letters and household accounts allow us to view the progress of some of the boys who were educated privately. A well-recorded case is that of Thomas Cromwell's son Gregory.[86] Born in about 1520, he was brought up away from home by a series of tutors from about the age of eight. First he was at Cambridge, although not as an undergraduate, then at the priory of Little Marlow in Buckinghamshire, and later again at Cambridge. The tutors sent reports about him from time to time, sometimes implying that they were an improvement on their predecessors. He seems to have been a slow learner. He studied the Latin 'accidence' or basic grammar and how to write. Occasionally he 'wrote' letters in English to his father, no doubt under the tutors' supervision. Two or three other boys of similar rank were boarded with him for company, one of whom (Nicholas Sadler) was more intelligent and able to bring Gregory on in his wake. By the mid-1530s, when he was in his teens, he had progressed somewhat but was not yet proficient in Latin. An account of his day in about 1533 states that his studies, which seem to have occupied the morning, began with a lesson on a Latin dialogue of Erasmus, *Pietas Puerilis* ('Youthful Piety'). This the tutor had translated for him into English so that he could compare the two languages. After that he wrote for one or two hours, and spent about the same amount of time reading Robert Fabian's *Chronicle*: a history of England in English. A more capable student would have been reading classical history in Latin. The tutor got round this by 'telling him some history of the Romans or Greeks' and getting him to repeat the story afterwards.

Gregory also followed other pursuits in the manner suggested by Elyot. He learnt French, good manners, and 'pastimes of instruments', in other words the playing of the lute and the virginals. He practised riding with his tutor. Like other Tudor boys, he exercised with the longbow, and this, the tutor claimed, 'suited him so well that he seems to be naturally gifted in it'. He profited from the wish of important people to keep in with his father. While in East Anglia he was invited to Lopham park in Norfolk, 'where he shot a buck and doe at his pleasure'. He went hawking and hunting. In Essex, where he had cousins, the earl of Oxford sent for him 'and let us see such game and pleasure as I never saw in my life'. And he underwent the usual religious exercises of someone of his rank, going to hear mass in a chapel every day before starting his lessons.

Another young gentleman whose education can be traced, albeit of less importance than Gregory Cromwell, was Francis Willoughby, born in about the 1540s. His father Henry Willoughby, an esquire, was killed by the rioters of Kett's Rebellion in Norfolk in 1549. Francis then became a royal ward until his uncle George purchased his wardship with that of his older sister Margaret and acted as their guardian, treating them well.[87] They had two servants to look after them. Francis studied Latin at Saffron Walden Grammar School in Essex, a respectable foundation that followed the curricula of Winchester and Eton. Here he ascended through reading the elementary poem *Cato*, a work of Terence, the psalter in Latin, Cicero's *Epistles*, the *Colloquia* of Juan Luis Vives, works by Erasmus, and the *Elegantiae* of Nicholas Valla – all requiring copies to be bought for him. He needed paper, ink, and an inkhorn, and learnt to write. Later he had lessons in arithmetic and the penmanship known as the 'Italian hand'. It seems that he learnt some Greek and Hebrew too, since grammars of both were bought for him for 2*s*. 4*d*. as well as a Latin-and-Greek dictionary. There are further mentions of French books, the cost of stringing his virginals, and payments of 2*s*. 6*d*. to two different men for teaching him to play. He received lessons in singing, acquired a song book, and learnt to dance.[88] He also had arrows and bowstrings for exercise. In due course he went to Cambridge, flourished, and died as a knight in 1597.

ELITE EDUCATION FOR GIRLS: SCHOOLING

As with boys, there was a tradition of writing about girls of high status and their desirable qualities that went back to the Middle Ages. One such work was *The Book of the Knight of the Tower*, composed by the French knight Geoffroy de la Tour Landry for his daughters in the 1370s. Caxton translated it into English and published it in 1483, two years before the Tudor era began. It is a series of stories, taken from romances and histories, explaining to the girls (after their mother had died) the importance of pursuing virtue (including modesty, devoutness, and moderation in food) and of avoiding vice (extravagant dress, cosmetics, and the seductive advances of young men). At times it is surprisingly frank. One story is about a man and woman who have sex in church beside the altar, causing them to be stuck together and suffer the embarrassment of being discovered. The book was still in circulation in 1534 when the Tudor writer John Fitzherbert observed wryly that it would teach people 'more vices, subtlety, and craft than they would ever have known without reading it'.[89]

During the 1520s, new works were produced for parents and daughters in England, marked by a blend of traditional and classical sources similar to that of Elyot's *The Governor*. In 1524 the Spanish scholar Vives produced a Latin work on *The Instruction of a Christian Woman*, dedicated to Queen Katherine of Aragon. It was translated into English by Richard Hyrde, one of the circle of Sir Thomas More, and published in 1529.[90] In this form it was reissued at least seven times in England up to 1592, making it a twin to *The Governor* in that respect.[91] Meanwhile Hyrde wrote an eight-page preface on the education of women for a translation of a work by Erasmus on the Lord's Prayer in 1524,[92] and Elyot composed *The Defence of Good Women* in the 1530s, published in 1540.[93]

The works of these writers were original in the emphasis that they placed on the literary education of women. La Tour Landry had observed briefly that it was good and profitable for women to learn to read (which meant primarily in their own language) but that it did not matter if they could not write.[94] The authors of the sixteenth century found inspiration in the scholarly ladies of antiquity, and felt that noble women nowadays might properly aim as high as men in terms of being able to read and write Latin and Greek. Vives praised Queen Katherine of Aragon and her sister Queen Juana of Castile for mastering Latin, as well as the daughters of Sir Thomas More (Fig. 41, p. 152).[95] Outside literary studies, however, the new authors were more cautious in what they advocated. Like La Tour Landry and medieval writers, they focused on female virtues rather than female skills. Vives discussed the importance of chastity, seclusion, modesty, devoutness, and obedience.[96] The artistic and physical accomplishments that girls in Tudor England are known to have acquired received far less attention than they did for boys in *The Governor*. Elyot's *Defence* mentioned only textile work and cookery. Vives agreed with both of these but he said nothing of music and deprecated the reading of romances, dancing, and attending jousts.[97]

There was a shortage of schools for girls compared with those for boys, other than at an elementary level of learning to read, and schools of the latter kind were unlikely to be used by the wealthy. The only large school for girls to be founded in the Tudor period was Christ's Hospital in London, which was opened in 1552 and had 396 pupils of both sexes in 1563, of whom 132 were girls.[98] But this was a charitable foundation, especially for orphans and the poor, and would not have attracted families of high status. By about the second half of the century, however, one can discern the emergence of small private schools for girls in towns that aimed beyond teaching mere reading. They have left little record, except in London in those cases where their

41. The daughters of Thomas More, including Margaret (later Roper: front row, second from the right), early examples of women learning humanist Latin.

proprietors were foreigners and appear in lists of aliens living in the capital. Such schools may have catered chiefly for citizens' daughters who could come on a daily basis, but wealthy citizens overlapped in status and lifestyle with the country gentry, and it is not impossible that some of the latter used schools of this kind. Several are mentioned in the late sixteenth century, run by women of French or 'Dutch' (Netherlands or German) origin. They are likely to have taught reading, writing, French, and needlework skills, as well as imparting the norms of good manners and proper behaviour.[99]

Most wealthy girls, in contrast, had their education in a domestic setting. Some were taught in their own homes by literate mothers, male tutors, or governesses. This was the case with the four Tudor royal princesses: the daughters of Henry VII, Margaret and Mary, and those of Henry VIII, Mary and Elizabeth. It was also true of the daughters of Sir Thomas More in London and Chelsea, as well as the future Queen Katherine Parr and her sister Anne Parr, in their mother's houses at Rye House and Blackfriars in

London.[100] If home education was impossible, there were two other choices. Up to the Reformation, some girls of rank were brought up in the larger and better-organised nunneries. Here they could be taught prayer, manners, reading, and perhaps French, as well as cultural skills like needlework. In 1536 thirty or forty gentlemen's children were said to be staying at Polesworth Abbey, Warwickshire, while St Mary's Abbey, Winchester, had twenty-six girls from local families including the daughter of Viscount Lisle.[101]

The other option was to send girls, usually when in their teens, to the household of a wealthier noblewoman or gentlewoman. There they acted as a kind of junior lady in waiting and practised similar skills to those above. Agnes, duchess of Norfolk, who was a widow from 1524 until her death in 1545, maintained large households at Horsham and Lambeth where she brought up the children of relatives and friends, including the future Queen Katherine Howard.[102] Among the gentry, Henry Willoughby's daughter Margaret went to serve Princess Elizabeth at Hatfield in 1556, and Richard Fermor's sister Mary to board with a Lady Gerrard in 1581.[103] There was the same hope, in such cases, as there was for noble boys. They would learn the manners and relationships of life in a great household, gain patronage, and perhaps come to the notice of other high-ranking families as a suitable choice for marriage.

The significant new feature of girls' education in the higher ranks of Tudor society was the mastery of classical languages. French had long been learnt by noble girls in England and this continued during the sixteenth century.[104] Latin, in contrast, had been studied only at a very basic level. Lady Margaret Beaufort, the mother of Henry VII, born in 1443 and as privileged a girl as any, regretted her inability to understand Latin to any great extent.[105] When Katharine of Aragon was about to come to England in 1498, she was advised to learn French because Margaret and her daughter-in-law Queen Elizabeth of York did not speak Latin or Spanish.[106]

The change began, or is at least evident, with the daughters of Henry VII and Elizabeth, round about 1500. Margaret, the elder of them (born in 1489), probably learnt humanist Latin like her brothers, although the identities of her teachers are not clear. Giles Duwes later claimed to have taught her French. Her younger sister Mary (born in 1496) was certainly taught

Latin by John Palsgrave, who was also competent in French, and it is possible that Thomas Linacre had some part in her education since he went with her to France in 1514, when she (briefly) married King Louis XII. Again, Duwes counted her as one of his pupils.[107] His credit with the royal family led to his further employment to teach French to Henry VIII's elder daughter Mary, born in 1516 and later Queen Mary I. When he published his textbook, *An Introductorie for to Lerne . . . Frenche* in 1533, he made Mary a character in a series of dialogues which illustrated conversation in the language. She learnt humanist Latin from Richard Fetherston, an Oxford and Cambridge MA,[108] and possibly also from Linacre, who dedicated a Latin grammar in English to her, *Rudimenta Grammatices* in 1523.[109] Vives too is likely to have given her some tuition during his visits to England in 1523 and 1527.[110]

Mary's younger sister, Elizabeth I (born 1533), had a later and more varied education, just as Edward VI's exceeded that of Henry Fitzroy (Fig. 42, p. 155). She was first taught, probably at an elementary stage, by Katherine Champernown, a lady of her household. Later, her Latin lessons were in the hands of William Grindal, a Cambridge graduate and pupil of Roger Ascham, Ascham being one of the leading educationists of Tudor England. After Grindal died in 1548 when Elizabeth was fifteen, Ascham took over her lessons himself, which by this time extended to the study of Greek. She also learnt modern languages. Her French tutor, shared with Edward VI, was the Frenchman Jean Belmaine, and her Italian instructor Giovanni Battista Castiglione. By 1544, at the age of eleven, she was able to write (or was helped to write) a letter in Italian to Queen Katherine Parr, and to do so in an elegant italic hand: it is her earliest surviving letter. She also seems to have learnt some Spanish. By 1545 she was capable of translating a French religious work into English, as 'The Glasse of the Synnefull Soul' for presentation to Katherine, and in the same year she made a corresponding translation for her father, King Henry. In this she turned Katherine's own 'Prayers and Meditations' from English into Latin, French, and Italian. Her linguistic powers remained with her throughout her life. As late as the 1590s, she amused herself in writing English versions of works by Horace, Plutarch, and Boethius, as well as being able to converse fluently in Latin when necessary.[111]

154

42. The learned Elizabeth I, aged about twenty-seven (*c.* 1560),
early in her reign.

The royal princesses were not alone in being taught to these higher standards. There are parallels in the families of the nobility and gentry. In that of Sir Thomas More, his daughter Margaret, later Margaret Roper, born in 1505, studied at home with her younger sisters under tutors: in her case in Latin and Greek. Each member of the family was encouraged to write to their father each day in Latin, and Margaret became as accomplished as a man in this respect.[112] Other wealthy girls who learnt Latin, and sometimes Greek, included the Parr sisters, Katherine and Anne, daughters of a courtier of Henry VIII;[113] Lady Jane Grey, born in 1537, daughter of the duke of Suffolk;[114] Mary Seymour, born in 1538, and her sisters, daughters of the duke of Somerset;[115] and Mary Fitzalan, born in 1539–40, daughter of the earl of Arundel. There are more examples later, too many to list. As the century wore on, Italian became popular and sometimes Spanish too. William Harrison could observe in 1587, 'How many gentlewomen and ladies there are that besides sound knowledge of the Greek and Latin tongues are thereto no less skilful in the Spanish, Italian and French, or in some one of them.'[116] Jane Grey, indeed, began to learn Hebrew.

Not all these women treated their classical studies as a mere educational trophy. Their studies fuelled their creative abilities as was the case with Elizabeth I. Several noble women were able to write Latin letters of high standard. Margaret Roper's were proudly shown to others by Thomas More, to the astonishment of Cardinal Pole himself.[117] The three daughters of Edward Seymour, duke of Somerset – Anne, Margaret, and Jane – composed 400 Latin couplets in honour of Queen Margaret of Valois, which achieved publication in France in 1550 and were even reissued.[118] Anne, the eldest of them, was capable of corresponding in Latin with the great Continental theologian, Jean Calvin.[119] Margaret Roper translated Erasmus's Latin *Treatise on the Paternoster* into English, published in 1525, while Mary Fitzalan, daughter of the earl of Arundel, compiled four collections of aphorisms in Latin taken from Greek and English sources, before her early death in 1557.[120]

It does not follow that all high-status families studied at this level. Honor, Viscountess Lisle (born in the 1490s into a family of gentry in Devon), does not appear to have known any foreign language well.[121] Anne Boleyn (born in 1507) lamented her own 'ignorance in the Latin tongue'.[122] The household school of the duchess of Norfolk in the 1520s and 1530s, where Katherine Howard grew up, seems not to have placed great emphasis on the classics. Grace Sharington's account of her own education in the 1550s and 1560s describes how she learnt to read and write in English, but she did not claim proficiency in Latin. Nor did she recommend it to her own daughters, although she advocated the reading of a variety of works in English: the Bible, Foxe's *Book of Martyrs*, chronicles, statutes and laws, and 'wise and witty sentences of philosophers'.[123] Elizabeth, countess of Rutland, went so far as to write to the countess of Bedford in 1588, on sending her daughter Bridget to be trained in courtly life, that 'her education has been barren hitherto, nor has she attained to anything except to play a little on the lute' and even that, because of a recent illness, 'she has almost forgotten'.[124]

ELITE EDUCATION FOR GIRLS: CULTURAL AND PRACTICAL SKILLS

Girls of status, like boys, were able to learn a range of skills beyond literary ones. Music had long been seen as a suitable recreation for them, however little educationists might mention the subject. Henry VII's daughter Margaret had a lute bought for her in 1501 when she was eleven, and her sister Mary got one at the same age six years later.[125] Mary had already learnt to play by then because she was only nine when King Philip the Fair of Castile visited Windsor Castle in 1506, for whom she 'played the lute and then the clavichord . . . very well, and she was of all folks there greatly praised'.[126] Henry VIII's daughter Mary I was described in 1527, when she was eleven, as skilled in music and dancing. Elizabeth I was able to play on the lute and spinet, and even wrote some compositions. A more typical girl of gentry rank, Margaret Willoughby, was given a pair of virginals in 1552, and tutors were paid 15s. to instruct her for three months.[127] William Cavendish of Hardwick encouraged his daughter Frances in musical skills. He paid her older brother 20s. for teaching her to play the viol, and promised (and paid) her 40s. for having five lessons with the viol and for learning to sing as well.[128] Grace Sharington, when married, not only played the lute each day but was capable of setting songs in five parts to be sung to its accompaniment.[129]

Girls also had lessons in dancing. Vives conceded that this was a popular pastime but expressed concerns about it: the Greeks had praised it but the Romans not. He disapproved of its modern forms which were 'full of shaking and bragging and uncleanly handlings, gropings, and kissings, and a very kindling of lechery'.[130] Elyot took a different, more positive view. Although he discussed it primarily in terms of the education of men, he made it clear that he endorsed it for women as well. 'In every dance, of a most ancient custom, there danceth together a man and a woman, holding each other by the hand or the arm, which betokeneth concord.' Dancing, he thought, brought about harmony between the two sexes, in which the contribution of each one combined to make the elements of nobility.[131] In practice, dancing was widely popular with young and old. In its elite forms, among the aristocracy, it was a skill to be learnt formally and carefully. The first dancing treatise in English, *The Manner of Dancing Base Dances*, was published in 1522, and there were teachers of the art. Francis Willoughby had lessons costing 3*s.* 2*d.* from one in 1554.[132]

Other skills acquired by noble and gentle girls related to the domestic duties they would have in adult life. Some knowledge of numbering and accounting may have been learnt. Margaret Willoughby, by her teens, was able to draw up bills of her own and her brother's expenditure to send to their guardian uncle.[133] Textile work was another occupation common to women of all classes, including the aristocracy. Vives recommended that a girl should not only learn her book but how 'to handle wool and flax'. He thought that craft work helped vary reading and promoted temperance. Classical women had done it, and it was suitable even for queens and princesses.[134] Harrison described how the older ladies of Elizabeth's court 'do shun and avoid idleness, some of them exercising their fingers with the needle, others in caulwork [i.e. netting], divers in spinning of silk'. 'Many of the eldest sort', he added, 'are skilful in surgery and distillation of waters.'[135] Grace Sharington studied surgery and medicine in her youth, as well as needlework.[136]

Finally there were physical skills. These were indeed more limited for girls than boys. Parents and governesses are unlikely to have forbidden the younger ones to run about and play like their brothers, but longer clothes impeded movement, and by the time of adolescence ideals of female behaviour had to be pursued. Nevertheless riding, especially on tractable horses known as palfreys, was an essential part of the wealthy lifestyle, necessary for travel and desirable for exercise. Most girls of the higher ranks must have learnt it and have worn appropriate clothes to do it.[137] Margaret Willoughby acquired a coat and hose for riding in 1552.[138] Pierre Erondelle, the teacher of French, could imagine a woman fishing with a line, and women were not barred from archery.[139] When Margaret Tudor, aged fourteen, travelled to

Scotland to be married in 1503, she stopped at Alnwick in Northumberland and killed a buck in the park there with her bow.[140] Women took part in hunting, either by standing to shoot as animals were driven past or riding in pursuit of them. Elyot commended hare-coursing for women without making it clear how they followed it: on foot at a vantage point or on horse-back.[141] When Roger Ascham visited Jane Grey at Bradgate Park, Leicestershire, in 1550 he found her at her book while all the gentlemen and women of the household were hunting in the park.[142] Elizabeth I enjoyed both shooting and riding. In 1591, for example, she is recorded, along with the countess of Kildare, as shooting deer with a crossbow at Cowdray in Sussex, and as late as 1600 she was spending every second day on horseback to hunt during a stay at Hanworth Park in Middlesex.[143]

Female education in Tudor England, as so often with women's history, is harder to reconstruct than that of men. It happened more informally and at home, generating far fewer records. Even at an aristocratic level it is often obscure, and this increases the lower one goes down the social hierarchy. Nevertheless it is clear that the aim of educational writers to promote virtue for women rather than skills fell wide of the mark. The wealthy were active in all the spheres of learning, culture, and physical pursuits, and it was not their abilities but the conventions of the day that stopped them taking their talents into professional spheres as men could do.

6

SPEECH, SONGS, AND STORIES

SPEECH

People in Tudor England knew that we learn to speak, when young, by listening to our elders and imitating them. Bartholomew Glanville's thirteenth-century encyclopaedia, still in print in Elizabeth's reign, observed that a nurse in a wealthy family not only cared for a child but 'lispeth and soundeth [her] words, to teach more easily the child that cannot speak'.[1] Another commentator, Elyot in 1531, stressed the importance of teaching speech to noble and gentry children. The nurse and other women in the nursery should use English 'which is clean, polite, perfectly and articulately pronounced, omitting no letter or syllable, as foolish women often times do of a wantonness, whereby divers noblemen and gentlemen's children . . . have attained corrupt and foul pronunciation'. He objected, in other words, to the use of 'baby talk' and feared that children of rank might grow up with rustic dialects.[2] In truth adults have always distorted words for young children, or mimicked their own distortions. 'Baby', 'daddy', and 'mummy' are such words, all in use in the sixteenth century. So was the term 'handy-dandy' for the hand, and possibly also 'pig-wig' for a pig.[3] Elyot need not have been concerned. In practice this is only a transitional phase, and children go on to master adult speech.

Educationists worried that the young learnt foul language. This was especially an issue in wealthy households where they came into contact with servants. Elyot wanted all men barred from the nursery except for physicians. 'For we daily hear, to our great heaviness, children swear great oaths and speak lascivious and unclean words by the example of other[s] whom they hear.' Even worse, he asserted, parents condoned the practice.[4] Others

160

thought the same, before and after him. A schoolmaster in Oxford during the 1490s complained that parents (he probably had in mind those of the prosperous classes) spoilt their offspring. 'If [the children] happen to call the dame [mother] "whore" or the father "cuckold" (as it lucketh [chanceth]), they laugh thereat and take it for a sport, saying it is kind [natural] for children to be wanton in their youth.'[5] Queen Elizabeth's tutor, Roger Ascham, recounted his shock at a gentleman's house in 1569 when 'a young child, somewhat past four year[s] old, could in no wise frame his tongue to say a little short grace, and yet he could roundly rap out so many ugly oaths, and those of the newest fashion . . . And that which was most detestable of all, his father and mother would laugh at it.' The reason, Ascham concluded, was that the child spent too much time with the family's serving men.[6]

How children spoke, unfortunately, is hardly ever recorded. The nearest we can reach it is in early Tudor school texts, where teachers were trying to get boys to understand Latin by translating everyday words and phrases. A few schoolboy sayings occur in the *Vulgaria* (sentences for translation) of the Oxford schoolmaster John Stanbridge, published in around 1500. Here we can eavesdrop on remarks like 'Reach me bread. I am weary of study. Thou stinkest. I beshrew thee. Thou art a false knave. Thou art worthy to be hanged. His nose is like a shoeing horn. What the devil dost thou here? I shall kill thee with thine own knife. Thou art a blab. He is the veriest coward that ever pissed.'[7] Another Oxford schoolbook of the same period contains some bits of dialogue:

A: What! What gear is this? Whose paper is this?
B: What would ye? It is mine.
A: While ye have so good stuff, I trust ye will give me one leaf.
B: Nay, for good, ye may think yourself well entreated if ye get so much as half one.[8]

Schoolboys, as we shall learn, took part in dramatic performances (Fig. 43, p. 162), and some Tudor plays include portrayals of children's speech. *Fulgens and Lucrece*, printed in about 1520, has two boy characters, A and B, who engage in lively repartee during the action. In *Nice Wanton* (1569), the two

43. A picture of the life of Sir Henry Unton (d. 1596), showing a banquet enlivened with an interlude performed by actors including children.

adolescents who go to the bad (Ismael and Dalilah) engage in the banter of which Elyot and Ascham disapproved. 'By Gog's body! Peace, whore! Knave's face! Come on, with Christ's curse!' Once formed, of course, the speech of Tudor children would have been similar to that of adults, except for shriller and more swift articulation.

RHYMES AND SONGS

A child today will hear much of its first 'literature' in the form of rhymes and songs. Some of these will be 'nursery rhymes': a relatively modern term for a traditional anthology, now largely fixed in terms of items and wordings, which is considered suitable for young children and chiefly for them alone. Others will be advertising jingles or adult lyrics, sung by parents to children or overheard. Much of this was true in Tudor England. At that date there was as yet no recognised body of nursery rhymes, which were first brought together and regularised in the eighteenth and nineteenth centuries. Some rhymes and songs were probably thought appropriate to be told or sung to children even in the Tudor age, but they were not standardised and might vary from place to place or generation to generation. Others belonged to adults, and reached children simply because they were heard being said or sung.

Only one Tudor writer has left us a helpful collection of this kind of material. Indeed we cannot reconstruct it more easily than was the case in the fifteenth century, when schoolboys were encouraged or tempted to write down English songs and rhymes in their notebooks and turn them into Latin.[9] The coming in of humanist Latin after 1480, as has been stated, gradually froze out such work in favour of the imitation of classical writers. The Tudor exception is the London clergyman William Wager (d. 1591), author of the play *The Longer Thou Livest, The More Fool Thou Art* (1569).[10] Its young anti-hero Moros quotes or refers to ten songs or rhymes which he learnt, he says, as a child on the lap of a 'fond' (foolish) woman who worked for his mother.[11] Apart from Wager's play we possess only accidental scraps until a new source becomes available in the reigns of James I and Charles I in the form of printed song books, with texts and notation. Their contents were mostly traditional ones, although they were sometimes re-edited for new audiences. Several of the songs that they printed were referred to by Moros or repeated themes that occur in other texts associated with children, so that they have some value in suggesting what was known by the young in Tudor England.

The body of rhymes and songs that emerges is a varied one. It includes little one-verse story vignettes about human beings of the type of 'Jack and Jill' or 'Humpty Dumpty', and similar stories about animals. Some items are satirical, others convivial, others riddling, and yet others lyrical or amatory. There are two or three little human tales. Two are quoted by Wager:

Tom a lin and his wife, and his wife's mother,
They went over a bridge all three together;
The bridge was broken and they fell in;
'The Devil go with all', quoth Tom a lin.

Martin Swart and his man, sodledum, sodledum,
Martin Swart and his man, sodledum bell.[12]

Both must have been more than single compositions known in one place. Rhymes about characters named Tom-a-lin or the like occur in later records: possibly as satire on Scotsmen.[13] Martin Swart or Schwartz was a German mercenary employed by Lambert Simnel, the pretender to the throne, and was killed at the battle of Stoke in 1487 by the forces of Henry VII. The fact that he was still remembered some eighty years later shows that the lines must have circulated: perhaps as a mocking gibe on the defeat of Simnel's rising.

A few other rhymes that children may have known seem to hover on the edge of Tudor literature. The poet John Skelton, writing in 1522–3, comments in one place:

And Mock hath lost her shoe:
What may she do thereto?

while in another he says, 'Though Jack said nay, yet Mock there lost her shoe.'[14] There seems to be a sexual innuendo in both cases – a maiden losing her virginity, but the rhyme is worth mentioning because it is close to one reported as being in the mouths of children in 1602. This occurs in a sensational account of a murder, and the mutilation of a small girl who witnessed it, making her dumb. Later the girl was rescued by another family at Bishop's Hatfield in Hertfordshire, and was playing with the daughter of the house when a cock crew. The other girl, 'mocking the cock with these words,

Cock a doodle doo,
Peggy hath lost her shoe,

called to her injured friend to do the same, causing her to speak and bring about the discovery of the murder.[15] The rhyme is next recorded, in the longer modern version, 'Cock-a-doodle-do, my dame has lost her shoe', in the eighteenth century.[16]

Allusions of a similar kind occur in Shakespeare's play *King Lear* of about 1605–6. They appear in the speeches of Edgar, who is disguised as a madman.[17] He quotes snatches of several songs and poems, including two works yet to be discussed which were known to children: *Bevis of Hampton* and 'Come o'er the bourn, Bessy'. A third of his songs goes:

Sleepest or wakest thou, jolly shepherd?
Thy sheep be in the corn;
And for one blast of thy minikin [dainty] mouth
Thy sheep shall take no harm.

This has a resemblance to the later nursery rhyme, first recorded in about 1760:

Little boy blue, come blow up your horn;
The sheep's in the meadow, the cow's in the corn.[18]

Edgar also quotes:

Child Rowland to the dark tower came,
His word was still, 'Fie, foh, and fum,
I smell the blood of a British man.'

These words were reproduced by Thomas Nashe in 1596, and later came to be associated with the Giant in the story of 'Jack and the Giant Killer'.[19] That story may well have been known in Shakespeare's time, although it did not take a published form until the eighteenth century. Both of the last two quotations seem to form part of the oral culture that Tudor children would have known, although they cannot be traced in print as children's literature until a hundred or more years later.

44. Two songs known to children. Above, 'Three blind mice'; below, 'Jack boy, ho boy', an ancestor of 'Pussy's in the well'.

Small children are fascinated by animals and the possibility of seeing them as human countertypes. Three or four animal rhymes or songs can be linked with Tudor England. One, about a fox raiding a farmyard and either catching or failing to catch a cockerel or a goose, gave rise to Chaucer's 'Nun's Tale' and appears in two lyrics of the fifteenth century.[20] A song on the subject, 'Tomorrow the fox will come to town', printed in 1609, shows that something similar must have been sung in Tudor times.[21] The text in question is one of four songs about animals scored by the musician Thomas Ravenscroft and included in his publications for amateur singers. The other three songs are all ancestors of later nursery rhymes (Fig. 44, above). The first is a round for three voices:

Three blind mice, three blind mice,
Dame Julian, Dame Julian,

The Miller and his merry old wife,
She scraped her tripe, lick thou the knife[22]

a more rustic but less violent version than the modern one. The second is a canon in unison:

Jack boy, ho boy, news, the cat in the well,
Let us ring now for her knell, ding dong, ding dong, bell.[23]

This is now known to us as 'Ding dong, bell, Pussy's in the well'. The third is a song for four voices, called 'The marriage of the Frog and the Mouse'. It too exists in later versions:

It was the frog in the well,
humble-dum, humble-dum,
And the merry mouse in the mill,
tweedle, tweedle twine.

The frog courted the mouse, after which they were married by a rat. Alas, the celebrations came to a tragic end, for 'then came in Gib our cat, and catcht the mouse even by the back', while the frog fell victim to 'Dick our drake' who 'drew [him] even to the lake'.[24]

Children were likely to hear convivial songs either at home or from ale-houses, where the typical lattice windows of Shakespeare's day would have allowed the noise of singing to spread well outside. Wager's Moros quotes what seem to be the opening lines of two of them.[25] 'There dwelleth a jolly foster [forester]' may be a version of the popular early Tudor song, 'I am a jolly foster', in which a forest ranger expounds his prowess at hunting and shooting 'both hart and hind'.[26] 'I come to drink some of your Christmas ale' is the kind of song sung by wassailers or beggars in the Christmas season. A third text known to children, but not to Moros, was 'Away the mare', scored by Ravenscroft in 1611 and explained as a song for servants who have been discharged and are looking for new masters:

Heigh ho, away the mare,

Let us set aside all care,

If any man be disposed to try,

Lo, here comes a lusty crew

That are enforced to cry anew,

'Master anew!'[27]

This is the song sung by the young boy Jack in the popular Tudor story, *The Friar and the Boy*, which we shall encounter later. It was not a song of children alone, of course, but one of the many that they must have known.

Riddles have always fascinated children, and examples occur in fifteenth-century school exercises.[28] One of Moros's songs may be a riddle unless it is a lyric:

The white dove sat on the castle wall,

I bend my bow and shoot her I shall,

I put her in my glove, both feathers and all.[29]

Two books of riddles were published in 1629 and 1631, the first of which aimed to appeal to 'any young man or child to know if he be quick-witted', while the second proclaimed itself as 'very meet and delightful for youth to try their wits'.[30] Some of the items are traditional, since they include the famous 'Two legs sat upon three legs, and had one leg in his hand', explained as a man sitting on a stool holding a leg of lamb which is stolen by a dog.[31] Others must be similar in form to Tudor examples because they also resemble medieval ones.[32] They may be in prose or in verse:

He went to the wood and caught it.

He sat him down and sought it,

Because he could not find it,

Home with it he brought it. [Answer: a thorn in the foot.][33]

Beyond the sea there is an oak

And in that oak there is a nest,

And in that nest there is an egg,

And in that egg there is a yolk
Which calls together Christian folk. [Answer: the clapper of a church bell.][34]

I am called by name of man
Yet am as little as a mouse;
When winter comes I love to be
With my red gorget near the house. [Answer: a robin redbreast.] [35]

The next is not a riddle but may have had a place in playground taunts or games:

Hitty pitty within the wall,
And hitty pitty without the wall;
If you touch hitty my toy
Hitty pitty will bite the boy.[36]

The answer is 'a nettle' which may, perhaps, have been flourished as a weapon. There is an analogous rhyme in a school exercise of about 1480, 'Hur, hur, the fool bears the bur', which could have been chanted along with the sticking of burs or goose-grass onto somebody's clothes.[37]

The rest of the songs in Moros's repertoire can be broadly described as lyrical or amatory, and are likely to be adult songs that children learnt by hearing them sung.[38] They include:

Come over the bourn, Besse,
My little pretty Besse,
Come over the bourn, Besse to me.

This song, also recorded in the late fifteenth century, includes a religious explanation: the bourn is the world, Besse is mankind, and Christ calls 'come over to me'.[39] It looks more likely that the song was originally a secular one that came to be moralised.

Broom, broom, on [Hive] hill,
The gentle broom on [Hive] hill,

is a quotation from a ballad found in later, mainly Scottish, texts. A knight lays a wager with a lady that she cannot meet him on Hive Hill without losing her virtue. He arrives first but falls asleep. She scatters broom flowers over his body and places her ring on his finger, to his discomfiture when he wakes up.[40] Another lyric runs:

> There was a maid came out of Kent,
> Dainty love, dainty love,
> There was a maid came out of Kent,
> Dangerous be,
> There was a maid came out of Kent,
> Fair, proper, small, and gent
> As ever upon the ground went,
> For so should it be.

This does not seem to be known elsewhere but is presumably a love-song that ended either in satisfaction or disillusionment. The next song,

> Robin, lend to me thy bow,
> Sweet Robin, lend to me thy bow,
> For I must now a hunting with my lady go,
> With my sweet lady go,

tells how Wilkin asks Robin for his bow to go hunting with his 'sweet lady'.[41] Finally,

> By a bank as I lay, lay, lay, lay,
> Musing on things past, hey ho,
> In the merry month of May,
> O somewhat before the day
> Methought I heard at the last, the last, the last,

was later set by Ravenscroft as a song for four voices. It describes how the listener lay on the ground in a melancholy mood until he heard the nightingale and was enthralled by her music.[42]

These and the other songs and rhymes represent only a tiny fragment of what children would have heard and sung, but they remind us that music penetrates everywhere. While few children, except for the wealthy or those in church choirs, would be taught to sing or play on instruments, all could have experienced sound through singing, through organs and choirs in churches, and sometimes through musicians playing in taverns, weddings, and fairs.

STORIES

Beyond the song and the riddle, children in Tudor England heard the spoken story: the traditional tale, the episode of family history, or the event of public importance. Even today these play a significant part in our upbringing, and the same must have been true in the past. The aristocratic Clifford family passed down a story about how Henry Lord Clifford, born in 1456, had to be concealed as a shepherd boy for fear of the Wars of the Roses. Allegedly he did not learn to read or write for several years, through fear of being discovered.[43] Another such family, the Scropes, may have retold how the lady of the family had to send her little boy and his nurse to hide in a poor man's house during the Pilgrimage of Grace in 1536.[44]

Adults could tell stories to children, children to one another or even to adults. In Shakespeare's *The Winter's Tale* (1611) Hermione, lady in waiting to the queen, asks the queen's son, Prince Mamillius, for a tale. 'Merry or sad shall it be?' asks the prince. 'As merry as you will.' 'A sad tale's best for winter,' says the boy, 'I have one of sprites and goblins.' The two sit down but we overhear only the first few words: 'There was a man dwelt by a churchyard . . .'[45] An earlier play, *The Old Wives' Tale* (1595), by Shakespeare's contemporary George Peele, takes the form of a folk tale. Three youths lost in a wood are given refuge in the house of the local smith. They too propose to relax, this time with 'a merry winter's tale'. One of them asks for 'the Giant and the King's Daughter', remembering that 'when I was a little one, you might have drawn me a mile after you with such a discourse'.[46] The smith's elderly wife begins to tell the tale in a rambling manner; then it suddenly turns into a play with actors.

Of all the vast repertoire of oral stories in early modern England, hardly anything was recorded. We hear of them only by chance. Stories resembling that of Mamillius are described by Reginald Scot in his brave attempt to debunk the popular belief in witches, *The Discoverie of Witchcraft* (1584). Much of the fear of the supernatural, argued Scot, began with the tales told to children by the maids in the house: by implication those of less education and more attachment to folklore. They have, he said:

> so terrified us with an ugly Devil having horns in his head, fire in his mouth, and a tail in his breech . . . whereby we start and are afraid when we hear one cry 'Bough'. And they have so frayed [frightened] us . . . with Robin Goodfellow, the sporne, the mare, the man in the oak, the hell-wain, the fire-drake, the puckle, Tom Thumb, Hob Goblin, Tom Tumbler, boneless, and other such bugs that we are afraid of our own shadows.[47]

The practice of adults silencing unruly children with stories of bogeys is confirmed in the pirated version of Shakespeare's *The Merry Wives of Windsor* (1602). 'Women to affright their little children say that he [Herne the Hunter] walks [in Windsor Park] in shape of a great stag.'[48] But not all tales of this kind need have been alarming. Shakespeare showed Puck or Robin Goodfellow as a comic and mischievous character in *A Midsummer Night's Dream*, while Tom Thumb became the miniature hero of humorous stories in print from 1630 onwards.[49]

Children could also hear more formal stories in more formal settings. The daily timetable drawn up for Prince Edward (V) in 1473 provided that, during his dinner, he should listen to the reading of 'such noble stories as behoveth to a prince to understand'.[50] Something of the same was done for Gregory, the son of Thomas Cromwell: not an easy boy to teach, as we have seen. His tutor in the 1530s reported that 'when he rides (which he often does) I tell him some history of the Romans and Greeks which I cause him to rehearse again in a tale'.[51] The tutor narrated a story; the boy repeated it to show that he understood it. Biblical stories were also told and became well known. Up to the Reformation, when church services including Bible readings were in Latin, the stories were recounted via religious dramas in English, especially in the towns. By the mid-1540s the Bible was being regularly read in churches in English, and children could hear the long series of stories that appear in the Old and New Testaments.

One other kind of story orally told should be mentioned: that of the stage play. As we shall see, some schools were acting plays from the very beginning of the Tudor age.[52] During its progress, dramas with secular subjects were a highly popular form of public entertainment in which new texts were constantly written, leading ultimately to the great works of the Elizabethan playwrights. Their audiences (and indeed their casts) included children, especially in the provinces where amateur or travelling players might not charge or charge very much. Richard Willis, whose memories of his schooling we have encountered, described a play that he saw as a child in Gloucester in about 1570. It is in fact the fullest account of watching an Elizabeth drama. When players came to Gloucester, the mayor would give them a reward for their first performance which was then free. Willis's father sat on a bench and the boy stood between his legs. The play was a morality drama called 'The Cradle of Security'. It featured a king who was drawn away from good counsel by ladies representing Pride, Covetousness, and Luxury. There were songs and a transformation scene in which courtiers and ladies all disappeared. The king woke from sleep to face his judgment and be carried away by wicked spirits. Seventy years later, Willis could still recall the play in vivid detail.[53]

READING

Reading gave those who acquired the skill personal access to stories without the need for a narrator. But reading in Tudor times did not mean doing so silently to the extent that is the case today. The process of reading might involve the mouth, so that people often voiced what they read. The habit may have begun in school, where so much time was given to pronouncing the alphabet as one looked at it, and similarly with syllables, words, and sentences. An Italian visitor to England in about 1500 noted that churchgoers in London took with them the office of Our Lady (the prayer book known as the Book of Hours) and recited it with a companion 'in the church, verse by verse, in a low voice'.[54] A service in such a church consisted of the formal liturgy articulated by the clergy accompanied by a murmur of voices, reading from different prayer books, by literate people in the congregation.

Reading orally to listeners was also well established. In monasteries up to 1540 one of the community read aloud from a text during meals, and we have seen this recommended in godly households in Elizabethan England.[55] Literate families are likely to have shared the written material they had through the spoken word. A creation characteristic of the later Middle Ages was the miscellany or 'commonplace book' in which a man or woman with access to written material made a personal anthology of texts that interested them. Some of these contain items appropriate for children.[56] An outstanding example in early Tudor England is that of the London grocer Richard Hill (*c.* 1490–1540), which has already been mentioned for recording the births and baptisms of his children.[57] It contains the texts of nearly 150 items: songs, short romances, and works of practical instruction.[58] Since Richard transcribed the pieces, they were primarily collected to serve his own purposes but it is reasonable to think that these included the education and entertainment of his family, including the five children who survived their infancy.

His anthology contains three lyrics that look likely to have been recited by or with children: the repetitive rhyme 'I have twelve oxen that be fair and brown', the nonsense lyric 'I saw a dog seething sauce', and a song to be sung by a schoolboy complaining of the pains of going to school (Fig. 45, p. 175).[59] There are also the youthful story of *The Friar and the Boy*, to be discussed shortly, and three poems about good behaviour, including John Lydgate's translation of the popular courtesy book *Stans Puer ad Mensam*. Hill therefore seems to have had his children in mind, or at least his sons, in collecting his material. If that is the case he may well have used the miscellany more widely with his family, reciting the 'adult' romances that it contains or allowing his children to read them.

Hill's book reminds us that, even in the sixteenth century, written texts could circulate in manuscript and be read by adults and children in that form. However, nine years before the first Tudor ascended the throne, William Caxton established the earliest printing press in England at

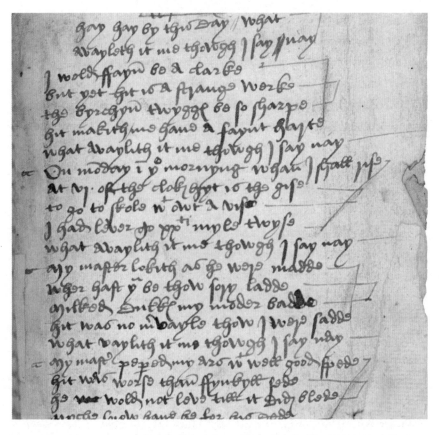

45. The sorrows of schoolboy life: a song recorded by Richard Hill
in his commonplace book.

Westminster in 1476. This did not suddenly revolutionise the production of books. There had long been a professional trade in copying them by hand, and Caxton had to proceed carefully, because printing tied up capital in stocks of books that might or might not sell. Nevertheless, the long-term result of printing was to make books cheaper and more plentiful, and this applied especially to the shorter and more popular literature that children were likely to read. At the very start of his English career, Caxton identified them (or their parents on their behalf) as one of his potential markets, and his opening list of titles included four short pamphlets for their use, all in English. Two were linked to schoolwork: a translation of *Cato* (the Latin collection of reflective observations intended to teach wisdom) and Lydgate's *Stans Puer ad Mensam*. The other two were moral fables: *The Churl and the Bird* and *The Horse, the Goose, and the Sheep*.

Not all Caxton's small productions may survive, but he did not apparently develop this line of his business very far, perhaps because such works were short, generated little profit, and did little to build his reputation. He later concentrated on publishing longer works of knowledge and fiction in English, primarily for adult purchasers and sometimes funded by them. Nevertheless, although these were not primarily children's books, most were able to be read by older children, at least, and it is very likely that this happened. In the category of non-fiction they included the anthology of wise sayings called *The Dicts and Sayings of the Philosophers*; a popular short encyclopaedia, *The Mirror of the World*; *The Book of the Knight of the Tower* for the instruction of girls; *The Fables of Aesop*, embellished with woodcuts; and *The Book of Good Manners*. For readers of fiction there were the comic stories of *Reynard the Fox*, Chaucer's *Canterbury Tales*, and the romances of *Jason*, *Blanchardyn and Eglantine*, Malory's *Le Morte D'Arthur*, and Virgil's *Eneydos*. In some of these Caxton tried to make links with young people. *Jason* was dedicated to Edward IV's young prince of Wales, Edward (V), and *Eneydos* to Prince Arthur son of Henry VII. The blurb for *The Book of the Knight of the Tower* claimed that it was especially suitable for the daughters of lords and gentlemen, and urged every gentleman or woman with children to acquire a copy.[60] Caxton also recommended *Blanchardyn and Eglantine* as appropriate for 'gentle young ladies and damsels for to learn to be steadfast and constant'.[61]

Caxton died in 1491. He was succeeded by his assistant, Wynkyn de Worde, who now had competition from another printer, Richard Pynson. Both men extended their range to publish not only substantial books of high status but also short popular works in English for general readers, sometimes in rival editions. These included two widely read medieval anthologies of stories, *The Seven Sages of Rome* and the *Gesta Romanorum*; the adventure tales of *Valentine and Orson*, *Guy of Warwick*, and *Bevis of Hampton*; as well as *A Little Gest of Robin Hood*, the chief account of the outlaw's exploits. Most of these titles were sold as a few sheets of paper, folded or for folding, and cost very little. By 1520 the Oxford bookseller John Dorne was selling *A Little Gest* for 2*d.* and the romances of *Robert the Devil* for 3*d.* and *Sir Eglamour* for 3½*d.*[62] Books in a similar format were also on sale at fairs and could even be purchased by children or adolescents with their own money, although they would soon become worn unless bound (which was expensive).[63] Like modern comics, many may have had a relatively short life. Hardly any copies have survived, and it is difficult to know how many editions were produced or how large the runs. Nonetheless it is clear that from 1500 onwards cheap works of fiction or news were increasingly available.

One category of printed book worth mentioning, since it is likely to have been attractive to children, is the jest-book: a collection of riddles or amusing stories. A very popular work of this kind was *The Friar and the Boy*: a 'fabliau' or comic tale in verse written by an anonymous author in the fifteenth century. After circulating in writing, it was published by Wynkyn de Worde between 1510 and 1513 as a small pamphlet of eight leaves, and continued to appear in print until 1820 (Fig. 46, p. 178). The hero, Jack, is the son of a wealthy farmer who remarries. His new wife is a shrew who dislikes the boy and arranges for him to be sent out to herd the animals. After befriending an old man, Jack is given three magic gifts, including a bow, a musical pipe, and a charm to make his stepmother fart loudly when she is angry. The story goes on to tell how the stepmother employs a friar to punish the boy, but the friar is made to dance in a thorn-bush. After more adventures, the whole village ends up dancing, the stepmother is disgraced in public, and Jack secures an amnesty for himself. The story is a humorous tale and scarcely anything more, which a child could read solely for the incidents in it and for the satisfaction of identifying with Jack: thumbing his nose at the adult world.[64]

Other short books of this genre came out through the sixteenth century. They included the pranks ascribed to the German trickster Till Eulenspiegel (1555), those of King Edward IV's jester John Scogan (1570), and *The Mad Men of Gotham* (1565), the last two of which were ascribed to the eccentric Tudor monk Andrew Boorde. They were generally short and therefore cheap, bringing them within the grasp of children to read and even to buy. And they

46. The earliest illustration in a printed Tudor book for children: the title
page of *The Friar and the Boy* (*c.* 1509), showing Jack with his pipe
and the friar dancing in the thorn-bush.

inspired one unusual work worth mentioning, although it dates from four
years after the death of the last Tudor monarch. *Dobson's Dry Bobs* (1607), by
an unknown author, is an amusing sequence of stories about a schoolboy,
George Dobson, said to have been the nephew of a canon of Durham
Cathedral and a pupil at a school in the city. He becomes the hapless butt of
pranks carried out by other boys, and the initiator of ones of his own. The
book is a curious oddity of its day: a *Tom Brown's Schooldays* or a *Verdant
Green* more typical of the nineteenth century. Its nearest models are the prose
stories of Thomas Deloney, except that his narrate the lives of merchant
heroes. *Dobson* survives in only one edition, perhaps neither meeting the
demands of adult readers nor, being quite long and densely printed, those of
children either.[65]

There must have been other stories that featured children as leading
characters: in oral folk tales told at home if not in printed form. Two with
youthful characters, both also boys, have survived in the famous Percy manuscript of songs and ballads. The manuscript was put together in the

seventeenth century, but each of these stories seems to date from before the Reformation because they mention the Catholic practice of confession. 'The Boy and the Mantle' is a ballad about a mysterious child who comes to King Arthur's court with a mantle that changes its colour according to the virtue of the woman who wears it. Queen Guinevere and the ladies of the court each try it on, with disastrous results that show their unfaithfulness. Only Sir Craddocke's wife survives the test and gets to keep the mantle as a gift.[66]

The other story is the ballad of 'Sir Aldingar', a tale with many analogies in European literature. Its titular character is a wicked knight who tries to seduce his queen and, when she rebuffs him, arranges for a leprous man to be found in her bed. The king orders the queen to be burnt and the leper hanged, but gives them a respite of forty days so that the queen may find a hero to fight her cause. Messengers are sent in all directions, but the only person willing to defend the queen is a boy aged only four, or apparently so. The queen is about to face the flames when the little one arrives dressed in miniature armour. He pulls out a sword and, with his first stroke, severs the legs of Sir Aldingar at the knees. Aldingar collapses, confesses his falseness, and dies with the queen's forgiveness. The leper becomes the king's steward, and we are left wondering whether the boy was real or supernatural.[67]

Three of the most popular printed stories of the sixteenth century, for readers of all ages, were *Valentine and Orson*, *Guy of Warwick*, and *Bevis of Hampton*. It is difficult to know the number of editions that appeared of any of them (some may not have survived), but *Valentine and Orson* was published in prose by Wynkyn de Worde in about 1510 and was still in print in the 1560s. The story, which originated in medieval France, tells how an empress of Constantinople gave birth to twin sons but, owing to false accusations, was cast from the court with her children. One, Valentine, was brought up by the king of France, and the other was reared by a bear and became a wild-man known as Orson. When grown up they met, fought, and made friends. Valentine tamed Orson and they set off on a succession of adventures ranging from France to India, which featured a giant, an enchanter, a green knight, and a magic wooden horse. Eventually they recovered their birthright and were crowned as emperors, until Valentine ended his life as a hermit – a characteristic medieval twist, like the retirement of Lancelot and Guinevere to be a monk and a nun in the Arthurian cycle of stories.[68]

Guy of Warwick has an English setting. It began as a French poem written in thirteenth-century England for the earls of Warwick, but came to be regarded as true history. Richard Pynson printed it in verse in 1500 and it continued to be published throughout the following century, eventually being retranslated into prose by 1600 (Fig. 47, below). Guy is the son of the earl's steward and falls in love with Felice, the earl's daughter. He must prove himself a warrior to gain her hand, and this demand creates a series of adventures including the killing of a dragon and a combat with a giant. Eventually the two lovers marry, but in later life Guy is afflicted by remorse for his deeds – that medieval twist again. He becomes a hermit near Warwick without his wife's knowledge, and they meet again only at his deathbed. In the fifteenth and sixteenth centuries, Guy's Cliff near Warwick contained a theme park in Guy's memory, where visitors could see his statue, enter the cave where he lived, drink water from a fountain, and (until 1549) attend mass in a chapel.[69]

47. The hero of *Guy of Warwick* (1609), in full armour, with a boar's head on a spear, accompanied by a lion.

Bevis of Hampton was another thirteenth-century French poem of English make, centred on Southampton in its case. Wynkyn de Worde published it in English verse in 1500 and it continued to appear in that format throughout the Tudor era. By 1585 it was accompanied by numerous woodcuts (Fig. 48, below), and one of the surviving copies contains annotations by children.[70] Again the story is a long and rambling one. It begins disturbingly. Bevis's father (like Hamlet's) is killed by a man who marries his (conniving) mother. He is sold to heathen merchants and taken to Armenia where he falls in love with Josian, the king's daughter, who gives him a magnificent horse named Arondel. A succession of mishaps follows for both of them, including fights with knights and monsters, imprisonments, and abductions. Bevis and Josian marry, but she is carried off and later gives birth to twin boys in a forest. Eventually all is resolved. His stepfather is cast into a vat of boiling lead and his mother throws herself from a tower. One of his sons becomes king of England and the other of Armenia. Bevis, Josian, and the horse all die on the same day and, with the usual religious conclusion, they are buried in a chapel while a monastery is founded to pray for their souls.[71]

48. A scene from *Bevis of Hampton* (*c.* 1560). Bevis storms his mother's house and attacks the stepfather who murdered his father.

ROBIN HOOD

These verse romances helped to inspire another popular group of tales, more particularly English and also in verse: about outlaws. The oldest, *The Tale of Gamelyn*, a work of the fourteenth century later ascribed to Chaucer, was not printed in Tudor England but it circulated in manuscripts and was utilised by Thomas Lodge in his romance of *Rosalynde* and, through him, by Shakespeare in *As You Like It*.[72] *Adam Bell*, set in 'the north country' with an episode in Carlisle, recounts the exploits of three outlaws: Bell, Clym of the Clough, and William Cloudesly. It was printed several times in the sixteenth century, perhaps as early as the reign of Henry VIII, and had a readership into the seventeenth.[73] But by far the most widely read work of this kind was *A Little Gest of Robin Hood*, 'gest' originally meaning an 'exploit' but coming by this time to be spelt as 'jest', implying also something for amusement. After its first appearance in about 1500, it was reproduced by various printers during the following century and its successor (Fig. 49, below). Later it came to be joined by other shorter

49. Robin Hood with his bow, and Little John with a pike, portrayed on the title page of *A Mery Geste of Robyn Hoode* (c. 1560).

ballads about the exploits of Robin and his men, but these mostly date from after 1600. Two brief plays about the outlaws were also published in about 1560, and two longer and more romanticised ones by Anthony Munday in 1601.[74]

The *Little Gest* is a fifteenth-century poem which has tried to fit together some older ballads of Robin Hood into an outlaw epic. It begins by featuring Robin as a romantic hero who hears mass three times every day (goodness knows where, in the forests) and (like King Arthur) refuses to dine until an unknown guest can be brought to share his table. The guest is Sir Richard at the Lee, a penniless knight who has been forced to mortgage his lands to an abbot and cannot pay by the due date of the loan. Robin gives him the requisite money on the surety of Our Lady, for whom both men have veneration, as well as new clothes. The abbot is shown up to be avaricious and merciless, but the lands are redeemed. Robin subsequently recovers the money by ambushing the abbot's cellarer. This, incidentally, is the only example in the *Gest* of robbing the rich to help the poor.

The focus of the story then shifts to the sheriff of Nottingham: an odd shift, because the earlier part of the *Gest* is set in Barnsdale, Yorkshire, not in Sherwood near Nottingham. Robin captures the sheriff and makes him swear to leave the outlaws alone in return for his freedom. The treacherous sheriff arranges an archery match in order to trap Robin, and tries to arrest him. Robin and the outlaws escape and take refuge with Sir Richard. They reach the forest, but the sheriff seizes the knight, whom they rescue. In the course of doing so Robin shoots the sheriff dead. Finally the king comes to deal in person with this lawlessness. He allows himself to be captured by the outlaws, is recognised, and forgives Robin and Richard, on condition that Robin comes to his court to live under supervision. Robin finds court life expensive; he gives away his money generously, becomes poor, and misses the forest. He escapes court by the subterfuge of wishing to make a barefoot pilgrimage to a chapel that he has founded in Barnsdale. He spends the next twenty-two years in the forest, until he is treacherously killed by the prioress of Kirklees while being bled for this health. His death is not described in the *Gest*, but features in a separate ballad.

The outlaw stories were not only read by adults. Their critics, as we shall see, believed that they were wildly popular with children, at least among boys, and it is not difficult to see what they had to offer young readers and listeners. They were unencumbered by the complications of love. The *Gest* contains no Marian, who came into Robin's stories only via dramatic versions during the sixteenth century. The outlaw tales appealed in those stages of life when we value comradeship. Young men in parishes used Robin Hood games as a way of associating together and raising money.[75] The characters in the stories were firmly divided into the good (Robin, Sir Richard, and the king) and the bad (the sheriff of Nottingham, Guy of Gisborne, various monks, and the prioress). The outlaws were described as 'yeomen': the class that included wealthy farmers and senior servants in households. This was a rank that many youths could aspire to reach, whereas casting the heroes as gentry would have made them less attainable.

Outlaw life is idealised as a carefree one without work, based on deer hunting which everyone would have liked to pursue but most could not. At the same time this life had the delicious sense of tension, danger, and impudence. Robin and the others cocked a snook at authority as represented by the sheriff of Nottingham. However much moralists disliked the stories, the Crown and the gentry saw no harm in them. Henry VIII himself enjoyed enacting scenes of Robin Hood. Far from being amoral criminals, the outlaws had a clear understanding of the social order, the duty to be polite to others, and the obligation of loyalty and obedience to the king. The hostility of the ballads to monks and nuns fitted well with the official view of such people after the Reformation. And perhaps most of all, the stories chimed with the respect for archery as the great English skill, which the Crown was so keen to preserve.[76]

It is worth pointing out, then, that although we tend to regard the sixteenth century as one of new writers of stories (Spenser and Shakespeare in verse; Greene, Nashe, and Sidney in prose), some of the most popular tales among adults and children were of medieval origin. Malory's *Le Morte D'Arthur* was published at least five times between 1485 and 1582. The medieval romance of *The Four Sons of Aymon* appeared at least four times up to 1554, and that of *Huon of Bordeaux* at least twice up to 1601. Not only that, the traditional stories went on including episodes from their Catholic past long after the Reformation: very obviously in the case of *The Friar and the Boy*. The 1565 edition of *Valentine and Orson* still ended with Orson's retirement as hermit, after which miracles were done in the place where he lived and he was eventually canonised as a saint.[77] A version of *Guy of Warwick* published in the same year had him buried richly, and many masses said on his behalf.[78] Only when new translations of *Guy* came out in 1600 and afterwards were the masses omitted. Bevis and Josian had a monastery founded to 'sing' for their souls as late as 1585.[79] Five years after that, *A Mery Geste of Robyn Hoode* still described the great outlaw as hearing three masses each day, venerating the Virgin Mary, and leaving the king's court to go 'barefoot and clothed in wool' on pilgrimage to his chapel.[80]

The earnest divines whom we shall now find attacking works of this kind are unlikely to have overlooked or forgiven such survivals from Catholic times. Children probably bothered less. One accepts, when young, the setting of a story as much as one does the plot, and when children today read about cooks and housemaids, evacuees and steam trains, this may only add to the romance and otherness of the experience.

ADULTS AND CHILDREN'S CULTURE

As literacy became more common, adults began to interest themselves in what children read for their recreation. This is apparent by the second half of the fifteenth century. An anonymous poem on good manners from about that period told the boy whom it was addressing to spend time reading, which would give him both learning and pleasure. It specified the masters of the late fourteenth and early fifteenth centuries: Chaucer, Gower, Hoccleve, and Lydgate.[81] The poet John Skelton, writing in the first decade of the sixteenth, complimented Joan Scrope, a young lady of his acquaintance, on the number of books she had read. These also included Chaucer and Gower, together with Caxton's translations of the *History of Troy*, *The Four Sons of Aymon*, and the romance of *Paris and Vienne*.[82] At about the same time, a reader of a manuscript of the romance of *William of Palerne* (a story of a prince and a benevolent werewolf) wrote a comment inside it, praising its medieval author for having written a book 'to keep youth from idleness'. He went on to recommend it for holy days and times of leisure.[83]

50. Boys fighting with daggers. Moralists worried that popular
literature encouraged youthful violence.

These were positive endorsements, but during the sixteenth century
negative attitudes evolved towards young people's reading and indeed their
other recreations, reflecting the sterner morality of the Reformation (Fig. 50,
above). A new trend is already apparent with John Fitzherbert's comment of
1523 that *The Book of the Knight of the Tower* taught more vices than virtues.[84]
Five years later, in 1528, William Tyndale, the future Bible translator,
launched what became a repetitive Puritan attack on popular literature. The
clergy, he declared, forbade the laity access to the scriptures while doing
nothing to dissuade them from reading 'Robin Hood and Bevis of Hampton,
Hercules, Hector, and Troylus with a thousand histories and fables of love
and wantons and of ribaldry, so filthy as heart can think, to corrupt the
minds of youth withal'. This was directly contrary to the words of St Paul
against 'fornication, uncleanness, filthiness, foolish talking, [and] jesting'.
No unclean person would have any inheritance in the kingdom of Christ.[85]

This view came to be widely shared by religious and educational writers.
Vives, in his treatise on the upbringing of girls in 1529, condemned the
reading of Arthur, Guy, Bevis, 'and many other . . . made only to corrupting
the manners of young folks'.[86] Miles Coverdale, also a Bible translator,
wished that his version of the Psalms, made in about 1535, would bring 'the
youth of England' to 'change their foul and corrupt *balettes* into sweet songs
and spiritual hymns of God's honour'. By *balettes* Coverdale had in mind not
only ballads but secular songs in general. 'I report me to every good man's

conscience what wicked fruits they bring. Corrupt they not the manners of young persons? I need not rehearse what evil examples of idleness, corrupt talking, and all such vices as follow the same, are given to young people through such un-Christian songs.'[87]

Another who took up this theme was Roger Ascham, in his book on archery, *Toxophilus*, published in 1545:

> In our fathers' time, nothing was read but books of feigned chivalry, wherein a man by reading should be led to none other end but only to manslaughter and bawdry. If any man suppose they were good enough to pass the time withal, he is deceived.

He accused the clergy not only of allowing such books but of creating them. 'These books (as I have heard say) were made the most part in abbeys and monasteries, a very likely and fit fruit of such an idle and blind kind of living.'[88] Five years after Ascham, the publisher Walter Lynne, recommending his edition of a German catechism, *The True Belief in Christ* in 1550, wished that all men, women, and children would read it instead of 'the feigned stories of Robin Hood, Clym of the Clough [*Adam Bell*], with such like'.[89] Hugh Rhodes said the same in 1577: parents should accustom their children to read the Bible and other 'godly books' and keep them away from 'feigned fables, vain fantasies, and wanton stories and songs of love, which bring much mischief to youth'.[90] As for Philip Stubbes, who wrote the most comprehensive Puritan attack against almost every possible kind of English recreation in 1583, he proscribed all amusing books (as opposed to godly and instructive ones) for reading on Sundays or any other days.[91]

Even writers who had no religious motive looked down on popular literature because it seemed unsophisticated and crude. In 1589 Thomas Nashe, an opponent of Puritanism, followed Ascham in accusing the 'abbey lubbers [monks] from whose idle pens preceded worn-out impressions of the feigned no-where acts' of the romances. He singled out 'Arthur of the Round Table' (presumably *Le Morte D'Arthur*), *Arthur of Little Britain*, *Sir Tristram*, *Huon of Bordeaux*, *The Squire of Low Degree*, and *The Four Sons of Aymon*. 'Who is it that reading *Bevis of Hampton*', he continued, 'can forbear laughing if he mark what scambling shift he [the author] makes to end his verses alike [rhyme his lines]'. He went on to quote some lame examples.[92] Shakespeare slyly took a similar line. Edgar in *King Lear*, while feigning his madness, quotes two characteristic lines from *Bevis*,

> Rats and mice and such small deer,
> That was his meat that seven year,

while the Bard described 'The Field of the Cloth of Gold' in *Henry VIII* as so magnificent that it was possible to think that even the fabulous story of Bevis could be believed.[93]

These writers are relevant to our subject, at least the Puritan commentators, because they saw the readers and singers of romances, ballads, and songs as including or especially the young: children and adolescents. This has not always been realised by scholars, notably in the debates of the 1950s about the extent to which the Robin Hood ballads were (allegedly) expressions of adult discontents about law enforcement and wealthy clergy.[94] The Puritan dislike of these popular tales may well have had an impact in godly families where parents imposed a strictly religious and moral diet of reading, as in that of Grace Sharington.[95] Fortunately for the history of English literature, not all families were so restrictive. A printed copy of *Bevis* still survives in the Bodleian Library, in which two boy owners of the sixteenth century scribbled their names and probably made the marks alongside certain passages that struck them.[96] At about the same time, Robert Ashley, the son of a gentleman of Wiltshire, who was born in 1565, was reading *Bevis, Guy, Valentine and Orson*, and 'The Life of King Arthur of Britain and the Knights of the Round Table', presumably Malory's book as there was no popular version. He too came to call them 'false and futile fables', but that was only in his adult life when he wrote some autobiographical reminiscences.[97] Most tellingly, the fact that publishers could go on issuing the classic tales of adventure throughout the sixteenth century shows that there was a large and continuing market for them. Indeed, the preface to *Huon of Bordeaux* in 1601 commended it as enabling the young to learn the valorous deeds of the past.[98]

There was, then, children's literature in the Tudor era. It has sometimes been argued that this was not the case: that children were merely casual readers of (or listeners to) works written for adults. Yet in principle children's literature can be traced back in England to about the year 1000, to the school dialogues of Ælfric of Eynsham and Ælfric Bata.[99] These and some other medieval authors were 'modern' in that they wrote for children, albeit works of education, and empathised with children, framing their works to interest their readers. Their tradition was still alive in the sixteenth century in the dialogues of Erondelle and Hollyband, and it was extended by the number of catechisms now written for children. The four books (two school texts and two fables) published by Caxton must also have been meant primarily for children to read, and much the same is true of *The Friar and the Boy* and *Dobson's Dry Bobs*. It was possible for an author to address a work to children, as Francis Clement did in *The Petie Schole* (1587) and John Carpenter in his catechism *Contemplations* (1601).[100] The number of recreational books written for children is indeed small by modern standards, but this surely reflects the fact that so many 'adult' works were seen as suitable for them and were popular with them. *Bevis, Guy, Orson and Valentine, Robin Hood*, and *Adam Bell* should arguably be called 'shared' not 'adult' literature. They were read by young and old. Cheaper versions, like the outlaw ballads, were within the scope of adults to buy for children and even for children to buy for themselves. The publishers of such works would have had both readerships in mind.

Indeed, the sixteenth century was not very different in this respect from more recent times. Literature has always been shared by the older and the younger. Much adult reading is suitable for children, and works meant for children may also be read by adults. Grown-ups with poor literacy have read children's comics, while their more literary counterparts have read what is written for children because they appreciate its artistry. There was, in short, Tudor literature for children both by intention and in practice, and they were able to access a wide range of written stories and other kinds of reading.

7

⟨ornament⟩

GROWING UP

YOUTH

Medieval and Tudor people agreed that human beings, at puberty, passed from childhood into the next stage of life: youth, the third of the seven ages. Youth had its own distinct features. On the positive side these were strength, vigour, and beauty; in a negative sense sexual desire and waywardness. The endowments of adulthood had appeared, but they were not yet balanced by its experience and discretion (Fig. 51, p. 191).

Youth raised more issues and gained more attention than childhood. Writers and artists portrayed it, as they hardly ever did childhood, because it had greater scope in terms of love and adventure, as well as in its appeal to adults. Secular lawmakers were more aware of it. Drafters of statutes and judges in courts had to decide at what age duties and penalties should be imposed. The fact that teenage men and women entered full-time employment raised further issues for regulation. The Church, too, since the twelfth century, had come to give more attention to adolescence than to childhood.[1] Little was required of children beyond baptism, confirmation, and the learning of basic prayers. From puberty onwards, however, young people were expected to attend church, go to confession, receive Easter communion, fast, and make the customary offerings. The Reformation abolished compulsory confession and delayed the rite of confirmation, but kept the other duties in the list.

At the same time, youth usually had something in common with childhood in being an age of dependence on adults. Most youths and maidens between puberty and marriage remained under the control of parents or

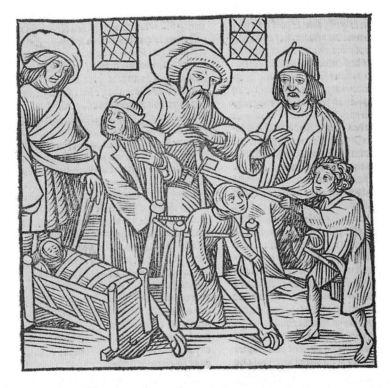

51. A version of the ages of man from the encyclopaedia *De Proprietatibus Rerum* (1499). It includes a baby, toddler in a walking frame, boy with hobby-horse and windmill, adolescent, and three adults.

employers. The latter were regarded as equivalent to parents in terms of the authority exerted and the obedience required. The word 'family' applied to an employer's living-in servants as much as it did to that employer's children. This gave youth a provisional and preparatory character, distinct from full adulthood. There was also a lack of clarity about when it ended. The law set various ages for the imposition of criminal punishments and the inheritance of property, ranging from about twelve to twenty-one. So, as is the case today, adolescents and young adults did not acquire rights and responsibilities at a single moment but over several years. Unlike today, however, Tudor England was not a country of equal rights. Social and legal differences meant that the young gained the attributes and privileges of adulthood at various ages. A wealthy heiress might marry and give birth to a child in her early teens. A male heir in wardship might not succeed to his lands until he was twenty-one, or an apprentice not finish his time in service until about the same age. A young man wishing to become a priest, both before and after the Reformation, had to wait until he was twenty-four.[2] And for most people, as we have seen, marriage was usually delayed till even later.[3]

Growing up alters one's self and one's relationships. Adolescence brings a different sense of being and of the world. There is a wish for change, and parental control grows more irksome. Dick, the schoolboy son of his family, complained of its constraints in the Elizabethan play *July and Julian*:

> Men [adults] may do what they list, God wot, so cannot we,
> For if I laugh my father a wanton calls me,
> If I be sad, my mother saith I am dumplish and surly . . .
> Both my parents and masters handle me so shrewdly.[4]

Moralists, on the other hand, insisted on the duty of children to respect their elders. 'Honour your father and your mother' was one of the Ten Commandments. Medieval clergy insisted upon it, and Reformation writers did not dissent. If anything, their emphasis was greater. After 1559 that very commandment, along with the others, was read in church every Sunday and was often displayed there with them on a board.[5]

Friction between children and parents was moderated, as we shall discover, by the practice of many young people leaving home at about the age of puberty to work elsewhere. But conflicts must have arisen, and writers were aware of the possibility. Shakespeare depicts poor relations between father and son (Henry IV and Prince Hal) in the two plays of *Henry IV*. The same is true in *As You Like It*. Here the orphan Orlando is in dispute with his elder brother Oliver, who has succeeded their father as head of the family. Marriage was another potential area of discord. It is gently touched on in *All's Well that Ends Well*, where the countess regrets her son's refusal of the bride selected for him by the king, and tragically so in *Romeo and Juliet*. It forms an element of comedies such as Shakespeare's *The Merry Wives of Windsor*, Thomas Dekker's *The Shoemaker's Holiday*, and the anonymous *Merry Devil of Edmonton*, in which fathers try to prevent loving attachments between young men and women to which there are no good objections.

Growing up can also produce strains with siblings. This is not an easy issue to summarise because there would have been so many variations between occasional, or long-term, friendship or friction. Shakespeare depicted brothers with close bonding: Henry V with his (Thomas, John, and Humphrey) in *Henry IV* and Guiderius and Arviragus in *Cymbeline*. Laertes in *Hamlet* is protective of, if rather domineering towards, his sister Ophelia. There are close cousin relationships between Celia and Rosalind in *As You Like It*, and Beatrice and Hero in *Much Ado About Nothing*. At other times Shakespeare set out to portray sibling rivalry: Edgar and Edmund in *King Lear*, Don Pedro and Don John in *Much Ado*. Admittedly Edmund and Don John are illegitimate, and to a Tudor audience equivocal figures. But there can be similar tensions between full brothers: Oliver, Orlando, and the two dukes in *As You Like It*, Prospero and Antonio in *The Tempest*, the historic brothers Edward IV, Clarence, and Richard III in the history plays, and (between sisters) Katherina and Bianca in *The Taming of the Shrew*. Francis Bacon thought that some of the blame for this belonged to parents. 'The difference in affection of parents towards their several children is many times unequal and sometimes unworthy.' In a house full of children, he observed, 'one or two of the eldest [would be] respected and the youngest made wantons. But in the midst some that are, as it were forgotten, who many times nevertheless prove the best.'[6]

Among the nobility and gentry, sibling relationships were complicated by the practice of primogeniture. This was the inheritance of property, and to some extent family headship, by the eldest surviving son. Apparent exceptions to this, in places such as Kent, applied only in cases of intestacy.[7] Primogeniture was unpopular with many people.[8] Thomas Wilson, the lawyer and diplomat, who wrote an account of *The State of England* in 1601, complained that by the convention the eldest 'must have all, and all the rest that which the cat left on the malt heap: perhaps some small annuity during his life or what please our elder brother's worship to bestow upon us if we please him'.[9] Some parents sought to moderate the imbalance by urging their eldest sons to care for the others. Thomas Howard, duke of Norfolk, did so in a letter to Philip, his heir, while he awaited execution for treason in 1572. 'Show yourself loving and natural to your brothers and sisters and sisters-in-law.'[10] The Yorkshire knight Sir William Wentworth repeated the duty to his son Thomas, later Charles I's earl of Strafford, in 1604. Thomas should love his brothers and sisters, assist them in honest matters, and advise them about their manner of living. Later, before his death, William mapped out their future careers which Thomas was to finance.[11] Inevitably, however, in adult life when siblings married and developed their own affairs, relationships often became more distant.

Real examples of sibling relationships are recalled in the memoirs of Robert Carey, earl of Monmouth (1560–1639). He was the youngest of the ten children – seven sons and three daughters – of Henry Lord Hunsdon, first cousin of Elizabeth I.[12] Robert seems to have been closest to his nearest brother, the sixth son Edmund, whom he fought alongside in campaigns in the Netherlands in the 1580s, to whom he clearly felt a loyalty. Relations with his eldest brothers were colder. William, so Robert claimed, fraudulently changed an entail so as to deprive him of property which he should have inherited. George supported William's widow against Robert in subsequent litigation. When Lord Hunsdon, who was captain of Norham Castle on the Scottish borders, proposed to obtain the reversion of the castle for Robert, the second eldest brother, John, objected to the proposal. These disagreements may have been magnified by the substantial age gap between Robert and his eldest siblings. Perhaps there was some jealousy as well, because Robert was (at least at times) in Queen Elizabeth's favour and active in the social life of the court. In the end he overtook all his brothers in worldly success, becoming the guardian of Charles I and being created earl of Monmouth.

WORK

The hard subsistence life of so many families meant that their children, once able to feel responsibility and avoid danger, were recruited into household chores and assistance with adult work. Early tasks included taking charge of younger siblings, water carrying, running errands, and light agricultural jobs in the countryside (Fig. 52, p. 195). The latter might include looking after

52. A girl driving a donkey: an example of the lighter tasks given to children.

domestic birds (fowls and geese), gleaning at harvest time, weeding, and gathering firewood or wild food such as berries, nuts, and mushrooms.[13] Scaring birds from the seeds and young crops was another activity: the writer Nicholas Breton described how, as dawn broke, 'the boy with his sling casts stones at the crows'.[14]

Girls might take on tasks in the home, freeing the mother for domestic or other part-time work. Their older brothers might lead the horses or oxen that drew the plough, directed by an adult (Fig. 53, p. 196). A rustic youth is pictured as saying in 1577, 'I did go to plough and cart, and kept the crows out of the field, and fetch[ed] home the kine and other such like things which appertain unto husbandry . . . My father did hedge and ditch, dig and delve, and did bring me up by the same trade.'[15] Boys, especially, could be useful assistants as messengers and couriers. In Derbyshire in 1598, the household accounts of William Cavendish contain numerous references to local lads running errands for their employers or doing small jobs. One regularly brought pigeons from a supplier, another carried a box and roll of papers, a third delivered a lock and key, a fourth helped to drive a troop of cattle. They were commonly employed in taking letters to the household from elsewhere, or vice versa.[16]

53. Youthful labour out of doors: a boy assists a ploughman in driving a team of two oxen.

In towns, where there were numerous specialised crafts, children grew up doing craft work to produce something that could be sold for money. The Norwich census of the poor in 1570 recorded one boy beginning to weave by the age of four, and others when they were five.[17] As we have seen, Tudor legislators thought that five was not too early an age to start work,[18] but such labour was more common in the city by about the age of nine. Both boys and girls are mentioned spinning yarn and carding wool, while knitting hose was common among girls. Other children (without indications of their sex) are described as weaving lace and making gloves. The work might be done along-side a parent, especially a mother, or independently of what the parents were doing. But not all the poor children of Norwich were used in this way. Some were at school although, as has been mentioned, the petty schools to which they went were often places for learning not only reading but textile skills.[19]

Thomas Wilson placed the starting age of work in English cities and towns quite early. 'Every child of six or seven years old is forced to some art whereby he [including girls] gaineth his own living and something besides to help to enrich his parents or master.' Again taking Norwich as an example, he stated that investigations there into what children from six to ten 'earned

54. Older girls were in demand for doing domestic tasks and food preparation. Here a dairymaid makes butter.

towards their keeping in a year' revealed 'that [the total] hath risen to £12,000 sterling which they have gained, besides other keeping'. This was done chiefly by knitting of fine jersey stockings, 'every child being able at or soon after seven years to earn 4s. a week at that trade'.[20]

Work was not only a necessity for children in poorer families. It was a principle in Tudor England that all should grow up to work (if not in school) rather than in idleness. As has been shown, society inherited the belief from the Middle Ages that there were two kinds of poor people: the deserving and the undeserving. This stimulated the parliaments of Elizabeth's reign to pass the statutes that provided for the support of the deserving poor, and tried to ensure that poor children should be brought up to work: by town and parish authorities if their parents could not, or failed to, do so.[21]

HOUSEHOLD SERVICE

In a judgment that has become famous, an Italian visitor to England in about 1500 reported back to his Venetian employers that the English had 'a want of affection . . . strongly manifested towards their children':

Having kept them at home till they arrive at the age of seven or nine years at the utmost, they put them out, both males and females, to hard service in the houses of other people, binding them generally for another seven or nine years. And these are called apprentices, and during that time they perform all the most menial offices; and few are born who are exempted from this fate, for everyone, however rich he may be, sends away his children into the houses of others whilst he, in return, receives those of strangers into his own. And on inquiring their reason for this severity, they answered that they did it in order that their children might learn better manners.

He commented tartly, 'But I, for my part, believe that they do it because they like to enjoy all their comforts themselves, and that they are better served by strangers than they would be by their own children.'[22]

The Italian observer's remarks invite criticism in more than one respect. He set the age for leaving home too low. While children might help their parents with work at home, only when they passed puberty were they worth employing and boarding in other people's houses. Few children appear to have left the parental household before the age of ten, and not many before fifteen.[23] Apprentices too were usually teenagers. Nor did he fully consider the gains from leaving home. Among the aristocracy, sending sons and daughters to another noble or gentle household introduced them to a wider experience of life and to patrons who might be able to assist them in future with careers or marriages. There is a good example of this in the family of Henry Lord Stafford, son of the ill-fated duke of Buckingham executed under Henry VIII in 1521. His son and heir Henry was sent to serve the lord chancellor, Thomas Wriothesley, and after his fall from power, to the duke of Somerset. Henry's younger brother Thomas was placed with another grandee, Sir William Paulet. The daughters went to the households of noble women: Margaret to the countess of Salisbury, Susanna to the duchess of Norfolk, Mary to the countess of Arundel, and Anne to the dowager Queen Katherine Parr.[24] Lower down in society, among the merchant class and the whole population below it, service with an employer developed skills to support one's future employment or (for a woman) one's own domestic life.

Going out as a teenager to live and work in another household was common at all levels of society in Tudor England.[25] The richer farmers in the countryside (those coming to be styled as yeomen) employed young men to live in as farm servants, handling the larger animals and agricultural tasks, while young women were needed for dairy and house work (Fig. 54, p. 197).[26] In towns, servants were used both to staff a business and to proclaim the status of their employer. Young people of this kind formed a significant presence in towns, constituting nearly a quarter of the population of Coventry in the 1520s.[27] Trades in which strength was required chiefly employed young men as artisans, while women found places with merchants as indoor servants or in the victualling trades as operatives, especially in bakeries and inns.[28] There seems to have been an increasing preference to employ women rather than men during the sixteenth century, perhaps because of a declining need for men servants to provide protection.[29]

A place as a young servant was sometimes found through a family connection. Wealthy people might employ a poorer relation as a favour, or a wealthy trader the child of a lesser operative in the same line of business. Those who had no such links would go to the more important fairs, known as 'hiring fairs', where would-be employers went to find servants.[30] In London, St Paul's Cathedral – a great centre of resort – had a similar function. Those in search of a job stood at 'the serving men's pillar' in the nave, and Shakespeare imagined Falstaff recruiting his factotum Bardolph there.[31] Work as a servant taught people basic skills and might lead to a close relationship with an employer. Women's personal maids seem to have sometimes become their confidants, at least if Tudor dramas may be trusted.[32] In law, however, servants had no permanent tenure. From at least the later Middle Ages, they were normally hired for only a year at a time, and this was confirmed by a parliamentary statute of 1563 which added that they themselves must give three months' notice before the end of the year if they wished to leave.[33] They might, of course, be employed indefinitely, but they had no right to be. The exception to this was apprenticeship. It too involved service in someone's house, but differed in that apprentices contracted to serve for several years and expected to be taught a skilled trade, enabling them to rise to the status of their employer. We shall consider them in the following section.

55. Another example of learning to work: a boy assistant watches a baker
loading bread into an oven.

The number of young servants and apprentices in most rural and urban
households usually ranged from one to four or more, but that of servants
increased greatly in the houses of the wealthiest merchants, gentry, and
nobility. Here they were kept not only to do useful tasks but to maintain the
dignity of their employers: 'idle serving men' as critics sometimes termed
them.[34] Up to the Reformation, bishops, abbots, and some other important
clergy also maintained large households with such men. The servants of the
wealthy differed in being mainly males, except for a small number of women
to attend on the lady of the house and look after the nursery, if these existed.
This masculine predominance survived from earlier times when important
people needed protection, especially if they were travelling. Moreover, as we
have noticed, the nobility and gentry were still a military class, expected to
take part in national defence and the keeping of law and order, with their
retinues to help them.[35]

The largest household of this kind was the royal one. A detailed account
of it drawn up in about 1471–2, just before the Tudor era began, identified
about fifty young people among its members, and there may have been
about sixty since the account is incomplete.[36] They fell into three groups.
First there were eight young noblemen known as 'henchmen' who were

learning manners and skills in an aristocratic setting like the other young people of high birth described in Chapter 5.[37] They had their own master to teach them social skills, athletics, and 'languages' (probably chiefly French), as well as access to a schoolmaster of Latin. In the early 1570s, Sir Humfrey Gilbert suggested the foundation of a royal 'academy' in London for the training of young noblemen and gentlemen. It would provide teaching in every major subject, from languages to philosophy, law, heraldry, and warfare. The cost would have been vast, and the proposal did not meet with support.[38] Instead, in 1571, Elizabeth did away with the post of schoolmaster of the henchmen, suggesting that the group of young men was at least downgraded if not wholly abolished.[39]

Lower in status were the eight choristers known as 'children of the chapel'. They joined with the priests and clerks of the royal chapel in performing the polyphonic music long fashionable among royalty and the aristocracy. As they needed to have unbroken voices, they were under the age of puberty. In return they received board, lodging, and education, learning music from one of the adults in the chapel and presumably studying Latin grammar from the schoolmaster maintained in the royal household.[40] Finally there were young menial servants, at least thirty-five and perhaps forty-five, who did the everyday work.[41] Some were termed 'pages' and some 'children', but they were probably all in adolescence or close to it. Five of them served in the king's great chamber, and three in the pantry, the saucery, and probably the kitchen and the stables. Every other department of the household had at least one.

They learnt the skills of the department through doing basic tasks. Thus the page of the wardrobe of beds (or as we would say bedding), which had to be moved when the court changed its residence, was charged with trussing up and looking after the bedding and helping to see it put into the carriages. The page of the chandlery (the department providing fuel and lights) had to bring in the wood and coal, while his counterpart in the cellar washed out barrels, cleaned pots and cups, and loaded them into the carriages for transport. All pages and children received board, lodging, and small wages, and they could expect to develop careers through their service. The account of 1471–2 states that they might be 'preferred to higher service', and for that reason they should be chosen from youths who were 'of clean [legitimate] birth, clean limbs, personable, and of good disposition'. This meant that they could be promoted to be 'grooms' or adult servants, and perhaps eventually the 'yeomen' or 'sergeants' who headed each department. The children of the chapel, when they reached the age of eighteen, also qualified for advancement to a household post and, if none was available, the monarch would send them to university until some other provision could be made for them.[42]

The royal family had, at times, one or more satellite households. These were created to look after the royal children, whose needs differed from those of the court and who did not perambulate around with it. In the late fifteenth and early sixteenth centuries some of these households had a political significance. Edward IV came to the throne in 1461 through the Wars of the Roses, in which the outlying areas of England – the Welsh Marches and the North – played an important part in disrupting the central government. He therefore tried to buttress his authority in these regions by sending his brother Richard (III) to rule the North and his young son Edward (V) as the royal presence in a council administering the Marches at Ludlow in Shropshire. Henry VII continued this policy by placing Prince Arthur at Ludlow in the 1490s, and Henry VIII did the same in the 1520s. He stationed Henry Fitzroy in Yorkshire as the figurehead of a council of the North, and his daughter Mary (I), his only legitimate child at the time, at Ludlow to embellish the council there. This policy then came to an end, partly through a lack of suitable children and partly through the development of royal government in the regions by other means.

The households of the nobility and wealthier gentry and clergy followed and, to some extent, imitated the pattern of the royal household. Their form among the nobility is probably well illustrated by a description of that of Henry Algernon Percy, earl of Northumberland, made in 1512.[43] It included about thirty boys or youths. Again they fell into three groups. The earl had four children at home: three sons and a daughter, all ten or under, with two nurses to look after the younger ones. He employed about nine young men of gentry status acting as upper servants and learning manners: henchmen, carvers, sewers, and cupbearers. These probably came from the families of his tenants or neighbours; two of the youths were maintained at their parents' expense. Such service gave cachet, provided experience of noble life, and carried an expectation of favour and patronage.

The second group consisted of the six children of the earl's private chapel. As in the royal chapel, they were needed to perform the polyphonic music now in vogue, and they also received board, lodging, and education. They learnt music from one of the adults in the chapel and could presumably study Latin with the schoolmaster and usher maintained by the earl in his household. Finally there were about nine or ten young menial servants. The seven main departments of the earl's household were the wardrobe, kitchen, scullery, bakehouse, brewhouse, stable, and 'chariot', meaning the wheeled transport. Each included a 'child'. Two other 'children' are mentioned: one in the nursery and one attending on the earl's brother. Again we are told about some of their duties. The child of the kitchen turned the broaches round the fire and kept the kitchen clean. The child of the scullery scoured the vessels used in the kitchen. The children of the bakehouse and brewhouse helped to make the bread and ale, while their colleague in the wardrobe did sewing and mending.

As with the servants of the royal household, there was probably the hope of promotion to an adult post when vacancies occurred, either in the household or on the earl's estates. This might then allow them to marry and live independently. A nobleman could benefit by planting such loyal followers around his sphere of influence. At the same time, it is probably unwise to regard all household service in so rosy a way. Peter Carew recalled becoming page to a gentleman who demoted him to be a mere lackey or servant and finally a muleteer. He had to be rescued by a relation and given a training appropriate to his rank.[44] An employer might look to replace his older staff with younger, cheaper recruits, or if he or she died the household might be dispersed. A writer in 1577 pointed out the disadvantages of life as a servant. 'The old proverb is true. A young courtier, an old beggar, for they say "Service is none heritage."' He quoted Aesop's fable of the greyhound. 'When age cometh on you, as did on the greyhound, then you shall not be esteemed, but ready to be set at liberty without comfort.'[45]

The early Tudor period was, perhaps, the heyday of the great noble household. Two developments in the sixteenth century made it somewhat less important for young people. One was the growing popularity of the university colleges as places to send a youth or even a boy to be educated and brought up. Along with them, the Inns of Chancery and the Inns of Court in London had become flourishing communities of young men learning law and doing so sociably in the company of others of wealthy status. There came to be less need to enter a noble household for the purpose. The other influence was that of the Reformation. It abolished the abbots, who had maintained private aristocratic households, and greatly cut down the wealth of the bishops. Its leaders were hostile to the celebration of mass in private chapels and to the performance of polyphony. Elizabeth insisted on keeping the traditional Chapel Royal with its choristers, but in most other households the religious staffing was reduced to a chaplain or preacher alone.

Nevertheless the employment of young men in menial posts continued. Well into the seventeenth century, noble and wealthy gentry households maintained their military aspect, proclaiming the power of their lords to the neighbourhood and on journeys elsewhere. William Harrison, writing in 1587, deplored 'our great swarms of idle serving men' who, he thought, impoverished their employers, caused the raising of rents, and indulged in bad behaviour.[46] We lack an exact account of the earl of Northumberland's household in the late sixteenth century, but it certainly continued to employ 'boys' in several of its departments: the kitchen, pantry, laundry, and coach-house.[47] Later still, under the early Stuarts, the author Richard Brathwait, drawing up rules for the government of an earl's household, still assumed the presence of gentlemen pages and boys in the kitchen.[48]

APPRENTICESHIP

Apprenticeship was another path from home to work in a household: in this case that of a craftsman, shopkeeper, or merchant (Fig. 55, p. 200). Although the word 'apprentice', by the sixteenth century, could be used of young people working in 'husbandry' or farming, the institution was traditionally linked to crafts or trade and based in towns. Historically, those who lived in towns were free in status, as compared with the former serfs of the countryside. Restrictions had long existed to prevent the children of peasants and labourers from being apprenticed in towns, because lords of manors would lose their rights over them, especially the power to command their labour. Serfs had to get their lord's permission to send a son to school or to be apprenticed, and to pay money for the privilege. This was notionally the case until as late as 1552: about the last time that a treatise on the holding of manorial courts included a question as to whether any serf had sent a child away for either purpose.[49]

Parliament too had once legislated to restrict the kind of people who could become apprentices. In 1388 the Statute of Cambridge forbade any labourer's son or daughter to be trained in a craft if they were required to serve at the plough.[50] In 1406 the Statute of Apprentices prohibited anyone from apprenticing a child in a town unless they owned land to the value of at least 20s. per annum, which also implied having free status.[51] By the Tudor era, these restrictions had been much reduced. A statute of 1563, reflecting the fact that serfdom had virtually disappeared, allowed most craftspeople to take apprentices irrespective of their parental condition. These included smiths, carpenters, millers, potters, thatchers, and so on. Even a peasant farmer could have an apprentice as long as he held at least half a ploughland in tillage: in other words a reasonably sized holding. The only limitations were in the more elite trades: clothiers (drapers and mercers), goldsmiths, and ironmongers. In their case parents could apprentice their children in a market town only if they earned £3 a year from property, or £2 in a city. The same applied to weavers in most of England.[52] The majority of apprentices were boys, but girls could be apprenticed in crafts involving textile skills such as tailoring and embroidery.[53]

Apprenticeship, when properly entered into, involved a contract between the master and the apprentice.[54] Its terms were regulated by a written indenture, so called because it was a document of two identical halves, each held by the party concerned. As an example we may take an indenture of 1566 by which William Johnson of Kingston-upon-Thames, then probably in his early teens, bound himself to Robert Paltock, tailor, of the same town.[55] He was to live with Paltock and be taught by him for seven years as an apprentice, followed by one year as a covenanted servant. The tailor was to teach him all his craft, hiding nothing, and provide him with lodging, food, drink, clothes, and shoes appropriate for a servant. He undertook to make small payments to Johnson during the first seven years, and wages of 30*s.* in the eighth.

In return Johnson promised to keep his master's secrets and not to waste or lend his master's goods without permission. He was forbidden to play with dice, cards, or unlawful games; to visit taverns or ale-houses except with his master's leave, to engage in fornication with any of his master's household, or to leave his employment or marry without consent. It was understood that any apprentice would do domestic tasks as well as those of the trade, notably the bringing of water to the house from a neighbouring well or conduit.[56] The working day could be a long one, although no longer than that of adult workmen. The statute of 1563 ruled that all artificers and labourers should work in winter from dawn to dusk. In summer, from March to September, their hours stretched from 5.00 a.m. to 8.00 p.m. Within this time they should be allowed two and a half hours for breakfast, dinner, and drinkings, making a day of about twelve hours: not that the dictates of law were the same as what people did in practice.[57]

Terms of seven years were common but they had their reward in due course. Not only did the apprentice learn his master's work, but, having completed his terms of service, he was recognised by others in his craft as competent to engage in it. In large towns where there were guilds of particular trades, he became a member of the guild, and he also qualified to be admitted as a 'freeman' or citizen. This made him more than a mere inhabitant, since he had freedom to trade and a voice (albeit a very small one) in city government. Guilds, however, could be exploitative of their new recruits. A statute of 1531 complained that they were exacting entry fees from ex-apprentices, varying from 4*d.* to 40*s.* It capped the fee at 2*s.* 6*d.*[58] Some guilds then circumvented the law by demanding money in order to open trading premises or to work as a freeman. A further measure was required in 1536 to stop that practice.[59]

MUSIC AND DRAMA

For a small number of children, mainly boys, there was a path to adulthood through music and drama. Religious houses in England had used boys to help with their worship for centuries. Cathedrals and some other large churches maintained groups of choristers. They were taught to sing plain-song, took small parts in the daily liturgy, acted as servers at the altar, and carried candles, incense, and holy water in processions. In return they received board, lodging, and some wages and fees.[60] Monasteries also supported groups of what are now known as 'almonry boys', but their roles were at first mainly limited to serving the monks at their daily masses.[61] Some choristers and almonry boys grew up to become clergy, but this was not required and many departed for secular life in their teens.

During the fifteenth century, the role of boys in great churches changed with the growing popularity of polyphony. This kind of music, sung by different voices in harmony, centred on the veneration of the Virgin Mary: a mass in her honour every morning and an anthem in the afternoon. It also featured in the regular services on special occasions. Such music required the participation of boy trebles, who thereby became essential to its perfor-mance, rather than being merely trainees and 'extras'.[62] The vogue for such music spread widely, extending into the larger monasteries and wealthy urban parish churches, where small choirs of a few men and boys would function on Sundays and festivals. Churches competed with each other to gain the best young singers. Cardinal Wolsey sought out boys for his private chapel from other places. The Chapel Royal, the monarch's personal place of worship, dispatched talent scouts with the same intention. At Wells Cathedral, the clergy paid the king's servants 6s. 8d. in 1492–3 not to take any of their choristers, and 10s. in 1504–5. In turn, in 1510, they tried to obtain their own royal licence to seize boy singers from nearby monasteries or other churches to serve in the cathedral.[63]

By about the 1520s there must have been a few thousand boys employed in this way, ranging from full-time choristers in cathedrals to part-time 'boys' or 'children' as they were known in monasteries and parish churches. As before, a few might become clergy but most did not. They left their roles when their voices broke, at about fourteen, having been taught reading, plain-song, polyphony, and sometimes Latin grammar as well. An interest in music might stay with them for the rest of their lives. Two personal records of choris-ters survive from the middle of the century. One is that of Thomas Tusser in the 1577 edition of his popular guide to agricultural work and sober living called *Five Hundred Points of Good Husbandry*. He was born at Rivenhall, Essex, in about 1524, the son of a minor gentleman. His father sent him to be a chorister at the college of St Nicholas in Wallingford Castle on the Thames: a church with a small establishment of canons, clerks, and boy singers. The reward would have been a free education, at least in reading and singing.

Tusser was unhappy at Wallingford, perhaps from homesickness but certainly from petty punishments or bullying: 'tozed [pulled] ears . . . bobbed lips, what jerks, what nips'. He remembered the conditions as spartan: bare robes, stale bread, penny ale. While there he was spotted and conscripted to join the Chapel Royal, after which he managed to move to the choir of St Paul's Cathedral, where he served under John Redford, whom he remembered as 'an excellent musician'. From London he went to Eton College, learning grammar under that mixture of humour, severity, and paedophilia, the schoolmaster-dramatist Nicholas Udall. He survived to enter Trinity Hall, Cambridge, and become a country gentleman, agricultural writer, and poet.[64]

The other chorister autobiography is that of Thomas Whythorne, born in 1528 to a father with property at Ilminster in Somerset. Thanks to the help of a clerical uncle near Oxford, he became a chorister at Magdalen College there and was taught in its song school and grammar school. He seems to have had a more placid schooling than Tusser: at least he does not mention feeling discomfort during the seven years that he spent there. Moreover, in the 1540s he was able to go on to practice music in the secular world. Through the good offices of a friend, he was introduced to the playwright and musi-cian John Heywood and became his scholar and servant. With Heywood he transcribed poems and music by contemporary writers, practised at playing the virginals, and learnt to compose verse in English. After three years he embarked on an independent life, taking a room in London to teach singing and instrumental playing, mastering dancing and fencing as well in order to draw more pupils. This led to a musical career throughout his life.[65]

Whythorne was wise to build a career outside the Church because, as he grew up, the Reformation was shutting down much of the making of tradi-tional liturgical music. Not only were services translated into English, rendering obsolete the Latin polyphonic settings, but the leaders of the Church, especially under Edward VI, disliked polyphony for obscuring the meaning and impact of texts by musical elaboration. Boy singers disappeared from the monasteries when these were closed, and after 1549 from many parish churches. However, choristers survived at the cathedrals, of which there were now twenty-two in England, along with Westminster Abbey, St George's Chapel Windsor, the private Chapel Royal of the monarch, and a few collegiate churches.[66] Moreover Elizabeth I was more attracted to traditional services and singing than her brother Edward. In the first year of her reign in 1559, royal injunctions were issued to the whole Church of England which commended 'the laudable science of music' in services, and sanctioned it to remain as long as it was 'modest and distinct' so that what was sung could be understood.[67]

This approval enabled cathedrals and their like to go on recruiting choristers, using them in the daily liturgy and in singing polyphonic anthems during morning or evening prayer, or both. Some parish churches too returned to having choirs, including boys, to perform such anthems on special occasions. There continued to be a demand for good singers, and both the Chapel Royal and St Paul's gained royal warrants allowing them to conscript boys from other churches.[68] In return the boys could expect assistance with their careers. In 1589 Elizabeth wrote to Wells Cathedral about John Pitcher, one of their former choristers, who had been recruited to sing in her chapel. His voice had now broken and she wished the cathedral to appoint him to an adult singing post. When the clergy there demurred, they were told in the strongest terms to comply with her wish.[69]

While the employment of boys as choristers diminished after the 1540s, there continued to be scope for them to practise music outside church. One opening was as part of a group of instrumentalists or singers, providing popular music for money on an occasional or regular basis. Two early seventeenth-century writers mention this. Samuel Rowlands, in 1612, portrayed a group of fiddlers visiting women drinking in a tavern, bringing a youth or boy who sings them songs.[70] A little later Nicholas Breton described how 'minstrels in the countryside beat their boys for false singing'.[71] Some girls may have made a similar career or sideline as singers and dancers, but the evidence remains to be collected. Young people in wealthy households had engaged in singing and instrumental playing since the Middle Ages, and this provided an opportunity

209

for musical boys to evolve into teachers as Whythorne did. In *The Taming of the Shrew* it is taken for granted that a wealthy man's daughters should have tutors for music as well as for literary subjects.[72]

A newer area for boys, spanning speaking and singing, came about through the development of professional drama during Elizabeth's reign, especially in London. This, like choral music, required the services of pre-pubescent boys with unbroken voices. The giving of dramatic parts to boys in amateur plays can be traced back to the twelfth century, and they were undertaking roles as women, girls, or boys in religious and morality dramas by the end of the Middle Ages.[73] Early Tudor 'interludes', as such plays were then called, like Henry Medwall's *Fulgens and Lucres* (1512) and the anonymous *The Worlde and the Chylde* (1522), contained parts for boys, girls, and women. *Jack Juggler*, printed in about 1562, advertised itself as 'a new interlude for children to play', in other words by them entirely. Such plays were often musical to the extent that they included songs as well as speech.

There came to be several kinds of places where child or youthful actors could perform. One was the great noble household, where young people were present and where plays would be staged at certain times of the year like the Christmas season (Fig. 43, p. 162). Sir Thomas More, when a boy of fourteen in the household of Cardinal Morton in the 1490s, was able to step into a play of this kind and make up his own part.[74] Another place was the grammar school. Here boys after the 1480s studied the classical plays of Terence and Plautus, and some schoolmasters now encouraged them to act in Latin or English to develop their linguistic and rhetorical skills. Such plays might be done in the school or staged before local worthies on special occasions. In sixteenth-century London, for example, we hear of performances of a public or semi-public nature in the sixteenth century from the boys of Eton, St Paul's, Merchant Taylors', Westminster Abbey, and Windsor Chapel.[75] James Whitelocke, later a knight, recalled acting at Merchant Taylors' with gratitude as having taught him 'good behaviour and audacity'.[76]

During the reign of Elizabeth I, some of these schools came to put on plays more frequently and although the actors remained schoolboys, they became accomplished in their performances.[77] The two main schoolboy companies were the 'Children of the Chapel [Royal]' and the 'Children of

[St] Paul's'. Both staged plays at Elizabeth's court at least once a year. They also did so in public at the Blackfriars Theatre, south-west of St Paul's Cathedral: intermittently in the 1570s and 1580s, and more permanently after 1600. Their early plays were representations of classical history or mythology, perhaps written by their schoolmasters, but by the 1570s they were attracting the attention of career dramatists in more original works. John Lyly wrote several plays for the 'Children of Paul's', some of which were published (Fig. 56, p. 212). Later on the two groups of boys acted works by Christopher Marlowe, George Peele, John Marston, and Ben Jonson. The revived performances after 1600 drew audiences and attracted Shakespeare's attention in *Hamlet*, written in about that year. Rosencrantz tells the Prince that: 'There is, sir, an eyrie of children, little eyases [hawks] that . . . are most tyrannically clapped for. These are now the fashion, and berattle [assail] the common stages [the public play-houses].' Hamlet asks, 'Do the boys carry it away [succeed]?' Rosencrantz replies, 'Ay, that they do, my lord, Hercules and his load too.'[78]

The popularity of the young actors at the Blackfriars caused them to come close to being professional players. Under Henry Evans, their manager from 1600, advantage was taken of the royal right to conscript boys for singing in order to get good actors. Once, however, Evans overreached himself. He kidnapped a boy called Thomas Clifton, who was a pupil at Christ's Hospital in London, intending to put him on the stage. The boy's father secured his release through one of the queen's privy councillors, and complained to the Court of Star Chamber. He alleged that Evans was recruiting boys merely for acting, whereas the right of conscription related only to singing. John Chappell had been taken from a private school, John Motteram from Westminster, and Nathan Field from St Paul's. Four others were apprentices. Field must have been a star performer since he acted in two plays by Ben Jonson: *Cynthia's Revels* and *Poetaster*. The court released young Clifton, censured Evans, and ordered him to surrender all his rights in the theatre or to organise plays, but he recovered his position under James I.[79] The Children of Paul's survived until about 1609 and those of the Chapel for some years longer. One of the latter, Salamon Pavy, was the subject of a poetic epitaph by Ben Jonson, lamenting his death at the age of thirteen.[80]

Sapho and Phao,

Played beefore the
Queenes Maieſtie on Shroue-
tewſday, by her Maieſties
Children and the Boyes
of Paules.

Imprinted at London
for Thomas Cadman,
1584.

56. The title page of John Lyly's drama *Sapho and Phao*, 'played by Her Majesty's Children and the Boys of [St] Paul's'.

Meanwhile, professional companies of adult players had developed during Elizabeth's reign, under the patronage of members of her court. This gave them status as servants of the nobility, which offered some protection, both in London and when travelling, against the hostility of Puritan town councillors and the laws against vagabonds. These companies, like the Lord Chamberlain's to which Shakespeare belonged, required boy actors too. Some played boys and pages, like the Princes in the Tower in *Richard III* or Falstaff's page Robin in *Henry IV Part II* and *The Merry Wives of Windsor*. A greater need was for them to undertake female parts, since women did not normally act on public stages until the Restoration. These boys were technically apprentices. They were articled to an adult actor for whom they did chores in return for teaching and the procuring of stage roles. In 1597 Philip Henslowe, the owner of the Rose Theatre in Southwark, bought a boy named James Bristowe from an actor, William Augusten, for the sum of £8.[81] This was in effect a transfer of an apprenticeship, the old master being paid to surrender his rights. Having finished their period of learning, the apprentices could become adult actors, but it is possible that some preferred to leave and follow other occupations.

TOWARDS ADULTHOOD

Adolescence is an age of comradeship. Younger boys and girls bond with others of their sex, of course, but adolescence brings the knowledge and power to do so more effectively. Youths and maidens past the age of puberty met together at work (in the same household or outside at such tasks as fetching water) and socialised together in recreations or (in the case of men) in making mischief. To that extent there was a 'youth culture' distinct from that of children and mature adults. At the same time, all adolescents lived with adults, worked with adults, and shared a good deal of life with them, including religious observances, community activities, and even recreations.[82]

Up to the Reformation, parish churches formed centres at which comradeship could develop. By 1485 many contained cohesive groups of 'maidens' and 'young men' (Fig. 57, p. 214). These were young people aged between puberty, when church attendance and obligations began, and marriage in the mid-twenties. After they married, women would join a similar group of 'wives'. Unlike religious guilds, which were usually run by adult men, the groups of wives, maidens, and young men controlled their own affairs.[83] The evidence about their activities comes chiefly from the accounts drawn up each year by parish churchwardens. Unfortunately these fail to tell us all that these young people did: the initiations and social events they might have held. Rather, they are restricted to recording the money raised for the church. The maidens gathered funds: we are not told how, whether by entertainment such as singing and dancing or making and selling food. They maintained a light before an image in the church and gave surplus money to church funds.

The young men did likewise. They too raised cash by brewing and selling ale, and by collecting money, especially around Plough Monday in early January. Most of all they organised and acted in Robin Hood plays.[84] These were popular over most of England in the first half of the sixteenth century and could take elaborate forms, involving an outlay on costumes, especially the 'Lincoln green' that the outlaws were said to have worn. The plays centred on combats and these, with the attendant touting for money, could be disruptive. Some towns tried to suppress them for this reason and, when the

57. Social bonding at church. The window donated by the 'sisters' (probably the young women of the parish) in St Neot church, Cornwall.

Reformation came, religion was another dampening force. Lights in churches disappeared and many Puritans disliked drama of any kind.[85] The plays gradually died out, and the groups of maidens and young men seem to have been less important in churches by the reign of Elizabeth.

Comradeship easily led to violence.[86] Tudor writers featured aggressive, vainglorious young men gathering together for drinking, gambling, lawlessness, and sex (Fig. 58, p. 215).[87] Roistering in taverns could be followed by vandalism and an urge to claim territory or pay off scores which might generate brawls with other groups. This was particularly the case in towns with many servants and apprentices, and most of all in London, where there were hundreds. Even Dekker's genial play, *The Shoemaker's Holiday* of 1600, shows how young artisans (in this case shoemakers) could suddenly erupt into quarrels with the famous cry of 'Clubs and prentices!' to bring out armed supporters.[88] Similar clashes could happen in the countryside between village communities. A visitor to the parish feast at Garsington in Oxfordshire deplored the bravado displayed there between the different parochial contingents, crying 'Hey for Garsington', 'Hey for Cuddesdon', and 'Hey Hockley'.[89]

58. A youth en route to the gallows bites his mother's nose in revenge for his bad upbringing, from William Caxton's translation of *Aesop's Fables* (1484).

Sometimes there was a greater (although not necessarily a higher) motive for violence. Cases are recorded where young men (and occasionally young women) took action to resist encroachments on their liberty.[90] This usually involved the pulling down of fences which kept them out of areas that they used for recreation. In 1513–14 young men joined other London people in doing so at Islington and other places outside the city where open fields had been enclosed with hedges and ditches, excluding recreational walking and the practice of archery. The king's council ordered the lord mayor to send the perpetrators home, but they carried their point to the extent that the hedges were not reinstated.[91] In 1598 anonymous letters were circulated to the apprentices of London complaining about the punishments meted out to young people by the city authorities: whippings and settings on the pillory. They were urged to gather in the fields on St Bartholomew's Day (24 August), a local holiday, 'with daggers and staves'. That afternoon the lord mayor would go there to attend a wrestling match, and they could 'be revenged of him'.[92]

The young also joined in attacks on unpopular groups, especially foreigners. The most famous example, the 'Ill' or 'Evil' May Day, took place in London in 1517. Anger had been growing in the city against the 'Dutch' (Germans or Netherlanders), French, and 'Lombards' (Italians) for their alleged arrogance and competitive trading. Assaults were made on them in the last days of April, causing the city authorities to imprison the perpetrators. As May Day was a holiday, Cardinal Wolsey and the king's council ordered all men to remain indoors with their servants that day. The order was not sufficiently publicised, and in the morning one of the city aldermen found two young men in Cheapside fencing with swords and watched by a large crowd. He told them to go home and, when they demurred, tried to arrest them. This caused the crowd to riot and cry 'Prentices and clubs!' Disorder spread; the rioters broke into the prisons and freed those locked up on the previous days. Thomas More tried to quieten the crowds, without success, and there were attacks on aliens and their houses. The riot lasted for about six hours and subsided only in mid-afternoon.

The authorities took draconian action. Suspects were arrested, bound in ropes, 'some men, some lads, some children of thirteen year', and tried on the following days. Fourteen (not necessarily the very young) were condemned for high treason and hanged, drawn, and quartered. Others were then reprieved, and on 22 May all the remaining prisoners (men and women) were brought to Westminster Hall before the king himself, wearing halters round their necks, where they were ceremonially pardoned.[93] The affair was still remembered in about 1600 when a group of dramatists, including Shakespeare, tried to include it in a play called *Sir Thomas More*. Shakespeare wrote the scene in which More spoke to calm the rioters. But recalling the event remained so sensitive that the censor, the Master of the Revels, ordered the removal of the whole 'insurrection', and it seems that the play was never performed.[94]

CRIME, SEX, AND MARRIAGE

Those administering justice had to consider what should be done to young people accused of crimes, like the thirteen-year-olds said to have been arrested in 1517. During the Middle Ages a rough scale of penalties had evolved in relation to youthfulness, although it was never exactly defined. Children below the age of seven were not considered capable of felony (serious crime). Between seven and twelve or fourteen, there was a presumption of incapacity although it could be set aside if that seemed appropriate.[95] Statutes punishing beggars in Tudor England did not apply to children under the age of fourteen.[96]

More serious crimes above or even around that age, however, could receive adult penalties. Employers were free to exert corporal punishment on their servants. That given by Thomas More has already been mentioned.[97] Grace Sharington recalled that 'I have seen my father [Sir Henry] with his own hands (for example's sake) scourge a young man naked from the girdle upwards, with fresh rods, for . . . a saucy and irreverent behaviour towards us his children', before expelling him from his service.[98] Civic authorities took similar action. The London diarist Henry Machyn reported a 'stripling' being whipped around the city in 1555 for speaking against the Church, another 'boy' in 1558 whipped at the post called 'the Reformation', and a third 'stripling' whipped in 1561.[99] These were perhaps unusually young for punishment, hence the diarist's interest. In 1538 a 'boy' servant of a courtier was found guilty of stealing his master's purse containing £11 in coins and a jewel. He was sentenced to be hanged next day and was actually on the scaffold wearing the noose when the king's pardon arrived, 'to the great comfort of all the people there present'.[100] But leniency of this kind was not universal: another 'boy' was indeed hanged at Tyburn in 1562 along with eight adults.[101]

Adolescence was a time of awakening sexuality. Youths might bond together and maidens together, but they also wished to meet the opposite sex. Dancing was a popular way of doing so.[102] It had numerous forms, hard now to reconstruct because they were learnt or copied physically rather than from written texts. The sole Tudor guide to the subject was translated from French and dealt only with what was known as the 'base dance'.[103] This was slow and intricate, hence Elyot's recommendation of it to aristocracy as embodying the ideals of noble life and marriage, although he also recognised the existence of alternative forms: bargenettes, pavions, turgions, and rounds.[104] Shakespeare in *Twelfth Night* mentions others: the cinquepace, galliard, jig, and coranto.[105] Wealthy people paid for their children to learn, boys and girls. One of the sons in the family of the earls of Rutland was taught by the king's minstrels and two others by a specialist dancing master.[106] London had professional instructors, like Whythorne, and there was an attempt in 1574 by the Crown to give three of them a monopoly of teaching in the capital.[107] This can hardly have been effective for long, however, since

217

it was noted in 1615 that dancing was taught, apparently freely, by musicians throughout the city.[108]

Dancing was equally popular lower down in society, where it must have been learnt by watching others or being taught by one's elders. Contemporary writers and artists liked to depict its plebeian forms as less refined than those of the higher ranks of society but in truth there could be vigorous or measured versions of it at any social level.[109] Anne Boleyn is recorded, while in her mid-teens in France, as dancing 'the English dances, leaping and jumping with infinite grace and agility'.[110] The historian John Stow, looking back on his youth in London in the 1530s and 1540s, recalled the popularity of dancing in the fields and that of maids by themselves in the streets, 'one of them playing on a timbrel, in sight of their masters and dames'. Writing towards the end of Elizabeth's reign, he thought that this, 'being now suppressed, worser practices within doors are to be feared'. In other words it had provided a benign release for sexual energy.[111]

The suppression that he mentions arose from a disapproval of dancing by moralists which can be traced back to the Middle Ages.[112] We have already noticed its presence in the writings of Vives.[113] This increased with the growth of Puritanism after 1559, and some of what we know about the popular forms of dancing comes from writers of that kind.[114] They associated it, as Stow did, with young unmarried servants. It was a popular activity on Sundays, in the holiday seasons of Christmas and Whitsuntide, and at weddings. There were recognised places where it was done. It was a cheap form of amusement because it needed only a single musician: piper, harper, or fiddler. Gentry sometimes paid for the music. To Puritans, of course, it broke the Sabbath and led to lewdness and vice, hence attempts to restrain or abolish it. These were more likely to succeed in towns with Puritan officials than in the countryside under the more tolerant gentry.

Beyond the social mixing of the sexes lay the attraction of private and intimate sexual relations. This area of life in Tudor England came under the oversight of the Church, through its system of bishops' and archdeacons' courts, as well as that of the secular authorities, especially guilds and borough courts in towns.[115] The Church permitted child marriages in this period. They were a small minority of such events and were typically contracted between families of property in order to gain some advantage.[116] We hear in Cheshire of a marriage between John Somerford, aged three, and Jane Brereton, a year younger, the children being carried to the ceremony in the arms of adults, who spoke all or most of the words assigned to the couple to say.[117] More commonly the participants were older and could say the words by themselves. The Church, moreover, regarded such marriages as provisional until the parties concerned reached puberty and had the mental and physical powers to consent to the marriage and consummate it. Records of such marriages are usually linked with legal proceedings in the Church courts, when one family changed its mind or one of the adolescents refused to go ahead with the match.

Permanent marriages could be made, with the consent of the partners, from the age of puberty, but were uncommon in adolescence except among the very wealthy. The normal time for marriage across the population, as has been shown, lay in the mid-twenties.[118] It was a firm belief in society that parents should be asked to consent to their children's matches, even if the children were young adults. In cases of guardians and wards, there was even a legal right of the former over the latter, unless the ward compensated the guardian for permission to marry at will.[119] When Thomas Cranmer drew up his new code of canon law for the Church of England in 1553, he sought to make all marriages take place in church and be dependent on parental approval.[120] Thomas Stockwood, minister of Tunbridge, published a pamphlet in 1586 'showing that children are not to marry without the consent of their parents, in whose power and choice it lieth to provide wives and husbands for their sons and daughters'.[121]

In practice it was difficult emotionally and economically for young people to ignore their parents in this matter, but Cranmer's code of law was never ratified. Throughout the Tudor era, the Church continued the medieval practice of recognising any marriage, whether it was made at or outside a church, if it could be proved that the parties had exchanged vows.[122] Determined young people could therefore marry at will, even among the gentry. Thomas Thynne and Maria Audley did so in 1594 when they were both sixteen. The cost, however, was great. His family did their utmost to undo the marriage, and the subsequent quarrels – it has been suggested – may have helped inspire the writing of *Romeo and Juliet*.[123]

The long interval between puberty and most people's weddings meant that sexual relations, if pursued, had to take place outside marriage. This had been forbidden by Church law for centuries. The Reformation made no difference in this respect; indeed the Reformers were stern enforcers of morality. When sexual relations came to light, the parties concerned would be summoned for examination and punishment before a Church court or that of a secular authority, especially in a town. By 1576 the Crown itself was intervening in extra-marital sex in order to handle the problem of illegitimate children born out of wedlock. A statute of that year allowed two justices of the peace to deal with such children. They could punish the mother and reputed father, and charge them for the upkeep of the child, with imprisonment as an option if they defaulted on their duty.[124]

Tudor moralists steadily preached the virtues of virginity and chastity. The Church authorities continued to try to enforce them as the Crown came to do. Employers insisted on abstinence from sex, as we have seen in William Johnson's indenture. This was effective to the extent that illegitimate births in late Tudor England amounted to only about 4 per cent.[125] Nevertheless, men and women were constantly brought into the Church courts for fornication, although the lack of records of their ages usually makes it impossible to identify which were adolescents or young adults. Moreover the Church authorities complained that sex between unmarried men and women was often condoned within society. The official set of homilies published in 1562 for reading in church on Sundays included one aimed at 'whoredom and uncleanness'. 'This vice [fornication] is grown unto such a height', it protested, 'that in a manner among many it is accounted no sin at all but rather a pastime, a dalliance and but a touch of youth, not rebuked but winked at, not punished but laughed at.'[126]

There is indeed some evidence that society tolerated intimate relationships between young people who were engaged to be married or even courting, if their families approved and saw the courting as leading to marriage.[127] Indulgence stopped where servants and apprentices had sex together or with their employers. Apprentices, in particular, were required to be chaste by their indentures. Sympathy might be extended to a maidservant seduced by her male employer or colleague. A letter in Henry VII's reign to the head of the Plumpton family in Yorkshire pleaded for a woman with a baby whose father was a Plumpton servant, the writer saying that he had supported her hitherto and asking the Plumptons to do so in future.[128] Male apprentices and servants, however, might be severely punished for sleeping with a maidservant or the mistress of the house. In London they could be paraded in a cart or whipped. In one case, where the apprentice had been found in bed with a maid and had apparently boasted of his exploits to others, the leaders of his trade, the Drapers' Company, ordered him to be thrashed in public, in their hall, and on his bare back by two men hooded to give them anonymity.[129]

Activities not involving the opposite sex seem to have received a similar kind of tolerance or inattention. Very little was written against masturbation, and the law did not penalise it.[130] Indeed Thomas Cogan, in a book on human health first printed in 1584 and often reissued, circumspectly commended it. Observing that carnal desires were natural to men and women, he argued that there were benefits in releasing them. 'The commodities which come from moderate evacuation thereof, are great.' They included, he thought, an appetite for food, better bodily health, stimulation of the mind and the senses, and the avoidance of 'lecherous imaginations and unchaste dreams'.[131] Homosexual activity between men had been regarded equivocally in the medieval Catholic Church. It was condemned by theologians, but in practice there was a caution about referring to it lest men be tempted in that direction.[132] In the mid-Tudor period it became more of an issue, probably under the influence of religious reform. In 1533 and 1563 parliamentary statutes were enacted which categorised it as 'buggery' and made it a felony with severe penalties.[133] This was followed by a few high-profile prosecutions with at least two executions, but cases rarely came before the normal legal authorities and it is highly unlikely that any adolescents featured in them unless they were victims of adults.[134]

William Harrison, as has been mentioned, associated unmarried household servants with whoring.[135] Prostitution went on in the towns, and indeed in the countryside. Licensed brothels existed until 1546: in London they were situated in Southwark, south of the Thames.[136] They survived the fear of syphilis, which troubled England in the early Tudor years, but Henry VIII suppressed them at the end of his reign, probably as part of the growing fervour of the Reformation against sexual sins.[137] Nevertheless unlicensed brothels continued to operate with fitful harassment from the authorities (Fig. 59, below). Shakespeare portrayed them in *Henry IV*, *Measure for Measure*, and *Pericles*, treating them and their inhabitants with some tolerance and assuming as much from his audience. The main barrier for the young in using them was the fees they charged, anything from 1*s*. to 5*s*.[138] This did not stop some apprentices resorting to them. Machyn noted the punishment of a male procurer in the pillory in 1556 for bringing prostitutes to apprentices who paid them out of their masters' goods, and this practice or the use of one's wages seems to have been quite common.[139] Contrarily it also became a custom after 1600 for apprentices to attack and sack brothels on Shrove Tuesday: not out of Puritanism, it seems, but from high spirits and lawlessness on that day, or even through the resentment of those who had been fleeced for money in such places.[140]

59. London in 1630, the greatest concentration of young people in England, with corresponding scope for violence and philandering. The brothel area in Southwark appears at the bottom left.

In the longer term adolescents could look forward to marriage. It was a long wait for most, however, since rarely before the mid-twenties was there a likelihood of a secure job for a man, an inheritance from parents, or their need to co-opt a son into running a farm or a business. In the meantime, adolescence might last for ten or fifteen years spent under parental authority or that of an employer elsewhere. Only with marriage did most men and women achieve the independence and dignity of becoming householders, with the resources to start a new cycle of life with a family of their own.

8

REFLECTIONS

Did childhood, as we understand it, exist in Tudor England? Assumptions have sometimes been made that children were regarded as small adults; that their childhoods were brief, loveless, and impoverished; and that, at best, the modern idea of childhood was only evolving in the sixteenth century.[1] The scope of this book will have shown the impossibility of such views. Children in the Tudor age, as always, differed from adults in their physique, mentality, and needs. Adults, as always, recognised the fact. Their concept of 'the ages of man' caused them to regard infancy, childhood, and youth as distinctive stages of life with their own characteristics. Treatises were written to advise on the upbringing of children, on their behaviour, and on their illnesses. The Church treated them differently from their elders. It welcomed them with baptism and later with confirmation. It exempted them from church attendance, fasting, and the payment of dues, as well as from confession while that institution was still in being. It thought that they were too young to receive communion. After 1549 it provided teaching for them in the form of the catechism. In the secular sphere the laws of England had long made special provision for the treatment of children as orphans and when convicted of crimes.

Adults with families provided for the special needs of their children. The rich employed nurses to feed and care for them. Cradles, walking frames, and small chairs were manufactured for the babies and toddlers of wealthy people. Appropriate food was given and clothes were made for their use. Their clothes, especially in families of status, might imitate those of adults, but that is so of children's dress today (Fig. 60, p. 225). Toys and books were purchased for their pleasure or profit. It was recognised that they had, to

224

60. Another Tudor family: Edmund Chapman, his wife, and children, from
Sibton, Suffolk (1524).

some extent, a culture of their own. Bartholomew Glanville, in a work still
thought worth reprinting in the 1580s, observed how 'they love talking and
counsel of such children as they be, and avoid [the] company of old men
[adult people]'.[2] They played by themselves, sometimes in their own distinctive games. They are likely to have had some words of their own (like those
for spinning tops). They possessed their own concepts of public space and
how to use it, which might differ from those of their elders.

We can glimpse all these things, but a clear and complete understanding
often eludes us. The source material available at present is fragmentary and

diminishes the lower one descends in the social order. Only one aspect of childhood, education, provides us with substantial records. Even that is mainly confined to treatises on education and to the functioning of grammar schools, attended by a minority of boys. Of the elementary schools that taught most children we know very little: even where precisely they existed. Other areas of life, those of the family, religion, and work, have left us much less of their interaction with the young. Lists of the games children played and the literary works they read can be made, but we are largely ignorant of how games were conducted and who read which books with what consequences. The historian is usually obliged to gather fragments of evidence and fit them together as best he may. In this respect it is easiest to chart the history of children of the nobility and gentry, some of which has survived in letters and household accounts.

Autobiographies and biographies were written in the Tudor era, but they are not now numerous. Those by Robert Carey, and those about Thomas Wolsey and Thomas More, have little or nothing to say on their childhoods. Their counterparts by Grace Sharington, Thomas Tusser, and Thomas Whythorne are chiefly concerned with their authors' education, and record little else about their formative years. Personal reminiscences, like Edward Herbert's and those that Peter Carew related to John Hooker, are rare indeed. Adult records about children are similarly scarce. The diary of Dr John Dee, with its observations on his children's health and accidents, is precious but unique in this respect; otherwise we are dependent on the occasional survival of private letters and financial accounts. One source is less helpful to us in most of the sixteenth century than in the fifteenth. Up to about 1530, schoolboys were dictated, or allowed to write sentences in exercise books about their everyday lives and pursuits. After that date, such exercises came to be replaced by translations from classical authors and, although vignettes of school life survive in dialogues for teaching modern languages, these were written by teachers rather than pupils.

There is also a difficulty in extracting childhood as a whole from social life as a whole. Child development and the experiences of childhood would have differed according to social status. Housing, food, dress, care, and education wrought disparities. Work would have impacted on poor children earlier than on the rich. Mental horizons would have varied, depending on literacy and the ability to travel. Because of these differences, it is hard to take children out of their social context and study them together as a group. It is easier to consider them along with the adults around them: in particular places or in specific classes of people.

A further problem is the gap between precept and practice. Laws and treatises laid down how children should be treated but they are no sure guides to what was being done. Home discipline was notionally something that should be applied to all young people, but there are as many complaints about its absence as there are precepts for its observance. Tudor society was a religious society, but it is far from clear that the observances recommended in the home (and often followed there by wealthy literate families) were observed by the poor. Even the statutory requirement to go to catechism classes after 1549 was apparently ignored by some people, as indeed one should expect of any religious duties. In education, the studies recommended by Sir Thomas Elyot for boys of high status were taught with some difficulty to real boys like Henry Fitzroy and Gregory Cromwell. Moreover the traditional division between the skills prescribed for noble boys and the virtues assigned to their sisters is misleading. Girls of this rank, as we have seen, studied languages, played music, danced, learnt to shoot with bows, and joined in hunting. Despite this, educationists ignored such activities or even condemned them.

Given these difficulties, it is impossible to state concisely what Tudor childhood was like, as opposed to collecting and presenting the scattered evidence about its various aspects. There was no standard child or childhood experience. Perhaps an easier question to ask is how far the treatment and experience of children in Tudor society were traditional, and how far in the process of change. Certainly much survived from the past throughout the Tudor years up to 1603. It was far from being the new age so often assumed. One long-established element was parental authority, demanding deference and obedience. Religious obligations were another, centring on the need to grow up learning about and embracing Christian beliefs, observances, and moral behaviour. The Reformation barred most rituals from church, but it could not remove the folk customs associated with baptisms and weddings:

processions, decorations, and the boy attendants of the bride. Outside church, the autumnal and winter customs continued of children dressing up or begging for food or money, and the taking of them for healing to holy wells. The Reformation also kept some established medieval practices: early baptism, confirmation, exemption from church attendance and fasting, and exclusion from communion until adolescence.

Many of the laws and conventions relating to childhood remained the same all through the sixteenth century. These included an approximate understanding of an age of criminal responsibility, conventions about the age of majority (differing according to the kind of property held), and the arrangements for the wardship of orphaned children with property. The institutions of education too were ancient ones. Elementary reading schools, free and fee-paying grammar schools, instruction in office skills and foreign languages, the learning of manners, and physical training all came to Tudor England from the Middle Ages. The need for many children to do light work, and for all to learn how to live and work as adults, was traditional too. So were some of the games that children played, and much of the literature that they read in the sixteenth century: *Bevis of Hampton*, *Guy of Warwick*, *Valentine and Orson*, stories of Robin Hood, and *The Friar and the Boy*.

At the same time, certain of these elements became significantly modified between 1485 and 1603. Parent and child relationships may not have been very different at the end of the period than at its beginning. But religion changed greatly due to the Reformation. The internal appearance of churches, the character of services, the coming in of the catechism, and the kinds of religious observances used at home altered for children during the middle of the sixteenth century. There were developments too in education. It is possible that elementary schooling became more widespread under the Tudors although the fact is difficult to establish. The way that grammar schools functioned, in terms of their classroom layout, hours of work, and examination methods did not greatly evolve. Their studies, on the other hand, certainly did. Medieval Latin was replaced by classical Latin, medieval religious authors by pagan classical ones, and practical Latin composition by the imitation of classical writers. Girls of noble and gentry families, who had hitherto learnt French but very little Latin, sometimes now came to equal their brothers in both subjects, and in some cases learnt other languages as well.

There were changes for the poor. The basic understanding of their condition – the concept of the deserving and undeserving poor – was an ancient one, and the giving of charity to them in casual informal ways continued throughout the sixteenth century. Monastic poor relief disappeared, but individual people went on providing occasional alms, as they had always done. However the mid- and later sixteenth century saw the creation of national and uniform procedures for relieving the poor and setting them to work, which had not existed before. Finally, there were changes to children's culture, hard though it is to chart them. The most obvious was the proliferation of material for reading. What in 1485 was a mixture of manuscripts and early printed books and pamphlets became, by 1603, a much wider and cheaper range of printed publications. Then there were changes in music and drama involving children: the decline of boy choirs and the rise of professional acting. Among adults there were periodic new fashions in hair styles, clothes, dancing, and reading which probably spread to children. Games may well have fallen in and out of vogue, especially playing-card games. Among exercises, archery certainly declined during the Tudor era. It is difficult to come to a conclusion about all this, to quantify and compare the extent of tradition and change for children in the sixteenth century, beyond saying that both had influence. Sixteenth-century

61. A last look at childhood: boys enjoying snowballing.

children lived in a world that inherited much from the past, while sharing in a journey away from that past.

Childhood has received little attention from historians of Tudor England and its activities. While there are indeed valuable studies devoted to specific aspects of the subject, it makes few appearances in wider social and cultural surveys. The chief exceptions are histories of education and biographies of the Tudor monarchs. This partly reflects the difficulty of collecting material, but also comes from an assumption – as old as academic history – that the history of any particular topic is a history of adults. Yet children required accommodation, food, clothes, furniture, medical care, and upbringing. They too were members of the Church, enjoyed recreations, studied, read books, featured in paintings and on monuments, went to work, and broke the law. They deserve to be considered as participants and influences in all aspects of history: family relationships, household economy, religion, culture, literature, art, and social institutions. Their needs, and sometimes their activities, had an impact on what adults did. We gain a narrower and poorer understanding of Tudor society if we do not include them (Fig. 61, p. 229).

NOTES

ABBREVIATIONS

BL	British Library, London
EETS, os, es, ss	Early English Text Society, original series, extra series, supplementary series
LPFD	*Calendar of Letters and Papers, Foreign and Domestic, Henry VIII*
NPG	National Portrait Gallery, London
ODNB	*The Oxford Dictionary of National Biography*
OED	*The Oxford English Dictionary*
R + number	English Short Title Catalogue, online
S + number	English Short Title Catalogue, online
STC	A. W. Pollard and G. R. Redgrave, *A Short Title Catalogue of Books Printed in England, Scotland, and Ireland, 1475–1640*, 2nd edn, 3 vols (London, 1976–91).
TNA	The National Archives, Kew

1 BIRTH AND INFANCY

1. BL, Cotton MS Julius B.XII, f. 56r, printed in Leland, iv, 249.
2. *ODNB*, Edward VI, article by Dale Hoak.
3. Orme 2001, 13.
4. Hill, p. xiii. There is a study of Hill's book by Heather Collier.
5. Orme 2021, 280.
6. Orme 2001, 16; Nicholas Orme, *Medieval Pilgrimage* (Exeter, 2018), 142, 149.
7. Scot, 205.
8. Doreen Evenden, *The Midwives of Seventeenth-century London* (Cambridge, 2000), 25–7.
9. Compare the medieval accounts in Batman, ff. 72v–74r.
10. Rösslin, f. 7v.
11. Ibid., ff. 16r, 18r, 19r.
12. Ibid., f. 13r–v.
13. Ibid., f. 14r–v.
14. Ibid., f. 20v.
15. *OED* s.n. birth-stool.
16. On what follows, see Rösslin, ff. 13r–v, 21r–25v; Lupton, 8.
17. *OED*, s.n. navel-string.
18. Rösslin, f. 52v.
19. Ibid., f. 53r.
20. Lupton, 18.
21. John Stow, *A Summarie of the Chronicles of England* (London, 1575; S1140), 508; Raphael Holinshed, *The First Volume of the Chronicles of England, Scotlande, and Irelande* (London, 1577; S3985), 1816; see also Machyn, 23, 281.

22. Shakespeare, *The Winter's Tale*, IV.iv.263–85.
23. *The True Reporte . . . of a Monstrous Childe Born at Much Horkesleye* (London, 1562; S117982); John Barker, *The True Description of a Monsterous Chylde Borne in the Ile of Wight* (London, 1564; S115322); William Elderton, *The True Fourme and Shape of a Monsterous Chyld . . . in Stony Stratforde* (London, 1565; S121741); H. B., *The True Descripcion of a Childe . . . Borne in the Parish of Micheham* (London, 1566; S117265); *The Forme and Shape of a Monstrous Child Borne at Maydstone in Kent* (London, 1568; S113123); *Of a Monstrous Childe Borne at Chichester* (London, 1581; S90354).
24. Gospel of John, iii.5.
25. Orme 2021, 302–6.
26. Ellis, *Original Letters*, third series, ii, 225–6; *ODNB*, Ralph Sadler, article by Gervase Phillips.
27. Orme 2021, 312–13.
28. On the form of the service, see ibid., 302–14.
29. Ibid., 314–16.
30. Lupton, 10.
31. Frere and Kennedy, ii, 39–40.
32. Roger Schofield, '"Monday's Child is Fair of Face": favoured days for baptism, marriage and burial in pre-industrial England', *Continuity and Change*, 20 (2005), 93–109 at 101.
33. E.g. in the case of John Dee's children (Dee, 6, 53).
34. Machyn, 277.
35. Below, pp. 95–9.
36. Brightman, ii, 744–7, 790–1.
37. Foxe, viii, 126.
38. *Somerset Medieval Wills, 1383–1500*, ed. F. W. Weaver, Somerset Record Society, 16 (1901), 319; *Somerset Medieval Wills, 1501–1530*, ed. F. W. Weaver, Somerset Record Society, 19 (1903), 212.
39. Camden, 32–3.
40. Ibid., 52–3, 56, 63, 71.
41. Brightman, ii, 778–9.
42. Hill, pp. xiii–xiv.
43. Stephenson, 162.
44. Ibid., 330.
45. Ibid., 526; compare 239, 289, 291, 320, 387, 429, 456.
46. On forenames, see E. G. Withycombe, *The Oxford Dictionary of English Christian Names*, 2nd edn (Oxford, 1950).
47. Nicholas Orme, *The Saints of Cornwall* (Oxford, 2000), 106, 127 169 187, 217, 222.
48. Below, pp. 138–9.
49. Camden, 31. Atalanta Walton was an ancestor of mine, born in the 1580s; for the others, see Stephenson, 19, 209.
50. Winchester, 16.
51. *ODNB*, Robert Ferrar, article by Glanmor Williams; Simon Heynes, article by C. S. Knighton.
52. Camden, 31, and see his following directory of names.
53. Winchester, 16.
54. Camden, 35.
55. Cotman, ii, part ii, 23, fig. XXXVI.
56. Camden, 31.
57. Rösslin, f. 56r. On wet-nursing in general, see Fildes 1988, especially 69–84.
58. Vives 1529, sig. C1r; Elyot 1530, sig. B2v.
59. Bray 256–7.
60. Erondelle, sigs G6v–G7v.
61. Elizabeth Clinton, *The Countesse of Lincolnes Nurserie* (London, 1622; S116629), 1–21.
62. Fildes 1988, 83–4.

63. A. Newdigate-Newdegate, *Gossip from a Muniment Room: being passages in the lives of Anne and Mary Fitton 1574–1618*, 2nd edn (London, 1898), 18, 22, 57, 68–9.

64. Fildes 1988, 79–80.

65. Dee, 12, 14, 16, 19–20, 36, 39, 43.

66. Rösslin, f. 56v.

67. Dee, 8, 21, 55. On the age of weaning, see also Pollock 1983, 219–21.

68. Wrigley and others, 508.

69. Rösslin, f. 59v.

70. Erondelle, sig. G6v; *OED* s.n. pap2.

71. Lupton, 13.

72. Batman, f. 74r.

73. *ODNB*, Arthur, prince of Wales, article by Rosemary Horrox; Edward VI, article by Dale Hoak; and Elizabeth I, article by Patrick Collinson.

74. Percy, 43.

75. Ibid., 73, 75, 78.

76. John Evans, 'Extracts from the Private Account Book of Sir William More, of Loseley, Surrey', *Archaeologia*, 36 part 2 (1855), 284–310 at 289. For the nursery of the Tollemache family of Suffolk, see Coleman, 19.

77. *The Works of Thomas Deloney*, ed. Francis Oscar Mann (Oxford, 1912), 103.

78. On what follows, see Buck, 17–64.

79. Rösslin, f. 54v.

80. *Lisle Letters*, v, 660.

81. Rösslin, ff. 55r–v.

82. Erondelle, sigs G6v–7v.

83. Ibid.

84. Reproduced in Buck, 19, 58, 62.

85. Orme 2021, 308; Hair, 103.

86. Orme 2001, 78; Hair, 106.

87. Tarbin, 396.

88. Orme 2001, 86–8; Tarbin, 396; *The Historical Collections of a Citizen of London in the Fifteenth Century*, ed. James Gairdner, Camden Society, new series 17 (1876), pp. viii–ix.

89. Orme 2001, 96.

90. Tarbin, 392–3.

91. Fildes 1990, Table 6.4.

92. Ibid., Table 6.5.

93. Ibid., Tables 6.1, 6.4.

94. Below, pp. 38–9.

95. Wrigley and others, 215, 250–1, 256.

96. Wrigley and Schofield, 189, 249, 255, 565

97. Lupton, 55, 74, 83, 89–90, 99, 102, 111–12, etc.

98. Hill, pp. xiii–xiv.

99. Stephenson, 117.

100. Ibid., 447.

101. *ODNB*, Elizabeth of York, article by Rosemary Horrox.

102. Ibid., Katherine of Aragon, article by C. S. L. Davies and John Edwards.

103. Ibid., Anne Boleyn, article by E. W. Ives.

104. Ibid., Jane Seymour, article by Richard Glen Eaves.

105. On infanticide, see Billington, especially 18–20, 137–45, 153–4, 206–10, 253–63.

106. *Statutes of the Realm*, iv, 1234–5.

107. Orme 2001, 99–100.

108. Below, pp. 120–1.

109. Nelson, 15–16. Admittedly p. 17 contains an account of an unkind mother.

110. Cotman, ii, part ii, 23, fig. XXXVII.

111. Below, pp. 58, 211.

2 THE HOME

1. Below, pp. 218–19.
2. O'Day 2018, 245.
3. Frere and Kennedy, ii, 39–40.
4. Wrigley and Schofield, 255; Wrigley and others, 130.
5. Wrigley and others, 250.
6. Stephenson, 132.
7. Ibid., 382.
8. Wrigley and others, 508.
9. Wikipedia (accessed 27 Feb. 2022).
10. Stephenson, 34, 76.
11. Lupton, 18.
12. O'Day 2018, 32.
13. Strong, 110.
14. K. B. McFarlane, *Hans Memling* (Oxford, 1971), 55.
15. Above, p. 25; J. Wilson, 360–79 at 363–7.
16. Strong, 110.
17. Ibid., 112.
18. NPG L231, Marcus Gheeraerts the Younger, 1596.
19. Strong, 277.
20. NPG 3914, unknown artist, *c.* 1602.
21. Barclay, eclogue 5, lines 280–5.
22. For a medieval view, see William Langland, *Piers Plowman*, ed. W. W. Skeat, 2 vols (Oxford, 1969), C.x.61–187, and for a Tudor one, Harrison, 180–1.
23. Myers, 70.
24. Latymer, 51, 54.
25. *The Crie of the Poore* (London, 1590; S118119).
26. Barbara Harvey, *Living and Dying in England 1100–1540: the monastic experience* (Oxford, 1993), 16–23.
27. *Report on the Manuscripts of Lord Middleton*, 332–67; Riden, i, p. clxxxix (index of entries).
28. Brightman, ii, 662–3.
29. *Statutes of the Realm*, iv, 413–14.
30. Ibid., iv, 595.
31. Ibid., iv, 610–11,
32. Lambarde 1601, 44–5.
33. *Churchwardens' Accounts of Ashburton, 1479–1580*, ed. Alison Hanham, Devon and Cornwall Record Society, new series 15 (1970), 178–90.
34. *Tudor Churchwardens' Accounts*, ed. Anthony Palmer, Hertfordshire Record Publications, 1 (1985), 92.
35. Wrigley and others, 219.
36. Myers, 118.
37. William Lyndwood, *Provinciale* (Oxford, 1679, repr. Farnborough, 1968), 26–7. Dispensations for ordination when illegitimate continued after the break with Rome in 1534, but seem to have petered out in about 1538 (*Faculty Office Registers 1534–1549*, ed. D. S. Chambers (Oxford, 1966), p. xxxix). No mention of illegitimacy is made in the Church of England's requirements for ordination from 1550 onwards (Brightman, ii, 930–1).
38. Except, oddly, if they were the illegitimate children of serfs, since they could not inherit parental serfdom. But that can have affected very few children in Tudor England.
39. On what follows, see Thornton and Carlton 2019, passim.
40. Ibid., 116.
41. E.g. *Cornish Wills 1342–1540*, ed. Nicholas Orme, Devon and Cornwall Record Society, new series 50 (2007), 132, 136.

42. *Robert Furse: a Devon family memoir of 1593*, ed. Anita Travers, Devon and Cornwall Record Society, new series 53 (2012), 31–2.
43. *ODNB*, Thomas Wolsey, article by Sybil M. Jack; Thomas Wynter, article by Julian Lock.
44. William Smith, *Hidden Lives: the nuns of Shaftesbury Abbey* (Gloucester, 2020), 110.
45. *ODNB*, Thomas Poynings, article by David Grummitt.
46. Ibid., article by J. H. Baker.
47. Ibid., article by Jonathan Hughes.
48. Ibid., article by David Grummitt.
49. Ibid., article by Beverley A. Murphy; below, pp. 143–4.
50. Shakespeare, *King John*, I.i.160–2, V.vii.110–18.
51. Below, p. 132.
52. Platter, 179; T. F. Kirby, *Annals of Winchester College* (London and Winchester, 1892), 509–10.
53. *Dean Cosyn and Wells Cathedral Miscellanea*, ed. Aelred Watkin, Somerset Record Society, 56 (1941), 107.
54. Erasmus 1532, sig. D4v.
55. Below, p. 134; George Wilson, *The Commendation of Cockes and Cock-fighting* (London, 1607; S111808), sig. C2v.
56. On what follows, see Buck, 81–173.
57. *OED* s.n. breech, v.
58. Riden, ii, 65–145 passim, 368–9.
59. Coleman, 33–4.
60. *Churchwardens' Accounts of Ashburton*, ed. Hanham, 178–90.
61. Nelson, 86.
62. Above, p. 25. Compare also NPG, Mary Tudor (by Michel Sittow), and Lady Anne Pope (by Marcus Gheeraerts the Younger).
63. *Lisle Letters*, v, 237.
64. Pollock 1993, 28.
65. Nelson, 22.
66. NPG, Lady Anne Pope (as above), Sir Walter Ralegh (unknown artist *c.* 1602).
67. *Manuscripts of the Duke of Rutland*, iv, 382, 384.
68. *The Rates of the Custome House* (London, 1550; S108742), s.n. bagges; idem (London, 1582; S111657), s.n. knives, purses.
69. Orme 2021, 263.
70. Nelson, 8.
71. Percy, 73.
72. *Lisle Letters*, iv, 499.
73. Harrison, 140.
74. E.g. Shakespeare, *Henry IV Part 1*, II.i.57–9.
75. Cogan, 184, 195.
76. Percy, 76, 79.
77. Ibid., 73, 75, 78.
78. Sneyd, 11; Hollyband 1583, 49.
79. Cogan, 184.
80. Hollyband 1583, 49, 157–70.
81. Cogan, 207.
82. Langland, *Piers the Plowman*, ed. Skeat, A.vii.267–73, B.vi.282–8, C.304–311.
83. TNA, SP 12/88 no. 53.
84. On the ages of man, see J. A. Burrow, *The Ages of Man: a study in medieval writing and thought* (Oxford, 1986); Orme 2001, 6–7; and Griffiths, 20–2.
85. Rhodes, sigs Aiir–iiiv.
86. *July and Julian*, 9.

87. Dee, 30–1.
88. Hooker, 3–11.
89. Nelson, 13–14.
90. Ibid., 1–2.
91. Erasmus 1532, sigs B8r–v, C2v.
92. Harrison, 449–50.
93. On the tradition, see Orme 1984, 81–111, and Jonathan Nicholls, *The Matter of Courtesy* (Woodbridge, 1985).
94. John Lydgate, *Stans Puer ad Mensam* (Westminster, 1476; S106482), modernised version *Table Manners for Children*, ed. Nicholas Orme and Lotte Hellinga (Salisbury, 1989; London, 1990); Rhodes, passim. Segar, passim, contains similar information with some variations.
95. Erasmus 1560.
96. *The Good Wife Taught her Daughter*, ed. Tauno F. Mustanoja, Annales Academiae Scientiarum Fennicae, series B, 61 part 2 (Helsinki, 1948), 158–75.
97. Below, pp. 150–1.
98. Pollock 1993, 27.
99. Orme 2021, 183–6.
100. Hollyband 1573, 90.
101. Ibid., 94.
102. Segar, sig. B1r.
103. On wiping or spitting using a cloth, see also Phillips, 118.
104. Similar advice is given in Hollyband 1583, 203–11.
105. Hollyband 1573, 62; idem 1576, sig. C1v; Bellot 1586, sig. B1v; Erondelle, sig. H1v.
106. *Lisle Letters*, v, 660.
107. *OED* s.n. master (sb) 22, miss (sb)2, mistress 14(b). For examples, see Ridon, ii, 39, 163, 317; iii, 278.
108. On feudal wardship, see Smith, 97–101, and Hurstfield, passim.
109. Dee, 16, 25, 28, 35, 38.
110. On this subject, see also Houlbrooke 1984, 138, and Newton, 153–82.
111. *A New Enterlude called Thersytes* (London, 1562; S111417), sigs Div–Diiir.
112. George Gifford, *A Dialogue concerning Witches* (London, 1593; S105690), sigs E3v–4r.
113. Batman, f. 72v.
114. Thomas Elyot, *The Castel of Helthe* (London, 1539; S365), sig. Kivr.
115. Thomas Moulton, *The Glasse of Helthe* (London, 1540; S104399), chapters xliii, cxxiii, cxxv.
116. Rösslin, book ii, ff. lixv–lxxixr.
117. Jean Goeurot, *The Regiment of Life . . . with the Boke of Children* (London, 1544; S105685).
118. *ODNB*, Thomas Phaer, article by Philip Schwyzer.
119. Phaer, *Book of Children* in Goeurot 1544, sigs Aiiv–iiir.
120. For the context, see J. S. Brewer, *The Reign of Henry VIII*, ed. J. Gairdner, 2 vols (London, 1884), i, 386.
121. *LPFD*, iii, part i, 499–504.
122. Shirley, 181–2.
123. *Report on the Manuscripts of Lord Middleton*, 407.
124. Wall, 19, 22–5. See also the case of Frances Cavendish in 1598 (Riden, ii, 39).
125. Harman 1567, sigs E8v, F4r.
126. Orme 2001, 104.
127. *ODNB*, Nicholas Udall, article by Matthew Steggle.
128. *Statutes of the Realm*, iv, 617–18.
129. Ingram 2010, 69.
130. Machyn, 17.
131. Ibid., 311. For other cases, see Griffiths, 316–24.

132. Below, p. 188.
133. Thomas Nashe, *The Terrors of the Night* (London, 1594; S110111), sig. E4r.
134. Herbert, 30.
135. Orme 2001, 48.
136. Dee, 1–2, 6, 39.
137. Above, pp. 27–8.
138. Shakespeare, *Romeo and Juliet*, I.iii.11–20.
139. Kirby, *Winchester Scholars*, 49 onwards.
140. Nelson, 1.
141. Hollyband 1576, sig. B7v.
142. Dee, 2.
143. Tusser, ed. Grigson, 202–3.
144. Below, p. 159.
145. Winchester, 109.
146. Dee, 12.
147. *A Register of the Members of St. Mary Magdalen College, Oxford*, ed. W. D. Macray, new series, 8 vols (London, 1894–1915), i. 30, 32–3, 61, 63; ii, 43.
148. Towns were often unpopular with rural people for the tolls charged on goods brought to market. Town and country rivalries among youths are mentioned in Barclay, eclogue 5, lines 407–10. On parish rivalries, see Orme 2021, 293, 295.
149. Orme 2021, 136.
150. Below, p. 85.

3 PLAY

1. Thomas More, *The Complete Works*, ed. A. S. G. Edwards and others, vol. i (New Haven and London, 1997), 3.
2. *The Worlde and the Chylde*, sig. A2v.
3. Wager, sig. A4r.
4. Shakespeare, *As You Like It*, II.vii.142–66. On the subject, see J. A. Burrow, *The Ages of Man* (Oxford, 1986), 5–54.
5. Studies of play in the later Middle Ages and Tudor period include Orme 2001, 164–97, and Lewis 2009, 86–108.
6. *The Worlde and the Chylde*, sig. A3r.
7. John Heywood, *The Play of the Wether* (London, 1533; S125019), sig. D3r.
8. Wager, sig. B1v.
9. *Pleadings and Depositions in the Duchy Court of Lancaster*, ed. Henry Fishwick, Lancashire and Cheshire Record Society, 32 (1896), 61–7.
10. Orme 2006, 157–8; Withals 1553, f. 67r.
11. Orme 2020a, 69. For the link between cock-fighting and 'victory' days, see also *LPFD*, iii, part i, 499–504.
12. Orme 2013, 386–7.
13. Nelson, 27.
14. Elyot 1531, book i, chapter 4.
15. Dee, 14.
16. *OED*, s.n. toy sb.
17. *Ratis Raving*, ed. J. R. Lumby, EETS, os 43 (1870), 57–8.
18. Breton, sig C2v.
19. *Promptorium Parvulorum*, 411; Wager, sig. C4v; *OED* s.n. blow-point.
20. John Gerard, *The Herball*, ed. Thomas Johnson (London, 1633; S122165), 750.
21. Horman, f. 147r.
22. *The Rates of the Custome House* (London, 1583; S111657), s.n. rattles.
23. Above, p. 25.
24. Shakespeare, *The Merry Wives of Windsor*, IV.iv.51.

25. *York Civic Records*, ed. A. Raine, vol. iii, Yorkshire Archaeological Society, Record Series 106 (1942), 70.
26. *OED*, s.n. babe, baby, poppet, puppet.
27. *Ortus Vocabulorum* (Rouen, 1520; S93059), s.n. pupa.
28. *Manuscripts of the Duke of Rutland*, iv, 384.
29. Winchester, 103.
30. Riden, ii, 127, 163, 244, 268, 331.
31. Withals 1584, sig. H8v.
32. Stubbes, i, 75; *OED*, s.n. maumet; Shakespeare, *King John*, III.iii.58.
33. Thomas Hariot, *A Briefe and True Report of the New Found Land of Virginia* (Frankfurt, 1590; S106427), plate viii.
34. William Turner, *The Seconde Part of William Turners Herball* (London, 1562; S102019), f. 46r.
35. *The Rates of the Custome House* (London, 1545; S100583), s.n. babyes; idem (London, 1582; S111657), s.n. puppets.
36. On what follows, see Forsyth and Egan, now the principal source for the subject. It includes an introduction and a catalogue of objects.
37. Hollyband 1573, 182; idem 1576, sig. D6v; Edmund Spenser, *The Shepheard's Calendar* (London, 1579; S111264), sig. E3v.
38. Forsyth and Egan, e.g. 29, 155.
39. Riden, ii, 317.
40. Helkiah Crooke, *Mikrokosmographia* (London, 1631; S107279), part ii, 4.
41. Thomas Blundeville, *A Newe Booke Containing the Arte of Ryding* (London, 1561; S103460), part ii, sig. D2v.
42. John Florio, *A Worlde of Wordes* (London, 1598; S102357), 443.
43. Orme 2001, 168.
44. E.g. Bodleian Library, MS Douce 276, f. 124v.
45. Shakespeare, *Twelfth Night*, I.iii.44.
46. Forsyth and Egan, 387–8.
47. *OED*, s.n. scopperil, spilcock, spilquern and whirlbone.
48. William Hawkins, *Apollo Shroving* (London, 1627; S106116), 5, 49, 51.
49. Gomme, passim.
50. *OED* s.n. handy-dandy; Florio, *A Worlde of Wordes*, 40.
51. Withals 1553, f. 68r; *OED*, s.n. pot, sub.3.
52. *OED*, s.n. cherry-pit, cherry-stone; Gomme, i, 66.
53. Thomas More, *The Complete Works*, vol. viii part 1, ed. L. A. Schuster and others (New Haven and London, 1973), 492.
54. *OED*, s.n. penny-prick.
55. Ibid., s.n. cob-nut; Gomme, i, 71–2.
56. Hollyband 1583, 129.
57. As reported in the nineteenth century (*OED*, s.n. cob-nut).
58. Ibid., s.n. ally (alley), marble, taw.
59. Jan Amos Comenius, *Orbis Sensualium Pictus* (London, 1659; R20487; repr. Menston, 1970), 276–7.
60. *OED*, s.n. check-stone.
61. *L'Histoire de Guillaume le Maréchal*, ed. P. Meyer, 3 vols, Société de l'Histoire de France (Paris, 1891–1901), i, lines 602–19; Gomme, i, 73.
62. Wager, sig. C4v.
63. *OED*, s.n. span-counter; Gomme, ii, 210.
64. *OED*, s.n. shove-board, shove-groat, shovel-board.
65. Shakespeare, *Henry IV Part II*, II.iv.188.
66. *OED*, s.n. merel.
67. Randle Cotgrave, *A Dictionarie of the French and English Tongues* (London, 1611; S107262), s.n. merelles; Gomme, i, 414–19.

68. Shakespeare, *A Midsummer Night's Dream*, II.i.98.
69. Eliot, part ii, 58; *OED* s.n. gresco, hazard, mumchance, passage. Hazard and passage are described in Charles Cotton, *The Compleat Gamester* (London, 1674; R23124), 167–73.
70. Horman, f. 280v.
71. *OED*, s.n. daly; *Promptorium Parvulorum*, 112.
72. Richard Huloet, *Abcedarium Anglo Latinum* (London, 1552; S117241), sig. K6v; *OED*, s.n. even, a. 12(d); odd 2(d).
73. *A New Enterlude for Chyldren to Playe, Named Jacke Jugler* (London, 1565; S109241), sig. A4r.
74. Chaucer, *Canterbury Tales*, VI (C) 463–9.
75. Withals 1574, f. 59r.
76. Horman, f. 282v; *OED* s.n. backgammon, tick-tack.
77. Elyot 1531, book i, chapter 26.
78. Strong, 112; *Manuscripts of the Duke of Rutland*, 371.
79. *OED* s.n. trump2; Cotton, *Compleat Gamester*, 114, on the similar game of 'ruff'.
80. Bellot, sigs E5v–7r.
81. Elyot 1531, book i, chapter 27.
82. *OED* s.n. loggat.
83. *OED*, s.n. mumble-the-peg.
84. Ibid., s.n. kayles, skayles, pin (section 8).
85. Ibid., s.n. closh.
86. Elyot 1531, book i, chapter 27; below, p. 92.
87. Woodfield, 81–159.
88. Hollyband 1583, 137.
89. *Tom Thumbe, His Life and Death* (London, 1630; S101741), sig. A3r–v.
90. Shirley, 182.
91. Bellot, sig. A6v.
92. *OED* s.n. spurn-point.
93. Shakespeare, *Henry V*, V.ii.139.
94. *OED* s.n. truss, sb (7), truss-a-fail.
95. Wager, sig. A4r.
96. Nelson, 27.
97. Withals 1553, f. 67v.
98. Castiglione, 42, 45, 97.
99. Michael Drayton and others, *Annalia Dubrensia* (London, 1636; S111583), sig. I2r.
100. On the subject, see Orme 1983.
101. Orme 2001, 141.
102. Oxford, Bodleian Library, MS Wood donat. 4, p. 384; Gomme, i, 231–8.
103. *OED*, s.n. base sb2, prisoners' bars, base; Shakespeare, *Cymbeline*, V.iii.19–20; Gomme, ii, 79–80.
104. *OED*, s.n. barley, barley-break; Gomme, i, 21–3.
105. Richard Huloet, *Huloet's Dictionarie*, ed. John Higgins (London, 1572; S119246), s.n. king-by-your-leave; Gomme, 1, 299.
106. *OED*, s.n. blind-man's-buff, hot cockles, king-by-your-leave.
107. Stow, i, 94.
108. Drayton, *Annalia Dubrensia*, sigs C2v, I2r.
109. Carew, ff. 75v–76v.
110. Withals 1584, sig. I5r, illustrated in Orme 2001, 331.
111. *OED*, s.n. stool-ball.
112. Ibid., s.n. trap-ball, knur (3).
113. Ibid., s.n. battledore (2).
114. Ibid., s.n. fives, tennis.
115. *Statutes of the Realm*, ii, 462. Gomme (i, 188) has this as a chasing game, but parliamentary legislation was more likely against games with equipment.
116. Gairdner, 292.

117. *Letters and Papers of John Shillingford, Mayor of Exeter 1447–50*, ed. Stuart A. Moore, Camden Society, new series 2 (1871), 101.
118. *OED* s.n. tennis (1).
119. Eliot 1593, part ii, 59–61.
120. Ibid.
121. Nichols, iii, 590.
122. Carew, ff. 73v–74r.
123. Ibid., ff. 74v–75v.
124. *OED* s.n. camp(1); Eamon Duffy, *The Voices of Morebath: reformation and rebellion in an English village* (New Haven and London, 2001), 138.
125. Elyot 1531, book i, chapter 27.
126. Mulcaster, 104.
127. Stubbes, 183.
128. Orme 2001, 182.
129. Carew, f. 124v.
130. *The Chronicle of Queen Jane*, ed. J. G. Nichols, Camden Society, old series 48 (1850), 67; *Calendar of State Papers Spanish, 1554* (London, 1949), 146.
131. On what follows, see Orme 2001, 184–9.
132. Breton, sig. C1r.
133. Mulcaster, 79; Orme 2001, 184, 186.
134. *OED*, s.n. jack-a-Lent; Breton, sig. D3v.
135. Orme 2001, 187.
136. Ibid., 187–8.
137. Elyot 1531, book i, chapters 16–18, 27; Ascham, 217; below, pp. 149–50.
138. Mulcaster, 51–105.
139. Below, pp. 147–8.
140. *Nice Wanton*, sig. A2r–v.
141. Hollyband 1576, 24; Stow, i, 95.
142. Nelson, 23–7.
143. Horman, ff. 277r–283v.
144. *The Merry Wives of Windsor*, IV.i.7–9; *July and Julian*, 22.
145. Leach, 270.
146. Maxwell-Lyte, 139–52.
147. Below, pp. 99, 106–7.
148. Whitford, sig. D4r.
149. Athene Reiss, *The Sunday Christ* (Oxford, BAR British Series 292, 2000).
150. John Hooper, *A Declaratyon of the Ten Holy Commaundementes* (London, 1550; S104197), f. 87v.
151. Stubbes, 137, 173–7, 183.
152. Orme 2021, 162, 164.
153. Below, p. 105.
154. *Statutes of the Realm*, ii, 462; iii, 25–6.
155. Ibid., ii, 569.
156. Ibid., ii, 462.
157. Ibid, iii, 25–6.
158. Elyot 1531, book i, chapter 27.
159. Ascham, vii–119.
160. Nelson, 23; Withals 1553, f. 67r.
161. *LPFD*, iii part i, 499–504,
162. *Statutes of the Realm*, iii, 837–41.
163. Ascham, 62.
164. *Statutes of the Realm*, iv, 548–9.
165. Fit John, sig. F4v.
166. Carew, ff. 72r–73v.

4 RELIGION

1. Above, pp. 6–7, 11.
2. Orme 2021, 318–20.
3. Hill, pp. xiii–xiv.
4. Ibid.
5. Orme 2021, 320–1.
6. Brightman, ii, 776–9, 790–1.
7. Ibid., ii, 790–1, 798–9.
8. Ibid., ii, 778–9.
9. Ibid., ii, 798–9.
10. Ibid., ii, 776–99.
11. Orme 2021, 180–2; Frere and Kennedy, ii, 6–8.
12. Orme 2001, 123.
13. Ibid., 214–15.
14. A. Hamilton Thompson, *Visitations in the Diocese of Lincoln, 1517–1531*, vol. i, Lincoln Record Society, 33 (1940), 23, 26, 29, 113.
15. Above, pp. 15, 57.
16. Nicholas Orme, *The History of England's Cathedrals* (Exeter, 2017), 170.
17. On adult non-attendance at church, see Orme 2021, 157–66.
18. Ibid., 76–9.
19. Below, pp. 206–8.
20. Orme 2021, 233–47.
21. *The Early English Carols*, ed. Richard Leighton Greene, 2nd edn (Oxford, 1977), 6.
22. Orme 2021, 259–60.
23. Ibid., 274–5.
24. Ibid., 289–94; Orme 2013, 93, 169–70.
25. Orme 2001 188–9, 232–3; Orme 2021, 257–8.
26. Orme 2021, 142, 263.
27. *Report on the Manuscripts of Lord Middleton*, 400, 404, 406.
28. *Manuscripts of the Duke of Rutland*, iv, 373, 408.
29. *Stratton Churchwardens' Accounts, 1512–1578*, ed. Joanna Mattingly, Devon and Cornwall Record Society, new series 60 (2018), 130–1, 141, 183, 185.
30. *Tudor Royal Proclamations*, ed. Paul L. Hughes and James F. Larkin, 3 vols (New Haven and London, 1984–9), i, 301–2; A. G. Dickens, *Reformation Studies* (London, 1982), 295–6.
31. Polydore Vergil, *Beginnings and Discoveries: Polydore Vergil's* De Inventoribus Rerum, trans. Beno Weiss and Louis C. Pérez (Nieuwkoop, 1997), 45
32. Thomas Deloney, *The Pleasant History of John Winchcomb* (London, 1619; S105311), sig. D3v. There is a picture of the boys in secular dress, holding the bride's hands, on the title page of Samuel Rowlands, *The Bride* (London, 1617; S2862). I am grateful to Tamsin Lewis for both these references.
33. Brightman, ii, 796–9.
34. *Bishop Still's Visitation 1594*, ed. Derek Shorrocks, Somerset Record Society, 84 (1998), 39, 41, 44–5, 63, 79–80.
35. On this subject, see I. M. Green, *The Christian's ABC: catechisms and catechizing in England, c. 1530–1740* (Oxford, 1996).
36. Jean Calvin, *The Catechisme or Maner to Teach Children* (London, 1560; S2539).
37. Nowell 1570.
38. *Statutes of the Realm*, iv, part i, 356–7.
39. Brightman, ii, 744–5; Rhodes, sig. A3v.
40. *Statutes of the Realm*, iv, part i, 657, 841.
41. Orme 2021, 183–4.
42. Orme 1989, 185.

43. Ellis, *Original Letters*, 3rd series, i, 335–7, 343–5.

44. Vives, book i, chapter 5.

45. W. A. Pantin, 'Instructions for a Devout and Literate Layman', in *Medieval Learning and Literature*, ed. J. J. Alexander and M. T. Gibson (Oxford, 1976), 398–400.

46. Whitford, sig. D4v.

47. Below, p. 126.

48. Orme 2021, 152.

49. On what follows, see Tara Hambling, *Decorating the 'Godly' Household: religious art in post-Reformation Britain* (New Haven and London, 2010), 93–120, 121–217.

50. Shakespeare, *Henry IV Part II*, II.i.142–3; *Merry Wives of Windsor*, IV.v.6–7.

51. Hamling, *Decorating the 'Godly' Household*, 98.

52. Pollock 1993, 28.

53. Ibid., 34.

54. *The Primer in English and Latin* (London, 1545; S108613).

55. 'I could make a wench [i.e. girl] so virtuous, she should say grace to every bit of meat' (Ben Jonson, [*The*] *Case is Alterd* (London, 1609, but written *c.* 1597; S121512), II.iii.3–8).

56. *The Primer* (London, 1545; S108613), sig. *6r–v; *The Primer Set Furth at Large* (London, 1559; S93628), sigs A1v–2v; *A Primer or Booke of Private Prayer* (London, 1568; S102106), sigs A7r–B2r.

57. Platter, 158.

58. *A Primer or Booke of Private Prayer*, sig. B2r; Hollyband 1576, sigs O3v–5r.

59. Hollyband 1573, 86–94, 136.

60. John A. F. Thomson, *The Later Lollards 1414–1520* (London, 1965), 89, 116.

61. *The Complete Works of St. Thomas More*, ed. J. B. Trapp, vol. ix (New Haven and London, 1979), 117–18.

62. Hall, *The Vnion of . . . Lancaster and Yorke*, 841; Foxe, v, 441–2.

63. Machyn, 91; Foxe, vii, 192–4.

64. On what follows, see Bossy, especially 121–65, and Underwood, especially 12–99.

65. *Statutes of the Realm*, iv, 356–7.

66. *The Christian Doctrine in Manner of a Dialogue* (London, 1597; S106750); Underwood, 52–3.

67. Underwood, 15.

68. Ibid., 12–16.

69. Ibid., 93–7; Beales, 40–7, 65–7.

70. *Statutes of the Realm*, iv, 657–8, 841.

71. Ibid., iv, 1075–82.

72. Underwood, 93–4.

73. On Catholic education in general under Elizabeth I, see Beales, 70–87.

74. Orme 2001, 124.

75. Ibid., 124–5.

76. Ibid., 124–6.

77. *The Great Chronicle of London*, ed. A. H. Thomas and I. D. Thornley (London, 1938, repr. Gloucester 1983), 294.

78. Orme 2021, 341–4.

79. Oxford, Lincoln College Archives, Computus 1, Calc. 6, which I owe to Professor R. N. Swanson.

80. Orme 2021, 344

81. For a recent summary of the case, see G. W. Bernard, *The Late Medieval English Church* (New Haven and London, 2012), 1–16.

82. Bray, 34–5.

83. *Later Writings of John Hooper*, ed. Charles Nevinson, Parker Society, 16 (1852), 31.

84. William Hubbock, *An Apologie of Infants in a Sermon* (London, 1595; S104267), 9, 23, 29.

85. William Hill, *The Infancie of the Soule* (London, 1605; S115206), sigs E4v–F1r.
86. See, for example, Machyn, 32, 39, 211, 255, 280.
87. Riden, ii, 367.
88. On this subject, see Brian and Moira Gittos, 'The English Medieval Churchyard: what did it really look like?', in *Monuments and Monumentality across Medieval and Early Modern Europe*, ed. Michael A. Penman (Donington, 2013), 31–44.
89. On the subject of children on brasses, see Page-Phillips, passim, and Orme 2020b, 77–86.
90. Below, pp. 23, 30.
91. *The Monumental Brasses of Essex*, ed. William Lack, H. Martin Stuchfield, and Philip Whittemore, 2 parts (London, 2003), i, 410.
92. *The Monumental Brasses of Buckinghamshire*, ed. William Lack, H. Martin Stuchfield, and Philip Whittemore (London, 1994), 251–2.
93. On this subject, see J. Wilson, 360–79 at 360–1, 367, and Phillippy, 17–38.
94. Orme 2021, 165.

5 SCHOOL

1. Pound, 17.
2. Bray, 346–7.
3. Clement, 9.
4. Ascham, 19.
5. Shakespeare, *2 Henry VI*, IV.ii.81–104.
6. Pound, 30, 60, 78.
7. Orme 2006, 166–7.
8. Clement, 7.
9. Herbert, 36.
10. Orme 2006, 57.
11. *OED*, s.n. battledore sb. (3), horn-book.
12. Orme 2001, 246–51.
13. Kempe, sig. F2r.
14. Orme 2001, 260–1; Pierre Du Ploiche, *A Treatise in English and Frenche right necessary and proffitable for al young children* (London, 1551; S116132), sig. L2r.
15. Thomas Morley, *A Plaine and Easie Introduction to Practicall Musicke* (London, 1597; S111843), 36.
16. Frere and Kennedy, ii, 6–8.
17. Anthony Wood, *The Life and Times*, ed. Andrew Clark, vol. i, Oxford Historical Society, 19 (1891), 46.
18. J. H. Lupton, *A Life of John Colet*, 2nd edn (London, 1909), 285–91.
19. Shakespeare, *2 Henry VI*, IV.ii.81–8.
20. Nicholas Orme, 'The Foundation of Rolleston School, Staffordshire', *Staffordshire Historical Society Transactions* (2022), 37–46.
21. Orme 2006, 68–73.
22. Humfrey Baker, *Such as Are Desirous . . . to Learne* (London, 1590; S3054).
23. Thomas Ingelend, *A Pretie and Mery New Enterlude Called the Disobedient Child* (London, 1570; S107422), sig. C2r–v.
24. Christopher Marlowe, *Doctor Faustus*, ed. John D. Jump (London, 1968), 44.
25. *The Lamentable Tragedie of Locrine* (London, 1595; S106301), sigs B4r–v, C4v–D1r.
26. Long gowns were still proper for schoolboys in 1584 (Withals 1584, f. K1v).
27. *LPFD*, ii, part i, 499; Hollyband 1576, sig. B7v.
28. Shirley, 183.
29. As late as the *Maner of Keping a Courte Baron* (London, 1552; S4222), sig. A3r.

30. 'Extracts from Proceedings of the Committee', *Norfolk Archaeology*, 4 (1895), 342–4.
31. Hooker, 3–11.
32. Orme 2006, 143–4.
33. Shakespeare, *Merry Wives of Windsor*, IV.i.5; *July and Julian*, 6.
34. Nelson, 40.
35. Hollyband 1576, sigs B8v, C3v.
36. Orme 2006, 144–5.
37. *July and Julian*, 9.
38. Hollyband 1576, sig. B8v. On punishment up to the early sixteenth century, see Parsons, passim.
39. Aubrey, 277–81.
40. Tusser, 203.
41. Parsons, 157–61.
42. Hollyband 1576, sig. C2v.
43. *July and Julian*, 9.
44. Orme 2001, 154–7.
45. Orme 1998, 76.
46. Willis, 97–9. For his identity, see Menna Prestwich, *Cranfield: politics and profits under the early Stuarts* (Oxford, 1966), 622 (index of entries).
47. Shakespeare, *Henry IV Part II*, IV.ii.104–5.
48. Segar, sigs A7v–8r.
49. Above, p. 78.
50. On the practice, see Thomas 1976, 21–30.
51. Shakespeare, *The Merry Wives of Windsor*, IV.i.11–72.
52. Willis, 101–3.
53. Nelson, 6, 8, 23, 26.
54. Orme 2013.
55. On this subject, see Orme 1984, 81–111.
56. Chaucer, *Canterbury Tales*, I (A) 79–100.
57. S 105376; STC 7635–7642.
58. Elyot 1531, book i, chapters 9–15.
59. The cultural studies are outlined in Elyot 1531, book i, chapters 7–8, 19–25, and the physical in book i, chapters 16–18, 26–7. A source was Plutarch (Elyot 1530, sig. D3r).
60. On dancing, see also below, pp. 217–18.
61. Below, p. 81; Orme 1983.
62. Below, pp. 92–4.
63. Castiglione, 35–77, 97–106.
64. Orme 1984, 22.
65. Ibid., 23, 155.
66. *ODNB*, Giles Duwes, article by Gordon Kipling.
67. Gallagher, passim.
68. On what follows, see Orme 1984, 24, 103, 155.
69. Nicholas Orme, 'John Holt (d. 1504), Tudor Grammarian', *The Library*, 6th series, 18 (1996), 283–305.
70. Above, pp. 40–1. On Fitzroy see *ODNB*, Henry Fitzroy, article by Beverley A. Murphy, and on his education in particular, Murphy, 85–109, 142–3.
71. *ODNB*, John Palsgrave, article by Gabriele Stein.
72. *ODNB*, Richard Cox, article by Felicity Heal.
73. Ibid., John Cheke, article by Allan Bryson.
74. Ibid., Jean Belmaine, article by Gordon Kipling.
75. Leland, v, 361–2.
76. Orme 2020b, 85–6.

77. *Lisle Letters*, iv, 498.
78. Elyot 1531, book i, chapter 13, based on Plutarch (Elyot 1530, sig. B4v).
79. Joseph Hall, *Virgidemiarum* (London, 1598; S103711), 38.
80. Below, pp. 200–1.
81. George Cavendish, *The Life and Death of Cardinal Wolsey*, ed. R. S. Sylvester, EETS, os, 243 (1959), 18–21, 29–30.
82. Orme 1984, 58; Ascham, 97.
83. Hurstfield, 119, 127.
84. Orme 1984, 82.
85. Below, p. 204.
86. On what follows, see *LPFD*, iv (ii), 1989, 2090–1, 2134; vi, 99, 154; viii, 233.
87. On what follows, see *Report on the Manuscripts of Lord Middleton*, 399–414.
88. Compare James Basset, learning to dance in 1537 (*Lisle Letters*, iv, 470).
89. Caxton, passim; Orme 1984, 107–9.
90. S105250, also published in Foster Watson, *Vives and the Renascence Education of Women* (London, 1912).
91. STC 24856–62.
92. S109306.
93. S366.
94. Caxton, 13, 122.
95. Vives, book i, chapter 4.
96. Ibid., book i, chapters 6–11.
97. Ibid., book i, chapters 3, 5.
98. On the history of the school, see G. A. T. Allan and J. E. Morpurgo, *Christ's Hospital* (London, 1984).
99. Gardiner, 198–9.
100. *ODNB*, Margaret Roper, article by Margaret Bowker; Anne Parr, Katherine Parr, articles by Susan James.
101. Orme 1984, 65. The disappearance of nunneries as places of education was regretted even by the Reformer Thomas Becon (Gardiner, 194–6).
102. *ODNB*, Agnes Howard, article by Catharine Davies.
103. *Report on the Manuscripts of Lord Middleton*, 409; Shirley, 182.
104. Gallagher, 115–25.
105. *The English Works of John Fisher*, ed. J. E. B. Mayor, part i, EETS, es 27 (1876), 292.
106. *Calendar of State Papers Spanish*, vol. i: *1485–1509* (London, 1862), 156.
107. *ODNB*, Mary queen of France, article by David Loades.
108. Emden 1974, 204.
109. Thomas Linacre, *Rudimenta Grammatices* (London, *c.* 1525; S104890).
110. *ODNB*, Juan Luis Vives, article by Charles Fantazzi.
111. Ibid., Elizabeth I, article by Patrick Collinson.
112. Ibid., Margaret Roper, article by Margaret Bowker.
113. Ibid., Anne Parr, Katherine Parr, articles by Susan James.
114. Ibid., Jane Grey, article by Alison Plowden.
115. Ibid., Jane Seymour, article by Jane Stevenson.
116. Harrison, 228.
117. *ODNB*, Margaret Roper, article by Margaret Bowker.
118. Gardiner, 178–9.
119. *Letters of John Calvin*, ed. Jules Bonnet, 2 vols (Edinburgh and London, 1855–7), ii, no. 245.
120. *ODNB*, Mary Howard, article by Stephanie Hodgson-Wright
121. *Lisle Letters*, i, 32.
122. Latymer, 63.
123. Pollock 1993, 23, 28–9, 34.

124. *The Manuscripts of the Duke of Rutland*, i, 250, 264.
125. *Excerpta Historica*, [ed. Samuel Bentley] (London, 1831), 126, 133.
126. Gairdner, 288–9.
127. *Report on the Manuscripts of Lord Middleton*, 407.
128. Riden, ii, 147, 278, 282.
129. Pollock 1993, 35. On music for girls, see also Erondelle, sig. F3v.
130. Vives, book i, chapter 13.
131. Elyot 1531, book i, chapter 21.
132. Orme 1984, 174; *Report on the Manuscripts of Lord Middleton*, 408.
133. *Report on the Manuscripts of Lord Middleton*, 406–8.
134. Vives, book i, chapter 3.
135. Harrison, 228.
136. Pollock 1993, 25.
137. See, for example, Leland, iv, 267.
138. *Report on the Manuscripts of Lord Middleton*, 406.
139. Erondelle, sig. N4v.
140. Leland, iv, 278.
141. Elyot 1531, book i, chapter 18.
142. Ascham, 201.
143. Nichols, iii, 553; iv, 130. In 1601 Anthony Munday imagined Queen Eleanor of Aquitaine shooting six fallow deer from a vantage point (*The Death of Robert, Earl of Huntington* (London, 1601; S110066), I.i).

6 SPEECH, SONG, AND STORIES

1. Batman, f. 74r.
2. Elyot 1531, book i, chapter 4, based on Plutarch (Elyot 1530, sig. B3r).
3. *OED* s.n. words mentioned, also pig-widgin.
4. Elyot 1531, book i, chapter 4.
5. Nelson, 12.
6. Ascham, 210–11.
7. *The Vulgaria of John Stanbridge and . . . Robert Whittinton*, ed. Beatrice White, EETS, os 187 (1932), 16–22.
8. Nelson, 42.
9. On this subject, see Orme 2001, 126–54, and idem 2011, 25–38.
10. *ODNB*, William Wager, article by Peter Happé.
11. Wager, sig. A3r.
12. Ibid.
13. Opie 1997a, 496–8.
14. *The Complete Poems of John Skelton Laureate*, ed. Philip Henderson, 4th edn (London and New York, 1964), 310, 389.
15. *The Most Cruell and Bloody Murther Committed by an Inkeepers Wife Called Annis Dell* (London, 1606; S113484).
16. Opie 1997a, 149–50.
17. Shakespeare, *King Lear*, III.iv.142–3, 186–8; vi.26, 42–5.
18. Opie 1997a, 113–15.
19. *King Lear*, III.iv.187–8.
20. R. H. Robbins, *Secular Lyrics of the XIVth and XVth Centuries*, 2nd edn (Oxford, 1955), 43–5.
21. Thomas Ravenscroft, *Deuteromelia* (London, 1609; S105060), 20.
22. Ibid., 12.
23. Thomas Ravenscroft, *Pammelia: Musicks Miscellanie* (London, 1609; S110598), 25.
24. Thomas Ravenscroft, *Melismata: Musical Phansies* (London, 1611; S105061), 21.
25. Wager, sig. A3v.

26. John Stevens, *Music at the Court of Henry VIII*, 2nd edn (Musica Britannica, 18; London, 1962), 50–1.
27. Ravenscroft, *Melesmata*, 6.
28. Orme 2013, 133–47.
29. Wager, sig. A3r.
30. *The Booke of Meery Riddles* (London, 1629; S104643); *A Booke of Merrie Riddles* (London, 1631; S114466).
31. *Booke of Meery Riddles* (1629), sig A3r.
32. On medieval English riddles, see Andrew Galloway, 'The Rhetoric of Riddling in Late-Medieval England', *Speculum*, 70 (1995), 68–105, and Orme 2013, 133–47.
33. *Booke of Meery Riddles* (1629), sig A3r
34. Ibid., sig. B5v.
35. *Booke of Merrie Riddles* (1631), sigs B1v–2r.
36. Ibid., sig. A8v; Opie 1997a, 246.
37. Orme 2013, 249
38. Wager, sig. A3r.
39. *Early Tudor Songs and Carols*, ed. John Stevens (Musica Britannica, 26; London, 1975), 27.
40. Child, i, 390–9.
41. Ravenscroft, *Pammelia*, sig. D2r.
42. Ravenscroft, *Deuteromelia*, sigs D4v–E1r.
43. *Clifford Letters of the Sixteenth Century*, ed. A. G. Dickens, Surtees Society, 172 (1957), 132, 137–8.
44. Ibid., 116.
45. Shakespeare, *The Winter's Tale*, II.i.21–32.
46. George Peele, *The Old Wiues Tale* (London, 1595; S110404), sig. B1r.
47. Scot, 152–3.
48. Shakespeare, *The Merry Wives of Windsor*, IV.iv.28–31 (Q version).
49. Above, p. 80.
50. Orme 1989, 185.
51. Ellis, *Original Letters*, series 3, i, 343–5.
52. Below, p. 210.
53. Willis, 110–13.
54. Sneyd, 23.
55. Above, p. 111.
56. On this subject, see Orme 2001, 276–8, and Hardman 2004.
57. Above, pp. 27–8.
58. Hill, pp. xxxiv–lix.
59. On these texts, see Orme 2011, 12–13, 25–38.
60. Caxton, 3.
61. William Caxton, *Caxton's Blaunchardyn and Eglantine*, ed. Leon Kellner, EETS, es 58 (1890), 1.
62. F. Madan, 'The Daily Ledger of John Dorne', in *Collectanea, First Series*, ed. C. R. L. Fletcher, Oxford Historical Society, 5 (1885), 79, 82, 149.
63. The romance of *The Four Sons of Aymon*, bound in parchment, cost 1s. 8d. (ibid., 115).
64. *The Friar and the Boy* (London, 1510–13; S119434); modernised text in Orme 2011, 72–83.
65. *Dobsons Drie Bobbes* (London, 1607; S113611); Avril S. O'Brien, '*Dobsons Drie Bobbes*: a significant contribution to the development of prose fiction', *Studies in English Literature 1500–1900*, 12 (1972), 55–70. I am grateful to Robert Kirkpatrick for directing me to this source.
66. Child, i, 2 57–74.
67. Ibid., ii, 33–48; modernised text in Orme 2011, 64–72.

68. Earliest complete printed text in *The Hystory of the Two Valyaunte Brethren Valentyne and Orson* (London, 1555; S101305).
69. *The History of Guy of Warwick* (London, *c.* 1500; S118960).
70. Orme 2001, 298–302.
71. *Syr Bevis of Hampton* (London, 1503; S111743).
72. *The Tale of Gamelyn*, ed. W. W. Skeat (Oxford, 1893).
73. Edited in *Rymes of Robyn Hode: an introduction to the English outlaw*, ed. R. B. Dobson and J. Taylor (London, 1976), 258–73.
74. On the early Robin Hood literature, see ibid., 1–230.
75. Below, pp. 213–14.
76. Above, pp. 92–3.
77. *Valentine and Orson* (London, 1565; S101305), chapter 118.
78. *Guy of Warwick* (London, 1565; S124774).
79. *Syr Bevis of Hampton* (London, 1585; S111932).
80. *A Merry Iest of Robin Hood* (London, 1590; S116951).
81. *Caxton's Book of Courtesy*, ed. F. J. Furnivall, EETS, es 3 (1868), 32–40.
82. *The Complete English Poems of John Skelton*, ed. John Scattergood (Harmondsworth, 1983), 87–92.
83. *The Romance of William of Palerne*, ed. W. W. Skeat, EETS, es 1 (1867), p. xxiii.
84. Above, p. 150.
85. William Tyndale, *The Obedience of a Christian Man* (Antwerp, 1528; S104871), f. 20r.
86. Vives 1529, sig. E4r–v.
87. Miles Coverdale, *Goostly Psalmes and Spirituall Songes* (London, *c.* 1535; S121127), f. 3r–v.
88. Ascham, pp. xiv–xv; see also ibid., 230–1.
89. Wolfgang Capito, *The True Beliefe in Christ and his Sacramentes* (London, 1550; S118691), sig. A2v.
90. Rhodes, sigs A3v–A4r.
91. Stubbes, i, 140–6.
92. Thomas Nashe, *The Anatomie of Absurditie* (London, 1589; S110083), sigs A2r, C1r–v.
93. Shakespeare, *King Lear*, III.iv.142–3; *Henry VIII*, I.i.35–8.
94. Listed in Dobson and Taylor, *Rymes of Robyn Hood*, 13 note 2.
95. Above, p. 110.
96. Orme 2001, 298–302.
97. Ronald S. Crane, 'The Reading of an Elizabethan Youth', *Modern Philology*, 11 (1913–14), 269–71; *ODNB*, Robert Ashley, article by John Ferris.
98. *Huon of Bordeaux* (London, 1601; S104310), preface.
99. On this subject, see Orme 2006, 44–6.
100. Clement, sig. A5r; John Carpenter, *Contemplations for the Institution of Children in the Christian Religion* (London, 1601; S114418).

7 GROWING UP

1. On this subject, see Nicholas Orme, 'Perceptions of Children in Medieval England', in *Childhood in History: perceptions of children in the ancient and medieval worlds*, ed. Reider Aasgaard, Cornelia Horn, and Oana Maria Cojocaru (London and New York, 2018), 318–33.
2. Orme 2021, 52; J. V. Bullard, *Constitutions and Canons Ecclesiastical 1604* (London, 1934), 38.
3. Above, p. 31.
4. *July and Julian*, 6.
5. Brightman, ii, 643.
6. Francis Bacon, *The Essayes or Counsels, Civill and Morall* (London, 1625; S100362), chapter 7.

7. Smith, 106–7.
8. Houlbrooke 1984, 41–3. On the plight of younger sons, see Thirsk.
9. T. Wilson, 24.
10. Neville Williams, *Thomas Howard, Fourth Duke of Norfolk* (London, 1964), 239.
11. *Wentworth Papers 1597–1628*, ed. J. C. Cooper, Royal Historical Society, Camden 4th series 12 (1973), 13, 54–5.
12. Carey, 6, 26, 32.
13. Ben-Amos, 40–5; Hindle, 25, 44, 210.
14. Breton, sig. E3r.
15. Fit John, sig. B1v.
16. Riden, ii, 34–5, 37–8, 42, 55, 135, 155, 195; Ben-Amos, 69–83.
17. Pound, 17 and passim.
18. Above, p. 38.
19. Above, p. 123.
20. T. Wilson, 20.
21. Above, pp. 36–8. Hindle, 194–7.
22. Sneyd, 24–5.
23. Phythian-Adams, 229; Ben-Amos, 39; Wrigley and others, 210.
24. *The Letter-Book of Henry Lord Stafford (1501–63)*, ed. Deborah Youngs, Collections for a History of Staffordshire, 4th series 25 (2012), 16–17.
25. On servants in Tudor England, see particularly Phythian-Adams, 204–20; Kussmaul, passim; and Goldberg 158–202.
26. Kussmaul, 34, 144.
27. Phythian-Adams, 204.
28. Goldberg, 189–202.
29. Ibid., 202.
30. Ibid., 177.
31. *St Paul's: the cathedral church of London*, ed. Derek Keene et al. (New Haven and London, 2004), 53; Shakespeare, *Henry IV Part II*, I.ii.52.
32. E.g. in Henry Medwall, *Fulgens and Lucrece*, and Thomas Dekker, *The Shoemaker's Holiday*; admittedly, a mistress talking confidentially to a maid was a useful device.
33. Goldberg, 173–4; *Statutes of the Realm*, iv, 415; Smith, 114.
34. E.g. Harrison, 119.
35. Above, pp. 140–1.
36. Myers, passim.
37. Ibid., 126–7.
38. Furnivall 1869, 1–9.
39. *ODNB*, Clement Adams, article by R. C. D. Baldwin.
40. Myers, 136–7.
41. Ibid., 118–96 passim, 228.
42. Ibid., 137.
43. On what follows, see Percy, 43, 308, 326.
44. Hooker, 3–11.
45. Fit John, sig. B2r–v. On discharged servants, see also above, pp. 167–8.
46. Harrison, 119.
47. G. R. Batho, 'The Household Accounts of Henry Percy Ninth Earl of Northumberland (1564–1632)', University of London, MA thesis (1953), 442–9.
48. Richard Brathwait, *Some Rules and Orders for the Government of the House of an Earle* (London, 1821), 3–4, 47.
49. *The Maner of Keping a Courte Baron* (London, 1552; S4222), sig. A3r.
50. *The Parliament Rolls of Medieval England*, ed. C. Given-Wilson and others, 16 vols (Woodbridge, 2005), parliament of September 1388, section 1.
51. Ibid., parliament of 1406, section 141.
52. *Statutes of the Realm*, iii, 414–22.

53. Ben-Amos, 135–45.
54. Smith, 113–15; Ben-Amos, 84–108. There is a good description of a London apprentice's life in 1577 in Fit John, sigs D3v, F4r–v, G1r.
55. Daly, 2–3.
56. For water carrying in London, see Fit John, sig. C3r, and Thomas Deloney, *The Gentle Craft* (London, 1637; S118250), sig. F3v.
57. *Statutes of the Realm*, iii, 414–22.
58. Ibid., iii, 321.
59. Ibid., iii, 654.
60. Orme 2017, 28, 45–6.
61. Bowers, 177–222.
62. Orme 2017, 80–2.
63. *Calendar of the Manuscripts of the Dean and Chapter of Wells*, 2 vols, Historical Manuscripts Commission (London, 1907–14), ii, 132, 182, 219–20.
64. Thomas Tusser, *Five Hundreth Points of Good Husbandry* (London, 1573), part ii, 27–32.
65. Whythorne, 10–18.
66. Eton College, Manchester collegiate church, Southwell Minster, and Winchester College.
67. Frere and Kennedy, iii, 12–13.
68. Chambers, ii, 17, 334.
69. *Manuscripts of the Dean and Chapter of Wells*, ii, 314.
70. Samuel Rowlands, *Tis Merrie when Gossips Meete* (London, 1612; S119875), sigs C2r, C3r.
71. Breton, sig. D1r.
72. Shakespeare, *The Taming of the Shrew*, II.i.98–159, III.i.1–79.
73. On what follows, see Orme 2020a, 62–76 at 71–6.
74. William Roper, *The Lyfe of Sir Thomas Moore, Knighte*, ed. E. V. Hitchcock, EETS, os 197 (1935), 5.
75. Chambers, ii, 63, 70–5.
76. *Liber Famelicus of Sir James Whitelocke*, ed. John Bruce, Camden Society, old series 70 (1858), 12.
77. A good deal has written about the boys' companies. The founding work was Chambers, ii, 12–76; more recently, see Gair 1982; Busse 2006, with bibliography on p. 98; and Ackroyd 2017.
78. Shakespeare, *Hamlet*, II.ii.336–57.
79. Chambers, ii, 43–5; Ackroyd 2017, 1–4.
80. Busse, 75–7.
81. Chambers, ii, 153–4.
82. Ben-Amos, 10–38, 191–200.
83. On these groups, see Orme 2021, 153–5
84. On the plays, see David Wiles, *The Early Plays of Robin Hood* (Cambridge, 1981) and Hutton, 1996, 270–4; for examples, see R. B. Dobson and J. Taylor, *Rymes of Robyn Hood* (London, 1976), 203–19.
85. Hutton, 1996, 273–4.
86. On this subject, see Griffiths, passim.
87. E.g. *Two Tudor Interludes: Youth and Hickscorner*, ed. Ian Lancashire (Manchester and Baltimore, 1980); *The Famous Victories of Henry the Fifth, 1598* (Malone Society reprints, 171 (2007)).
88. Dekker, *The Shoemaker's Holiday*, V.ii.35; compare Griffiths, 161–9.
89. Aubrey, 293. On parish rivalry before the Reformation, see also Orme 2021, 295.
90. On this subject see Phillips, 2, and John Walter, 'Faces in the Crowd: Gender and age in the early modern English crowd', in Berry and Foyster, 96–125 at 109.
91. Hall, 568.

92. *Trevelyan Papers, Part II: A.D.1446–1643*, ed. J. Payne Collier, Camden Society, old series 84 (1863), 101.
93. Hall, 586–91.
94. William Shakespeare and Others, *Collaborative Plays*, ed. Jonathan Bate and others (London, 2013), 350–3.
95. Orme 2001, 321–5.
96. *Statutes of the Realm*, iii, 242–3; iv, 448–9, 593.
97. Above, p. 113.
98. Pollock 1993, 28.
99. Machyn, 97–8, 164, 266.
100. Charles Wriothesley, *A Chronicle of England during the Reigns of the Tudors*, ed. W. D. Hamilton, vol. i, Camden Society, new series 11 (1875), 73.
101. Machyn, 280.
102. On dancing in Tudor England, see Ward and Howard and, albeit with a focus of France, McGowan, especially 95–101, with a good bibliography, 299–316.
103. 'The Maner of Dancynge of Bace Dances', translated by Robert Coplande, subjoined to Alexander Barclay, *The Introductory to Wryte and to Pronounce Frenche* (London, 1521; S110897).
104. Elyot 1531, book i, chapter 21.
105. Shakespeare, *Twelfth Night*, I.iii.117–27.
106. *Manuscripts of the Duke of Rutland*, iv, 281, 382; for girls, see Erondelle, sig. F3v.
107. *Calendar of Patent Rolls, 1572–5* (London, Public Record Office, 1974), 258.
108. Appendix by Sir George Buck to John Stow, *The Annales or a Generall Chronicle of England* (London, 1615; S117596), 986.
109. McGowan, 192, 194–5.
110. Agnes Strickland, *Lives of the Queens of England*, 12 vols in 6 (Philadelphia, 1857), iv, 129.
111. Stow, i, 94–5.
112. E.g. G. R. Owst, *Literature and Pulpit in Medieval England*, 2nd edn (Oxford, 1966), 383–4, 393–5.
113. Above, p. 157.
114. Information gathered from Thomas Lovell, *A Dialogue between Custom and Veritie Concerning the Use and Abuse of Dauncing and Minstrelsie* (London, 1581; S109641), and Christopher Fetherston, *A Dialogue against Light, Lewde, and Lascivious Dauncing* (London, 1582; S112556).
115. Ingram 2017, 15.
116. Furnivall 1897, passim.
117. Ibid., 25–8.
118. Above, p. 31.
119. Hurstfield, 130.
120. Bray, 248–9.
121. Stockwood, title page, sig. A6r.
122. Orme 2021, 359–60.
123. Wall, pp. xxv–viii.
124. *Statutes of the Realm*, iv, 610.
125. Above, p. 39.
126. *Certain Sermons* [*The Book of Homilies*] (London, 1562; S 124871), sig. T4r.
127. Ingram 1987, 225–37; Ben-Amos, 200–5; Ingram 2017, 98.
128. *The Plumpton Letters and Papers*, ed. Joan Kirby, Royal Historical Society, Camden 5th series 8 (1996), 103.
129. Ingram 2017, 286, 299–301.
130. Ibid., 33.
131. Cogan, 247.

132. E.g. John Mirk, *Instructions for Parish Priests*, ed. Gillis Kristensson, Lund Studies in English 49 (Lund, 1974), lines 223–5; *Selections from English Wycliffite Writings*, ed. Anne Hudson (Cambridge, 1978), 25 lines 27–8, 152.
133. *Statutes of the Realm*, iii, 441, 655, 725, 749; iv, 72, 447.
134. Ingram 2017, 34–8. Those executed included Walter Lord Hungerford, 1540 (*ODNB*, article by D. J. Ashton), and Humfrey Stafford, 1607 (*The Arraignment . . . of Humfrey Stafford* (London, 1607)).
135. Harrison, 119.
136. Stow, ii, 54–5.
137. Ingram 2017, 146–72.
138. Griffiths, 220.
139. Machyn, 104; Griffiths, 213–18.
140. Griffiths, 151.

8 REFLECTIONS

1. On this issue, see Orme 2001, 3–6.
2. Batman, ff. 72v–73r.

BIBLIOGRAPHY

This list does not include some works cited only once, which will be found in the notes.

Ackroyd, Julie. *Child Actors on the London Stage circa 1600: their education, recruitment and theatrical success* (Eastbourne, 2017).

Amussen, Susan Dwyer. *An Ordered Society: gender and class in early modern England* (New York, 1988).

An ABC for Children (London, c. 1570; S126832).

Ascham, Roger. *English Works*, ed. William Aldis Wright (Cambridge, 1904, repr. 1970).

Aubrey, John. *Brief Lives and other Selected Writings*, ed. Anthony Powell (London, 1949).

Barclay, Alexander. *The Eclogues of Alexander Barclay*, ed. Beatrice White, EETS, os 175 (1928).

[Batman, Stephen.] *Batman vppon Bartholome his Booke* De Proprietatibus Rerum (London, 1582; S106624).

Beales, A. C. F. *Education under Penalty: English Catholic education from the Reformation to the fall of James II 1547–1689* (London, 1963).

Bellot, Jacques. *Familiar Dialogues for the Instruction of Them that Be Desirous to Learne to Speake English* (London, 1586; S114666).

Ben-Amos, Ilana Krausman. *Adolescence and Youth in Early Modern England* (New Haven and London, 1994).

Berry, Helen, and Foyster, Elizabeth (eds). *The Family in Early Modern England* (Cambridge, 2009).

Billington, Josephine. *Infanticide in Tudor and Stuart England* (Amsterdam, 2019).

Bossy, John. *The English Catholic Community 1570–1850* (London, 1975).

Bowers, Roger. 'The Almonry Schools of the English Monasteries, *c.*1265–1540', in *Monasteries and Society in Medieval Britain*, ed. Benjamin Thompson (Stamford, 1999), 177–222.

Bray, Gerald (ed.). *Tudor Church Reform: the Henrician canons of 1535 and the* Reformatio Legum Ecclesiasticarum, Church of England Record Society, 8 (2000).

Breton, Nicholas. *Fantasticks: serving for a perpetuall prognostication* (London, 1626; S104782).

Brightman, F. E. *The English Rite*, 2nd edn, 2 vols (London, 1921; repr. Farnborough, 1970).

Buck, Anne. *Clothes and the Child: a handbook of children's dress in England 1500–1900* (Carlton, Beds. and New York, 1996).

Busse, Claire M. '"Pretty Fictions" and "Little Stories": child actors on the early modern stage', in *Childhood and Children's Books in Early Modern Europe, 1550–1800*', ed. Andrea Imml and Michael Witmore (Abingdon and New York, 2006), 75–101.

Calendar of Letters and Papers, Foreign and Domestic, Henry VIII, 22 vols (London, 1864–1932).

[Camden, William.] *Remaines of a Greater Worke Concerning Britain* (London, 1605; S107408).

Carew, Richard. *The Survey of Cornwall*, ed. John Chynoweth, Nicholas Orme, and Alexandra Walsham, Devon and Cornwall Record Society, new series 47 (2004).

Carey, Robert. *The Memoirs of Robert Carey*, ed. F. H. Mares (Oxford, 1972).

Castiglione, Baldassare. *The Book of the Courtier*, trans. Thomas Hoby (London, 1928, based on the London edition of 1588).

Caxton, William. *The Book of the Knight of the Tower*, ed. M. Y. Offord, EETS, ss 2 (1971).

Chambers, E. K. *The Elizabethan Stage*, 4 vols (Oxford, 1923).

Chaucer, Geoffrey. *The Riverside Chaucer*, ed. Larry D. Benson, 3rd edn (Oxford, 1989).

Child, Francis James (ed.). *The English and Scottish Popular Ballads*, 5 vols (New York, 1882–5; repr. Cambridge, 2015).

Clement, Francis. *The Petie Schole* (London, 1587; S105102).

Cogan, Thomas. *The Haven of Health* (London, 1584; S105007).

Coleman, Moira (ed.). *Household Inventories of Helmingham Hall 1597–1741*, Suffolk Records Society, 61 (2018).

Collier, Heather. 'Richard Hill – a London compiler', in *The Court and Cultural Identity*, ed. Evelyn Mullaly and John Thompson (Cambridge, 1997), 319–29.

Coote, Edmund. *The English Schoole-Maister* (London, 1596; S113558).

Cotman, John Sell. *Engravings of Sepulchral Brasses in Norfolk and Suffolk*, 2nd edn, 2 vols (London, 1839).

Cressy, David. *Literacy and the Social Order: reading and writing in Tudor and Stuart England* (Cambridge, 1980).

Daly, Anne (ed.). *Kingston upon Thames Register of Apprentices 1563–1713*, Surrey Record Society, 28 (1974).

Davies, M. G. *The Enforcement of Apprenticeship, 1565–1642* (Cambridge, MA, 1956).

Dee, John. *The Private Diary of Dr. John Dee and the Catalogue of his Library of Manuscripts*, ed. John Orchard Halliwell, Camden Society, old series 19 (1842).

Eliot, John. *Ortho-epia Gallica* (London, 1593; S121992).

Ellis, Henry. *Original Letters, Illustrative of English History, First, Second, and Third Series*, 11 vols (London, 1969).

Elyot, Thomas. *The Education or Bringinge Vp Children, Translated out of Plutarche* (London, 1530; S94753).

Elyot, Thomas. *The Book Named the Gouernour* (London, 1531; S105376).

Emden, A. B. *A Biographical Register of the University of Oxford A.D.1501 to 1540* (Oxford, 1974).

Erasmus, Desiderius. *De Civilitate Morum Puerilium*, trans. Robert Whittington (London, 1532; S105527).

Erasmus, Desiderius. *The Ciuilitie of Childehode*, trans. Thomas Paynell (London, 1560; S2112).

Erondelle, Pierre. *The French Garden* (London, 1605; S101691).

Fildes, Valerie. *Wet Nursing: a history from antiquity to the present* (Oxford, 1988).

Fildes, Valerie. 'Maternal Feelings Re-assessed: child abandonment and neglect in London and Westminster, 1550–1800', in *Women as Mothers in Pre-Industrial England*, ed. Valerie Fildes (London, 1990), 139–78.

Fit John, John. *A Diamond Most Precious, Worthy to be Marked* (London, 1577; S117750).

Fletcher, Anthony. *Growing Up in England: the experience of childhood 1600–1914* (New Haven and London, 2008).

Forsyth, Hazel, and Egan, Geoff. *Toys, Trifles & Trinkets: base metal miniatures from London, 1200–1800* (London, 2005).

Foxe, John. *Acts and Monuments*, ed. J. Pratt, 4th edn, 8 vols (London, 1877).

Frere, W. H. and Kennedy, W. M. (eds). *Visitation Articles and Injunctions of the Period of the Reformation*, 3 vols, Alcuin Club, 14–16 (1908–10).

Furnivall, F. J. (ed.). *Queene Elizabethes Achademy: a book of precedence*, EETS, es 8 (1869).

Furnivall, F. J. (ed.). *Child-Marriages, Divorces, and Ratifications, &c., in the Diocese of Chester, A.D.1561–6*, EETS, os 108 (1897).

Gair, W. Reavely. *The Children of Paul's: the story of a theatre company* (Cambridge, 1982).

Gairdner, James (ed.). *Memorials of King Henry the Seventh* (London, Rolls Series, 1858).

Gallagher, John. *Learning Languages in Early Modern England* (Oxford, 2019).

Gardiner, Dorothy. *English Girlhood at School: a study of women's education through twelve centuries* (Oxford, 1929).

Goldberg, P. J. P. *Women, Work, and Life Cycle in a Medieval Economy: women in York and Yorkshire c.1300–1520* (Oxford, 1992).

Gomme, Alice Bertha. *The Traditional Games of England, Scotland, and Ireland*, 2 vols (London, 1894–8; repr. London, 1984).

Gouge, William. *Of Domesticall Duties: eight treatises* (London, 1622; S103290).

Griffiths, Paul. *Youth and Authority: formative experiences in England 1560–1640* (Oxford, 1996).

Hair, Paul. *Before the Bawdy Court: selections from Church court and other records* (London, 1972).

Hall, Edward. *The Vnion of . . . Lancaster and Yorke, 1548*, [ed. Henry Ellis] (London, 1809).

Hardman, Philippa. ' "This Litel Child, His Litel Book": narratives for children in late-fifteenth-century England', *Journal of the Early Book Society*, 7 (2004), 51–66.

Harman, Thomas. *A Caveat for Commen Cursetors* (London, 1567; S112487).

Harrison, William. *The Description of England*, ed. Georges Edelen (Ithaca, NY, 1968).

Henricks, Thomas S. *Disputed Pleasures: sport and society in pre-industrial England* (New York and London, 1991).

Herbert, Edward, Lord. *Autobiography of Edward Lord Herbert of Cherbury*, ed. Sidney L. Lee (London, 1892).

Heywood, Colin. *A History of Childhood*, 2nd edn (Cambridge, 2018).

[Hill, Richard.] *Songs, Carols and other Miscellaneous Poems from the Balliol MS. 354, Richard Hill's Commonplace-Book*, ed. Roman Dyboski, EETS, es 101 (1908).

Hindle, Steve. *On the Parish? The micro-politics of poor relief in rural England, c.1550–1750* (Oxford, 2004).

Hollyband, Claudius. *The Frenche Littelton* (London, 1576; S11901).

Hollyband, Claudius. *The French Schoolemaister* (London, 1573; S109618).

Hollyband, Claudius. *Campo di Fior* (London, 1583; S109614).

Hollyband, Claudius. *The Italian Schoole-maister* (London, 1597; S117053).

[Hooker, John.] *The Life and Times of Sir Peter Carew*, ed. J. Maclean (London, 1857).

Horman, William. *Vulgaria* (London, 1519; S106246; repr. Amsterdam, 1975).

Horrell, Sara, and Humphries, Jane, 'Children's Work and Wages in Britain, 1280–1860', *Explorations in Economic History*, 73 (2019).

Houlbrooke, Ralph A. *The English Family, 1450–1700* (London, 1984).

Howard, Skiles. *The Politics of Courtly Dancing in Early Modern England* (Amherst, MA, 1998).

Hurstfield, Joel. *The Queen's Wards: wardship and marriage under Elizabeth I*, 2nd edn (London, 1973).

Hutton, Ronald. *The Rise and Fall of Merry England: the ritual year 1400–1700* (Oxford, 1994).

Hutton, Ronald. *The Stations of the Sun: a history of the ritual year in Britain* (Oxford, 1996).

Ingram, Martin. *Church Courts, Sex and Marriage in England, 1570–1640* (Cambridge, 1987).

Ingram, Martin. 'Child Sexual Abuse in Early Modern England', in *Negotiating Power in Early Modern Society*, ed. M. J. Braddick and J. Walter (Cambridge, 2010), 63–94.

Ingram, Martin. *Carnal Knowledge: regulating sex in England, 1470–1600* (Cambridge, 2017).

July and Julian, ed. Giles Dawson, Malone Society, 95 (1955).

Kempe, William. *The Education of Children in Learning* (London, 1588; S109252).

Kussmaul, Anne. *Servants in Husbandry in Early Modern England* (Cambridge, 1981).

Lambarde, William. *The Dueties of Constables* (London, 1601; S113603).

Latymer, William. 'William Latymer's Chronickille of Anne Bulleyn', ed. Maria Darling, in *Camden Miscellany XXX*, Royal Historical Society, Camden 4th series 39 (1990).

Leach, A. F. *A History of Winchester College* (London, 1899).

Leland, John. *J. Lelandi antiquari de rebus Britannicis Collectanea*, ed. Thomas Hearne, 2nd edn, 6 vols (London, 1770, repr. 1970).

Lewis, Carenza. 'Children's Play in the Later Medieval English Countryside'. *Children in the Past*, 2 (2009), 86–108.

The Lisle Letters, ed. Muriel St. Clair Byrne, 6 vols (Chicago and London, 1981).

Lupton, Thomas. *A Thousand Notable Things of Sundrie Sorts* (London, 1595; S106342).

McGowan, Margaret M. *Dance in the Renaissance: European fashion, French obsession* (New Haven and London, 2008).

Machyn, Henry. *The Diary of Henry Machyn, Citizen and Merchant-Taylor of London, from A.D. 1550 to A.D. 1563*, ed. J. G. Nichols, Camden Society, old series 42 (1848).

Manuscripts of His Grace the Duke of Rutland, 4 vols (London, Historical Manuscripts Commission, 1888–1905).

Maxwell-Lyte, H. C. *The History of Eton College*, 4th edn (London, 1911).

Mulcaster, Richard. *Positions* (London, 1581; S112928).

Murphy, Beverley Ann, 'The Life and Political Significance of Henry Fitzroy', University of Wales, PhD thesis (1997).

Myers, A. R. *The Household of Edward IV* (Manchester, 1959).

Nelson, William (ed.). *A Fifteenth Century School Book* (Oxford, 1956).

Newton, Hannah. '"Very Sore Nights and Days": the child's experience of illness in early modern England, *c*.1580–1720', *Medical History*, 55 (2011), 153–82.

Nice Wanton, A Preaty Interlude called (London, 1560; S102099).

Nichols, John Gough. *The Progresses and Public Processions of Queen Elizabeth I*, ed. Elizabeth Goldring and others, 5 vols (Oxford, 2014).

Nowell, Alexander. *A Catechism or First Instruction and Learning of Christian Religion* (London, 1570; S119860).

O'Day, Rosemary. *The Family and Family Relationships, 1500–1900: England, France and the United States of America* (Basingstoke, 1994).

O'Day, Rosemary. *An Elite Family in Early Modern England: the Temples of Stowe and Burton Dassett, 1570–1656* (Woodbridge, 2018).

Opie, Iona and Peter. *The Oxford Dictionary of Nursery Rhymes*, 2nd edn (Oxford, 1997a).

Opie, Iona and Peter. *Children's Games with Things* (Oxford, 1997b).

Orlin, Lena Cowen. *Elizabethan Households: an anthology* (Washington, DC, 1995).

Orme, Nicholas. *Early British Swimming 55BC–AD1719, with the First Swimming Treatise in English, 1595* (Exeter, 1983).

Orme, Nicholas. *From Childhood to Chivalry: the education of the English kings and aristocracy 1066–1530* (London, 1984).

Orme, Nicholas. *Education and Society in Medieval and Renaissance England* (London and Ronceverte, WV, 1989).

Orme, Nicholas. *Education in Early Tudor England: Magdalen College Oxford and its school 1480–1540*, Magdalen College Occasional Paper, 4 (Oxford, 1998).

Orme, Nicholas. *Medieval Children* (New Haven and London, 2001).

Orme, Nicholas. *Medieval Schools* (New Haven and London, 2006).

Orme, Nicholas. *Fleas, Flies and Friars: children's poetry from the Middle Ages* (Exeter and Ithaca, NY, 2011).

Orme, Nicholas. *English School Exercises 1420–1530* (Toronto, 2013).

Orme, Nicholas. *The History of England's Cathedrals* (Exeter, 2017).

Orme, Nicholas. 'Display, Ceremony and Performance in English Schools, *c*.1300–1530', in *Performance, Ceremony and Display in Late Medieval England*, ed. Julia Boffey (Donington, 2020a), 62–76.

Orme, Nicholas. 'Schoolmasters and Pupils on Brasses before the Reformation', *Transactions of the Monumental Brass Society*, 21 (2020b), 77–86.

Orme, Nicholas. *Going to Church in Medieval England* (New Haven and London, 2021).

Oxford Dictionary of National Biography, ed. C. Matthew and B. Harrison, 60 vols (Oxford, 2004), updated electronic version (including further biographies): http://www.oxforddnb.com

Oxford English Dictionary, ed. J. Simpson and E. S. C. Weiner, 2nd edn, 40 vols (Oxford, 1989).

Page-Phillips, John. *Children on Brasses* (London, 1970).

Parsons, Ben. *Punishment and Medieval Education* (Cambridge, 2018).

Pelling, Margaret. 'Child Health as a Social Value in Early Modern England', *Social History of Medicine*, 1 (1988), 135–64.

Percy, Thomas (ed.). *The Regulations and Establishment of the Household of Henry Algernon Percy* (London, 1770).

Phaer, Thomas. *The Regiment of Life* [by Jean Goeurot], *whereunto is added a treatise of the Pestilence, with the Boke of Children, newly corrected and enlarged* (London, 1550; S109504).

Phillippy, Patricia. 'A Comfortable Farewell: child-loss and funeral monuments in early modern England', in *Gender and Early Modern Constructions of Childhood*, ed. Naomi J. Miller and Narmi Yavneh (Farnham, 2011), 17–38.

Phillips, Kim M. *Medieval Maidens: young women and gender in England, 1270–1540* (Manchester and New York, 2003).

Phythian-Adams, Charles. *Desolation of a City: Coventry and the urban crisis of the late Middle Ages* (Cambridge, 1979).

Platter, Thomas. *Thomas Platter's Travels in England 1599*, ed. Clare Williams (London, 1937).

Plutarch. *A President for Parentes, teaching the vertuous training vp of children*, trans. E. Grant (London, 1571; S110518).

Pollock, Linda. *Forgotten Children: parent–child relationships from 1500 to 1900* (Cambridge, 1983).

Pollock, Linda. *With Faith and Physic: the life of a Tudor gentlewoman, Lady Grace Mildmay 1552–1620* (London, 1993).

Pound, John F. (ed.). *The Norwich Census of the Poor, 1570*, Norfolk Record Society, 40 (1971).

Promptorium Parvulorum, ed. A. Way, 3 vols, Camden Society, original series 25, 54, 89 (1843–65).

Report on the Manuscripts of Lord Middleton (London, Historical Manuscripts Commission, 1910).

Rhodes, Hugh. *The Boke of Nurture . . . with Stans Puer ad Mensam* (London, 1545; S104530).

Riden, Philip (ed.). *The Household Accounts of William Cavendish, Lord Cavendish of Hardwick, 1597–1607*, 3 vols, Derbyshire Record Society, 40–2 (2016).

Rösslin, Eucharius. *The Byrth of Mankynde*, trans. Thomas Raynald (London, 1540; S116014).

Scot, Reginald. *The Discoverie of Witchcraft* (London, 1584; S116888).

Segar, Francis. *The Schoole of Vertue* (London, 1557; S110652).

Shakespeare, William. References to his plays are taken from the individual volumes and editorial notes of the Arden Shakespeare, 2nd edn.

Shirley, Evelyn Philip. 'Extracts from the Fermor Accounts', *Archaeological Journal*, 8 (1851), 179–86.

Smith, Sir Thomas. *De Republica Anglorum* (London, 1583; S117628; repr. Menston, 1970).

Sneyd, Charlotte Augusta (ed.). *A Relation . . . of the Island of England . . . about the Year 1500*, Camden Society, old series 37 (1847).

Statutes of the Realm from Magna Carta to the End of the Reign of Queen Anne, 10 vols (London, Record Commission, 1810–24).

Stephenson, Mill. *A List of Monumental Brasses in the British Isles*, 2nd edn (London, 1964)

Stockwood, John. *A Bartholomew Fairing for Parents* (London, 1586; S105880).

Stow, John. *A Survey of London*, ed. C. L. Kingsford, 2 vols (Oxford, 1908).

Strong, Roy. *The English Icon: Elizabethan and Jacobean portraiture* (London, 1969).

Stubbes, Philip. *Anatomy of the Abuses in England*, ed. F. J. Furnivall, 2 vols (London, 1877–82).

Tarbin, Stephanie. 'Caring for Poor and Fatherless Children in London, c.1350–1550', *The Journal of the History of Childhood and Youth*, 3 (2010), 391–410.

Thirsk, Joan. 'Younger Sons in the Seventeenth Century', *History*, 54 (1969), 358–377.

Thomas, Keith. *Rule and Misrule in the Schools of Early Modern England* (Reading, 1976).

Thomas, Keith. 'Children in Early Modern England', in *Children and their Books: a celebration of the work of Iona and Peter Opie*, ed. Gillian Avery and Julia Briggs (Oxford, 1989), 45–77.

Thornton, Tim, and Carlton, Katharine. *The Gentleman's Mistress: illegitimate relationships and children, 1450–1640* (Manchester, 2019).

Tusser, Thomas. *Five Hundreth Points of Good Husbandry* (London, 1573; S1388); modern edn, *Five Hundred Points of Good Husbandry*, ed. Geoffrey Grigson (Oxford, 1984).

Underwood, Lucy. *Childhood, Youth and Religious Dissent in Post-Reformation England* (Basingstoke, 2014).

Vives, Juan Luis. *A very frutefull and pleasant book called the Instruction of a Christen Woman*, trans. Richard Hyrd (London, 1529; S95706).

[Wager, William.] *The Longer Thou Liuest the More Fool Thou Art* (London, 1569; S102098).

Wall, Alison D. *Two Elizabethan Women: correspondence of Joan and Maria Thynne 1575–1611*, Wiltshire Record Society, 38 (1983).

Ward, John M. 'The Maner of Dauncying', *Early Music*, 4 (1976), 127–42.

Warnicke, Retha M. 'Lady Mildmay's Journal: a study in autobiography and meditation in Reformation England', *Sixteenth Century Journal*, 20 (1984), 55–68.

Whitford, Richard. *A Werke for Housholders* (London, 1530; S105123).

Whythorne, Thomas. *The Autobiography of Thomas Whythorne*, ed. James M. Osborn (Oxford, 1961).

Willis, R[ichard]. *Mount Tabor, or private exercises of a penitent sinner* (London, 1639; S120175).

Wilson, Jean. 'The Noble Imp: the upper-class child in English Renaissance art and literature', *The Antiquaries Journal*, 70 (1990), 360–79.

Wilson, Thomas. 'The State of England Anno Dom. 1600 by Thomas Wilson', ed. F. J. Fisher, in *Camden Miscellany XVI*, Royal Historical Society, Camden 3rd series 52 (1936).

Winchester, Barbara. *Tudor Family Portrait* (London, 1955).

Withals, John. *A Shorte Dictionarie for Yonge Beginners* (London, 1553; S95893); augmented edn by Lewis Evans (London, 1574; S102200); further augmentation by Evans (London, 1584; S105750).

Woodfield, Charmian. 'Finds from the Free Grammar School at the Whitefriars, Coventry, c.1545–c.1557/8', *Post Medieval Archaeology*, 15 (1981), 81–159.

The Worlde and the Chylde: Here begynneth a propre newe interlude of the worlde and the chylde, otherwyse called Mundus et infans (London, 1522; S108266).

Wrigley, E. A., and Schofield, R. S. *The Population History of England 1541–1871: a reconstruction*, revised edn (London, 1989).

Wrigley, E. A. and others. *English Population History from Family Reconstitution 1580–1837* (Cambridge, 2010).

INDEX